CHANGING TIMES

LIFE IN 1950s NORTHERN IRELAND

GW00655980

PETER SMYTH

COLOURPOINT BOOKS

Published 2012 by Colourpoint Books
an imprint of Colourpoint Creative Ltd
Colourpoint House, Jubilee Business Park
21 Jubilee Road, Newtownards, BT23 4YH
Tel: 028 9182 6339
Fax: 028 9182 1900
E-mail: info@colourpoint.co.uk
Web: www.colourpoint.co.uk

First Edition
First Impression

Designed by April Sky Design, Newtownards
Tel: 028 9182 7195
Web: www.aprilsky.co.uk

Printed by GPS Colour Graphics Ltd, Belfast

ISBN 978-1-78073-044-8

Front cover: Laurence Olivier launches UTV in 1959 and opens a new world of
entertainment. (Courtesy of the *Belfast Telegraph*)
Rear cover: In a field near Belfast the first Minis are demonstrated to admiring crowds
in 1959. (Photographer: Arthur Campbell, Public Record Office in Northern Ireland,
document number D4122/B/103694)

*About the author: Peter Smyth is a retired senior civil servant.
He holds a PhD in History from Queen's University Belfast, and has
written articles for various academic and professional publications.*

CONTENTS

PREFACE

THE TASK OF the conscientious historian is to portray as accurately as possible the events of yesteryear, and to comment on those events in a way which adds to our collective understanding of the period under review. That is a difficult undertaking in itself, but it becomes even more so when the place being studied is Northern Ireland and the period being described is within the living memory of many potential readers. Much of what I am presenting in this book as some kind of broad universal truth will be at odds with what individuals will recollect – accurately or mythically – from personal experience, and some readers may be inclined to use any such discrepancies as the jumping-off point for anathematising the entire project. I can only acknowledge in advance that the risk exists, and that I have attempted to minimise it by checking very carefully the newspapers, books, periodicals, official files and conversations I have drawn on for the raw material, but it would be naïve to pretend that my account will correspond with every individual reality. It is possible to envisage the book being flung into a corner by an irate reader because I state that floodlights were first used at a football match at Grosvenor Park towards the end of 1952, when any sane person knows as an unassailable fact that it was at the Oval in October 1953 that this significant development took place. The irate reader will curse himself for having wasted good money on what purports to be a history book when if he had wanted to read fiction he would have bought a novel. I can only hope that on the other hand there may be an equal or greater number of readers for whom detecting suspected authorial oversights will bring about an intoxicating glow of intellectual superiority, sufficient to enliven their conversation in pubs and at dinner tables for months to come.

Besides trying to avoid factual inaccuracies, I have attempted to steer clear of the minefield that is Northern Irish politics. Of course it is impossible to do so, but this is not a political history and as far as possible it seeks to avoid making political points. As an example of the sensitivities involved, one has only to think of the Derry/Londonderry debate. In the 50s, almost everyone, irrespective of religion or political persuasion, referred to 'Derry' and usage throughout this book reflects that to some extent. I have adopted the modern academic device of using 'Derry' for the city, and 'Londonderry' for the County or the parliamentary constituencies, but it is unrealistic to expect that either form is proof against giving offence. But apart from wishing to avoid causing offence by making political references, the book deals with the changes which took place in everyday life in Northern Ireland during the 1950s, and the reality was that by the end of the decade the political landscape remained almost unchanged from what it had been. The handful of Northern Ireland Labour Party MPs elected to Stormont in 1958 mounted a more imaginative and sustained criticism of government policies than anything the weary and disorganised Nationalist Party could muster, but the fundamental issue of the state's constitutional status remained as entrenched as it had been 40 years previously. If civil society underwent change, the political world was resolutely unprogressive. Trying to explain why that should have been is not within the scope of this work.

Politics do get an oblique airing in the chapter on education. For the authorities in both the Protestant and Catholic Churches, the education of children was regarded as essential to their moral wellbeing, and the shape of the entire education system cannot be understood without an awareness of the influences the churches exerted on it. But any references to religion invariably drag political considerations in their wake. The record of the Northern Ireland government in the field of education in the 1950s was admirable in many ways, but it was not devoid of political calculation, and that bias cannot be airbrushed out. Education has a direct bearing on the values of citizenship which help to shape society, and any objective analysis of the educational process must take account of all the factors which helped to shape it.

A problem of a different order is posed by references to money. The pre-decimal currency used in the 50s made sense to those accustomed to its use, but to modern eyes it is both archaic and illogical, with coins like farthings and halfpennies so insignificant in contemporary value as to have no decimal equivalent, and others like guineas (gn) which had not actually existed as a unit of currency since 1816 and which even now survive only as notional prices for the purchasing of racehorses. I have tried to make accurate translations of 1950s prices into their modern equivalents, even though it can be a fairly meaningless exercise when the sums involved are small. The effort has been made however, because in the 50s small variations in prices were important to people who had very little disposable income, and it would be wrong to take a cavalier attitude to their preoccupation with what seem to us to be trivial amounts. In general I have tried not to clutter the text with figures although on occasions statistics are necessary to define a trend, estimate costs or measure the scale of change. It is not a problem as such, but it has to be acknowledged that the book is Belfast-centric. That is a function of the city being (more or less) the seat of government, the centre of industry and population, the home of broadcasting, the main generator of wealth, the producer of the more informative newspapers, and the place with the most and the brightest lights. That explanation is offered in full recognition of the fact that thousands of people in Northern Ireland in the 50s lived lives which were largely untouched by the more metropolitan values of the city, and whose interest in Continental holidays, the latest films, the newest model in contemporary vacuum cleaners, or the *dernier cri* in swagger coats was considerably less than zero. But sooner or later everyone was influenced by these trends and ideas, even if indirectly. For instance, posturing Teddy Boys and Girls wearing duffel coats who got the point of jazz were a largely urban phenomenon, but teenage rebelliousness and the reaction against authority was a trend which swept through society at all levels. It is not disrespectful to the remoter rural areas that they receive scant mention here, but recognition of the fact that Belfast did, by and large, set the trends that everyone else duly followed.

The theme running through the book is that the 1950s represented the decade when fundamental changes occurred to our way of life in Northern Ireland – as of course was the case in many other parts of the world. Change is nowadays so much a part of everyday existence that it is taken for granted, and it is difficult to grasp the extent to which the war years and their aftermath shook up assumptions which to that generation had seemed immutable. In the course of the 50s expectations altered in regard to housing, transport, entertainment, food, health, leisure time and education. The family as a social unit came under strain, and authority began to be questioned in ways which would have been unthinkable even a decade previously. Above all, perhaps, the introduction of the welfare state. While it relieved the misery of thousands of the poorest members of society, it also undermined the sense of self-reliance which had once held communities together, and introduced instead a sense of personal entitlement which became increasingly at odds with such traditional concepts as duty, morality, the virtues of hard work for its own sake, and the obligation to help others. Much was gained in the 1950s, and much was also lost.

Part of the charm of nostalgia is that it allows us to take an affectionate look at the past while simultaneously feeling grateful that we don't have to live there; and even if it were possible to do so, I don't suppose there are many people reading this book who would want to return to the 1950s. As we move ever further away from those years however, I hope this account of the decade will show that the image in the rear-view mirror is not without interest.

Finally, I should like to acknowledge all those who, either officially or privately, consciously or inadvertently, contributed to the writing of this book. John Killen and the staff of the Linenhall Library; Ian Montgomery, his colleagues and the Deputy Keeper of the Records in the Public Record Office of Northern Ireland; Michelle Ashmore in the Ulster Folk and Transport Museum; Paul Carson in the *Belfast Telegraph*; the newspaper section of Belfast Central Library; the National Archives at Kew; the McClay library at Queen's University – all of them provided not only information, but advice and guidance on how it might be used to best effect, and I am happy to record my gratitude. My thanks go, too, to Malcolm Johnston and the professionals at Colourpoint who ensured that my words were made manifest. In the wider world I would like to acknowledge the contribution made by virtually everyone of a certain age with whom I have lunched or dined over the past few years, and who (with varying degrees of subtlety) I petitioned for recollections of bygone days, or who served as a sounding board for my evolving suppositions. Two people in particular deserve special mention however. Trudy Hodkinson provided the encouragement and impetus in transferring my text from PC screen to publisher; and my wife Yvonne, who endured with fortitude and forbearance my frequent absences, physical as well as cerebral, while the book was in gestation, but who realised early on that my infatuation with the 1950s was unlikely ever to divorce me permanently from the cheerful felicities of contemporary life.

THE WAY WE WERE, THE WAY WE ARE

THE 1950s WERE the grey decade lodged uneasily between the retrospective glamour of the Second World War and the colour TV vision of the Swinging Sixties. Even the weather was grey. "The year 1952 was dry and rather dull with mean temperatures somewhat below average ..." "The year 1954 was notably dull, cool and wet with frequent and at times severe gales." "The year 1957 was notable for an exceptionally mild March ... [but a] dull wet summer and autumn." Such were among the summaries presented in the government's *Ulster Year Book*, and they seem to set the tone for our perceptions of the entire decade. Perhaps for that reason it is a period which has largely been ignored by historians, yet the six decades which have since elapsed have seen more advances impacting on our lives than any comparable period of history. Many of the developments which influence the way we live now were set in motion in the years following the War, and it is salutary to remind ourselves of the way we were.

What the 50s had and didn't have might include the following:

They didn't have satellite TV, personal computers, mobile phones, U-Tube, social networking, ATMs, credit cards, digital cameras, X-boxes or the myriad of electronic devices which have removed the need for face-to-face interaction. Electronic sophistication then was a 2-channel TV set with a black and white picture, a portable wireless with a 5-pound dry battery, and a Kodak camera costing almost £2 which took eight 'snaps' on a roll of film. People attended dancehalls, visited 'the pictures' twice a week, smoked in every conceivable place, listened to the wireless, drank in pubs which closed at 9.00 pm in many towns, and paid for their pleasures after abstruse calculations in pounds (£), shillings (s) and pence (d). They didn't have a 24/7 lifestyle, and would have regarded as insane anyone who aspired to such an existence. Dammit, they didn't have a lifestyle. They also used thin, shiny toilet paper.

The 50s didn't have supermarkets, food from around the world, or barcodes. They had yet to discover the delights of widespread drug abuse, an obesity epidemic, health clubs and fitness suites, plastic surgery, recreational shopping, clingfilm or electronic locking on cars. Rationing lasted until 1954, and because domestic refrigeration was rare the grocer's, butcher's and bakery had to be visited on a daily basis. 'Calories' were a new concept, pizza was an exotic treat, as were potato crisps and Coca Cola served cold. Both old people and young wore clothes appropriate to their age. Children dressed in hand-me-downs, women wore corsets and permed their hair, men wore hats, smoked pipes and were good at putting up shelves, and most people over 40 had full sets of dentures. Shoes were polished regularly and sent to the cobbler to be mended. The idea of insurance for domestic pets would have been greeted with incredulity.

The 50s didn't have widespread divorce, never mind gay marriages and civil partnerships. They lacked awareness of human rights and equality legislation, were largely immune to the requirements of health and safety and were not subject to regulation by the European Union. There were no football millionaires and no cult of celebrity, and ethnic diversity was a term applied by Belfast people to those who came from Fermanagh. Religious observance remained strong in the 50s, as did the belief in corporal punishment in schools, as well as flogging and capital punishment in prison. Doctors, bank managers, magistrates and senior civil servants defined middle class respectability; while policemen and teachers were part of the pantheon of authority which, along with parents and older people, commanded automatic respect from the young. 'Teenagers' were a new breed, and Teddy Boys were regarded as the advance battalion of a fully delinquent society. Conscious of its status as the sole university in Northern Ireland, Queen's did not award degrees in printmaking or media studies.

The 50s didn't have three-car families, motorways, or a limitless choice of exotic foreign holidays. Cars were old, expensive and unreliable, accidents were frequent, speed limits and driving tests were a new-fangled nuisance, and road signs constituted a form of pandering to tourists. Getting on a plane was an event for which the passengers got dressed up, large parts of Europe were unreachable or out of bounds, trains were pulled by steam engines, the tram from Fintona Junction into the town was hauled by a mare called Dick, and Butlins at Mosney was an exciting alternative to Portrush. Bus conductors carried leather pouches which jingled with coins and they dispensed tickets from an ingenious machine worn on the chest. Horses still provided the locomotive power for delivery carts in towns, drinking troughs stood in convenient roadside locations, and the streets smelled of harness, sweat and fresh manure.

There were slums, overcrowding and deplorable living conditions, and even in new houses central heating was virtually unknown. Gloss paint required endless stirring, dripped and had a strong petrochemical smell. Kitchens were not cluttered with gadgets, linoleum was the floor-covering of choice, and bedrooms were not regarded as gardens of earthly delight. Sex did exist, but had not yet been identified as the defining component of a successful life. There were family doctors who made house calls, and matrons who ruled hospital wards. There were collar studs, there were prices quoted in guineas, and apart from the city centre, Belfast's street lighting was provided by 16,000 gas lights. Milk in glass bottles was delivered to the front door, fish and chips were sold wrapped in newspaper. There were rolls of sticky flypaper, and clothes that smelled of mothballs. Boys in short trousers had scabs on their knees, climbed trees and had toy armies of lead soldiers. Girls played with skipping ropes and improbably pink dolls. And everyone had a grandmother who carried a permanent supply of Imperial mints.

In his novel *The Go-Between* published in 1953, LP Hartley offered as an opening sentence, "The past is a foreign country, they do things differently there." His protagonist was looking back 50 or 60 years to the beginning of the twentieth century and reflecting on the changes which had taken place in society over that period. Given the accelerating pace of change in the decades since Hartley was writing, we should find, in the terms of his dictum, that Northern Ireland in the 50s not just foreign, but positively alien. If we don't find that, it is because the things that they did differently there are the things that have shaped the society into which we have evolved. Those foreigners are our ancestors.

CHAPTER 1

EVERYONE'S COMING TO TOWN

NORTHERN IRELAND IN the early 50s was a green and pleasant land of 3.4 million acres, with something like 90% of it given over to agriculture in some form, mostly tillage and pasture, but with grazed mountains and woods making their contribution too. There were around 88,000 farms, more than one-third of them in the one to 15 acre category, and 14,000 of between one and five acres. Only a bare handful of farms were over 200 acres. The typical rural landscape consisted of a patchwork of small fields, dotted with whitewashed cottages with thatched, or in increasing numbers, slated or corrugated iron roofs. Farming gave employment to 160,000 people, including owners, family members and workers engaged on either a full-time or temporary basis. That was twice as many as were employed in the textile industry, and three times that in engineering, the major pillars of the local economy.

In many cases, because of the small size of the holdings farming was regarded less as an industry, and more a way of life that had been passed down from father to son over several generations. It was never formalised, and there were countless variations, but the typical setup involved the eldest son delaying his marriage until he was in his 30s when the father could begin, without loss of authority, to hand over the running of the family acres. In some areas, like the Castlederg valley in County Tyrone, the practice was still observed of dividing land among all the sons in a family, which led to economically unsustainable holdings, because unless the farm was highly specialised, even a small family could not be sustained on less than 10 acres. Surveys undertaken during the 1940s revealed that a startlingly high proportion of landowners had been born on the family farm, and had chosen wives from among women belonging to the same broad locality. Bringing a woman into a house which was already occupied by the groom's mother was felt to be one factor behind the high proportion of farmers who remained unmarried.

Start-up costs for a farm were comparatively high. A 44 acre farm in Fermanagh, boasting a one-storey house with thatched roof, a kitchen and four rooms but no sanitary arrangements, cost £735. When stocked with five cows at £147, a horse, donkey, harness and carts, the additional costs were another £200. In more prosperous areas, costs were even higher, and there were few people from outside the agricultural community who felt tempted to invest in farming as a business venture. Some larger farms specialised in milk or livestock, but most were mixed units keeping a few cows, pigs or sheep and hens, and growing potatoes, corn and barley. It was a way of life which had not changed significantly since the turn of the twentieth century. Particularly among small farmers, continuity and a conservative outlook were built into the genetic makeup, while innovation and new methods were resisted. Evening classes by the Ministry of Agriculture failed to attract enthusiastic crowds, and the benefits of weed control or crop rotation went largely unheeded.

Change was coming however, and the fate of the flax industry, at one time almost the defining feature of Northern Irish agriculture, was in that respect almost symbolic. When the wartime boom receded, Irish linen retained its reputation as a high-quality product, but against cheap imports of textiles from the Far East, and the introduction of artificial fibres, the industry declined remorselessly. This was despite substantial government subsidies, and despite, too, some imaginative experiments to see if linen could successfully be combined with the new fibres. From the farmer's point of view the decline in demand for flax must have been a mixed blessing, because it was a labour-intensive crop where the returns were often incommensurate with the effort. Flax was regarded as a 'chancy' crop, with unpredictable yields. When it was ripe in late July or early August it was harvested by physically pulling the plants out of the soil, in order to preserve as much as possible of the fibrous outer layer, which would in due course be transformed into linen thread. After pulling, the flax was immersed in water-filled ponds or dams for around two weeks in a process known as 'retting' to allow the outer layer to be loosened from the inner woody stalk; then, amid a pungent smell which carried across the countryside, it was dumped beside the dam to dry. When dry it was removed to the water-powered scutch mill, where it was passed through rollers and beaten by wooden paddles until the woody stalk disintegrated into dust and the cleaned fibre could be collected for sale at 2s (10p) for 14 pounds weight. By the mid-50s chemical retting and electrically driven mills were easily able to handle the much reduced output of flax, and for years afterwards the countryside was littered with dried-up dams and the shells of small, abandoned scutch mills. There were over 80,000 acres of flax cultivated in 1945, and by 1959 that was down to a mere 40 acres. It is a sign of the significance of flax that its blue flower retains for Northern Ireland the same kind of symbolic value as the

Welsh daffodil or the Scottish thistle, even though there are few people today who would recognise it in its natural state. It was another example of an industry in which Northern Ireland had once been dominant, now overtaken by post-war developments.

Yet in the broader sense agriculture continued to be a vital industry. The most visible manifestation of this was the quantities of produce which had been shipped to Britain on a daily basis throughout the War, and which in the early 50s still constituted a crucial element in the British government's food production programme. In 1951 the official figures for the year were 224,000 head of cattle, 123,000 sheep, 43 million dozens of eggs (around one-fifth of all the eggs consumed in Britain), 18,000 tons of bacon and ham, plus (during the summer) 72,000 gallons of milk per day, together with substantial quantities of potatoes and apples. In 1953 this trade was worth almost £60 million, or around a quarter of Northern Ireland's total export earnings. (There was some debate about whether the 78,000 gallons of whiskey which had been exported in 1947 could be counted as agricultural produce, despite grain being the basis of its production. It was worth £170,000, or just over £2 a gallon.) The wartime effort had not only increased production, it had, despite many grumbles and much resistance, enforced a degree of modernisation and improvements to the entire infrastructure of the industry. The Agriculture Act of 1947 introduced regular reviews of prices, and ensured guaranteed markets for the main sectors of production. Income streams could be roughly predicted, crude financial planning became possible, and in many cases farming was beginning to be regarded as a business.

Apart from exports, in the days before refrigerated transportation the role of agriculture lay in supplying the towns with fresh food. In the case of Belfast milk came mostly from herds in south Antrim – Carnmoney had a high reputation – and the Castlereagh hills, though supplies were lifted by lorries and transported from within a 50 mile radius of the city. Around Lurgan and the south-east corner of Lough Neagh was the main area for supply of eggs, because that represented the limit for transporting fresh produce into Belfast. Armagh concentrated on fruit and poultry. More specialised crops like tomatoes, or even flowers, were rare because of the investment which would have been required in building glasshouses. The market gardeners in north Down, around Comber and Newtownards, had their carts on the road early for the weekly journey to the Belfast markets for 8.00 am, although motorised transport was beginning to allow more frequent trips. Beef, pork and fresh meat came from the abattoirs and slaughterhouses at the city docks where thousands of animals were herded daily for shipping to Britain. To an extent we would find improbable today, much of the food which made its way onto plates was locally produced.

Agriculture had a salience in daily life. The Prime Minister, Sir Basil Brooke (later Lord Brookeborough) was a gentleman farmer in Fermanagh, and at times gave the impression that he preferred ditching and draining to the task of running the country. Whether they liked it or not his guests at Colebrooke were usually exposed to agricultural pursuits by way of rest and relaxation. Ploughing competitions were held throughout the province and attracted thousands of spectators who were willing to be entertained by the sight of horses and tractors turning the soil in an artistic manner. The Ford Motor Corporation ran county championships to boost the use of the Ford ploughing system, with finals being held at Shaw's Bridge near Belfast. Ploughing competitions were often international events, attracting contestants from Europe and beyond, although occasionally complaints were made and interpreters had to be engaged to ensure that Northern Irish horses were responsive to instructions delivered in imperfect English. Every town of any size had its annual agricultural show. The biggest was Balmoral Show, which was a major social event and was exceeded in spectator numbers – 20,000 a day being customary – only by Royal visits. As the *Belfast Telegraph* remarked in the days when readers appreciated a lyrical note in the editorials, "a few miles from the rim of the city will bring us back to the green lanes with their fragrant hawthorn and the good brown earth with its springing corn". Another commentator made the same point in a different way, remarking that "to a person standing in Wellington Place or on the Queen's Bridge in the centre of the capital, the vista is not one of smoky factories, but of mountains and pasture." Advertisements appeared in all the Belfast papers for milking machines, cattle feedstuffs, day-old chicks, TVO (tractor vaporising oil), tractors and farm machinery. The animal crematorium Burnhouse advertised itself as "the farmer's friend", collecting and disposing of worn-out or dead horses and cows, paying 12s 6d (62½p) per hundredweight for live horse meat and around half that for cattle. Life in the towns and cities was not lived sealed off from what was going on in the country.

Indeed the country was in the habit of coming to town. Marts in Belfast's Oxford Street saw daily auctions of the livestock which had been driven to the docks for shipping to Britain. The figures quoted for 1951 represented nearly 1,200 animals per working day. The drovers, known colloquially as 'cow wallopers', were a breed unto themselves, living, working and fighting to different rules from the rest of society. It was not accidental that the lower end of Victoria Street/Corporation Street was known as Cow Lane. There is an atmospheric photograph in the *Belfast Telegraph* in October 1953 of two sheepdogs herding sheep down Botanic Avenue, with only two parked cars to negotiate. There was a cattle yard or holding pen near Botanic Avenue, from which cattle broke out from time to time to disrupt the traffic in Bedford Street. In 1954, in response to complaints from Belfast Chamber of Commerce about Wild West scenes, the police introduced a cattle driving system for Oxford Street – and cows were given priority over traffic – but there were still reports of women and children running for cover as the cow wallopers drove their herds to the ships, leaving traumatised vehicle owners in their wake. Cleaning the streets afterwards must have been a considerable task. Similar scenes took place in Derry as cattle were loaded for Heysham, and in Enniskillen as animals from south and west were assembled for transportation by train. The same disruption took place on a smaller scale in every market town in Northern Ireland as farmers attended monthly marts for buying and selling stock, except then it was not regarded as an alien intrusion so much as an inevitable element of life in what was still (almost) a predominantly agricultural and rural community.

Although the numbers were declining swiftly, by the early 50s there were still more horses in Belfast than in most UK cities, a celebrated example being the one which pulled the mower in the City Cemetery. *Belfast Telegraph* delivery vans, UTA (Ulster Transport Authority) freight carts, rubber-wheeled bread vans and milk floats were still horse-drawn until well into the decade. There are references to the Belfast Horse Fair being held in 1951. In 1957 one carrier still had 60 horses in his stables and felt that his competitors who were moving into motorised transport would look very foolish in a few years' time. But the battle against the internal combustion engine had already been lost and it was generally recognised that horses and heavy traffic did not mix because incidents of horses being startled and causing collisions with cars were rising. By 1958 there were only six horse troughs left in the city and those were being removed. Not all animal life vacated the city however. Belfast Corporation in 1953 refused to amend the 1894 by-laws which permitted keeping pigs on private property, despite claims that in the most densely populated areas of the city piggeries now constituted a health hazard; and carts collecting domestic kitchen refuse for use as pig food were slow to yield their territory. Towns in Northern Ireland in the early 1950s not only looked different, they sounded and smelled different.

But here too change was taking place. In 1951 the population of the province was almost 1.4 million, with just under half of it living in the country. Belfast had 440,000 people within its boundaries, Derry had

50,000, Bangor 21,000, Portadown, Lurgan, Lisburn, Ballymena, Newry, Newtownards, Larne and Coleraine from 17,000 to 11,000. Those were the big towns. Then there were another 19 settlements, including the more prosperous market towns, ranging from Armagh with a population of 9,000, through to Newcastle with 3,000. Below that, the population of industrial villages like Sion Mills or Waringstown was largely made up of workers in the local factory; and even further down the scale were the numerous small villages with only a few hundred inhabitants, which acted as retail centres for their neighbourhood. In other words, the urban population was concentrated in one large and one medium city, and the rest in small towns. By 1961 some 54% of the population had become urbanised, and the trend continued. By 2001, with a total population of 1.7 million, Belfast's share had gone down due to a redrawing of the city's boundaries, but virtually every one of the towns mentioned had seen significant increases, Lisburn with 72,000 and Bangor with 58,000 being the most prominent. In 1951, there was only one town with a population greater than 20,000, but 50 years later there were nine. The other significant factor was that the migration was in most cases towards the east of the province, as the gravitational pull of Belfast and its hinterland became almost unalterable.

This reflected the phenomenon known as the drift from the land. A number of factors were involved. Mechanisation on farms was an obvious one, illustrated by the growth in the numbers of tractors from 550 in 1939 to 7,300 by the end of the War. In parallel was a decline in the number of horses, shrinking from 49,000 in 1950 to 26,000 five years later. A tractor represented significant capital outlay initially – a basic Ferguson model cost around £350–400, a Nuffield £2–300 more – but it didn't require feeding when not in use. With tractors came a range of agricultural equipment of a sophistication and efficiency that horse-drawn machines could never match. Almost overnight, farming became less labour-intensive and there was no longer the need to retain all the family members to work the land. If anything, the need now was to avoid a surplus of labour on the farm. Since mechanisation worked best on larger spreads, amalgamations of farms increased, and as family holdings were sold off, more people moved to the towns for employment in factories and shops.

Another factor was money. The amount of land under tillage had expanded enormously during the war years, but by the late 40s farmers were increasingly turning to livestock, because on small farms producing cattle, sheep or pigs for sale was the only feasible means of generating an adequate income. In the post-war years production of milk, eggs, bacon and fresh meat all rose significantly, while the acreage of land under the plough decreased. The greater part of this output was purchased by the Ministry of Food at British prices, and some farmers enjoyed a period of relative prosperity, but it was recognised in the local Ministry of Agriculture that farming as an industry was not developing as fast as in Britain, and that the post-war boom was unsustainable. In the late 40s a specialised dairy farm with 17 cows in north Down, with a guaranteed market in Belfast, made a profit of £87 a year when all expenses, including labour, were paid. Official figures from the Ministry of Agriculture claimed that an income of £240 could be made on a 30 acre farm and £400 on larger holding, but the amount of profit would have been considerably smaller. Official figures also suggested that only market gardeners and milk producers in north Down or larger mixed farmers in north Antrim would have a turnover of more than £800 a year, and in the poorer areas even such modest figures would have been unattainable. For thousands of small farmers keeping body and soul together was an achievement, and official reports abounded in statistical assessments of the amount by which the income of rural families was above or below the poverty line. Despite the provisions of the embryonic welfare state, there were times of hardship when many rural families were saved from actual want by the charity of neighbours. When a skilled worker could make a steady wage of more than £4 a week in a woollen factory in Lisbellaw in County Fermanagh, there was little incentive to continue scratching a living from the reluctant soil of the home farm.

Finally, housing conditions in rural areas were primitive. An official report in 1944 reckoned that of 160,000 rural houses throughout Northern Ireland around 25% were overcrowded and 11% totally unfit for habitation. In poor areas like Fermanagh, out of a housing stock of almost 12,000, those figures could be as high as 21% overcrowded and 37% unfit. At Hannahstown in the high land north of Belfast, thousands of people had moved to temporary huts to escape the Blitz in 1941 and some were still there in the early 50s, with families of five and six living in wooden boxes five feet high, and rooms of less than 20 square feet. On the farms, the government's Farm Building Scheme gave 50% grants towards the building or renovation of piggeries, barns, calving houses, silos and the like, and meant that in many instances the byre and the dairy were cleaner and of sounder construction than the farmer's home. Over 90% of houses had no electricity or gas, and a similar proportion had no running water or toilet facilities. Even in a prosperous area like north Down only 4% of farm houses had a bathroom; while in Fermanagh, where the water table was high and drainage difficult, 96% of all houses were without running water or sanitation. Some of these Fermanagh houses were still built with mud walls, and others had water sources which were so polluted by farmyard effluent that it was said people drank tea to mask the taste of the boiled water. The Silent Valley reservoir was only opened in August 1952 and during the previous month a prolonged spell of dry weather led to severe water restrictions in towns as geographically separated as Omagh, Antrim, Portadown and Portrush, with many people reverting to the local wells once more. The *Belfast Telegraph* in 1955 suggested that "the village pump may soon be a thing of the past", although even a comparatively large town like Newry still had a town water cart which supplied Daisy Hill hospital during dry spells, and Lurgan hospital relied on the local Fire Brigade to pump additional supplies. In the mid-50s villages like Ballywalter, Greyabbey, Portaferry and Kircubbin were still without piped water, and it would be years before all the small villages in Fermanagh and Tyrone were connected to the mains.

The Housing on Farms legislation passed in 1950 and 52 gave grants for new and reconditioned houses, and conditions began to improve. Ranges replaced open hearths for cooking, slates and corrugated iron replaced thatched roofs, the latter acquiring connotations of social inferiority. For every romantic who mourned the passing of the whitewashed cottage with its green-painted half-door and small windows, with cooking accomplished over a turf fire, there were dozens of realists who had no regrets about leaving damp and draughty rooms, walls built of rough stone held together by lime mortar, smoking fires and primitive kitchens, where water was carried in, one white enamel pail at a time. The embrace of the modern had its negative sides of course. The ruins of deserted cottages were scattered throughout the countryside, with little attempt made to rescue and preserve what was attractive about them, while new bungalows in inappropriate styles began to spring up along the main roads, leading to complaints about pebble-dashed suburbia being transported to the countryside. Poorer land which had been cultivated to meet the demand for wartime food was allowed to fall out of use and revert to rough grazing once more. As output increasingly turned towards pasture rather than tillage, even the appearance of the countryside altered. As early as 1945 the Planning Advisory Board was warning that ribbon development, the destruction of woodland and the renewed growth of private motoring were threatening the countryside as never before. The Board's Report noted with regret that "scenes once typical of the beauty of Ulster have ceased to be so, not so much from any deliberate intention to despoil as from lack of taste and of a sense of responsibility." How those deficiencies were to be removed however was a larger issue than the Board felt able to address.

With mechanisation came less inter-dependence, and less neighbourliness. In most rural areas two horses were necessary in order to operate the larger items of machinery, and those with a single horse each pooled their resources. In Fermanagh it was called 'cooring', in Down it was 'partnership', in Antrim 'neighbouring' or 'morrowing', but in all parts it was dying out as tractors became more common. Similarly, the hiring fairs which traditionally had been held in early May and November when agricultural labourers signed up for a six-month period of service had given way to short-term arrangements under which workers could be laid off during slack periods and receive National Assistance. The dances which used to be held to mark the end of a task involving communal labour – in parts of County Down it was known, appropriately, as a 'punch dance' – declined for the same reason. It was noted that, although farmer and labourer still worked side by side in the fields, on the more affluent farms they now ate at separate tables in the house. The gradual spread of rural electrification made numerous farming tasks easier, but it altered the ambience of the countryside, tidying it up and scrubbing it clean, and according to some authorities eliminating the once-universal belief in fairies and ghosts. The *ceilidh* houses where the menfolk of the neighbourhood would gather to talk over local affairs, often observing a rigid social pecking order, fell out of use. Fair days and harvest festivals were disappearing. Lighting a bonfire on Midsummer's Night and celebrating with old Irish songs and dances, which was a custom probably dating back to pagan times, was still celebrated near Portglenone in 1950, but was another tradition felt to be at risk. As one commentator noted: "The base of the older social life, the system of mutual aid between neighbours, has now ceased to be essential with the introduction of improved [farm] implements and greater wealth ... Once the necessity to work together has disappeared ... the customs of the age also vanish."

Bureaucracy was taking the place of custom. By the middle of the decade legislation had been brought in to give agricultural workers seven days' holiday a year, together with six additional days to be selected from a list of 11 public holidays. Soon afterwards consideration was being given by the government to introducing health and safety measures on farms, because the growing use of machinery and potentially dangerous chemicals was making the farmyard more hazardous than before. It was acknowledged that there would be objections from the preponderance of farms which were still run on a family basis, but if agriculture was to become a professionally organised industry, the keeping of records would be essential. Somewhere on the horizon an organisation called the

European Common Market was beginning to make itself known. By the early 60s 16,000 acres of land had fallen out of cultivation, and the 160,000 people who had worked on the land at the beginning of the decade were down to 115,000, with no sign of the trend ceasing.

But if rural housing was primitive, some conditions in towns could only be described as appalling. Inevitably the worst examples were from the cities where people were crowded together in slums which bore a resemblance to Dickensian London. A family of 11 was reported living in a cowshed on Belfast's Springfield Road. In Lonsdale Street (now demolished but near Carlisle Circus) 437 people lived in 26 houses – an average of 17 per house; and in another part of same street 74 families (176 adults, 109 children under 10) were accommodated in 16 houses. 18 people were reported occupying a small 'parlour house' off the Ormeau Road. Derry's Bogside was a honeycomb of lanes, alleyways and houses 150–200 years old, populated in part by children of dubious parentage who were regarded as an inevitable part of a seaport population. In another area of the city a family of 13 was found living in a house so decrepit that the road had to be cordoned off during the inspection in case the vibration from passing traffic would cause it to collapse. In Larne a survey of 180 houses found only nine with baths, 15 with inside toilets. In 1960 Derriaghy village outside Lisburn had rows of mud-built cottages 200 years old. The population density in Belfast was almost 30 people per acre, compared with Bristol's 17 and Edinburgh's 14; but within that overall figure some of the inner city areas had densities well in excess of 100, and in one ward almost 160, with 80% of the houses either overcrowded or unfit for habitation. All was not gloom however: in 1951 it was decided that in keeping with the 'progress and respectability' of Fintona in County Tyrone, with a population in the low hundreds, its lanes and alleys should in future be designated as 'Terraces' and 'Villas'.

The Government realised the gravity of situation – the 1951 census showed that overcrowding was at virtually the same level as in 1937 – and did not attempt to ignore it, but there were limits to the efforts which could be made to deal with the problem. A survey undertaken in 1943 showed that 70% of all existing houses in Northern Ireland were in need of repair to a greater or lesser extent, and it was estimated that at least 100,000 new houses would be required to deal satisfactorily with the situation. Although the criteria as to what constituted fitness seemed to be variable, in Belfast alone there were 12,000 homes deemed unfit for human habitation. The damage caused to the housing stock in Belfast by the Blitz of 1941 had added to pre-existing problems, the Unionist government having firm views on the undesirability of government intervention in matters such as housing, but there were serious obstacles to improving the situation with any rapidity. As was the case in cities in Britain in the early 50s, shortages of cement, steel and construction materials imposed strict limitations on the amount of reconstruction which could be undertaken. On top of that was the question of priorities – besides houses, schools, hospitals and roads were also desperately needed. Pre-fabricated houses or 'pre-fabs' were intended as a temporary measure of relief, but all too often were occupied beyond the lifetime of their design specification, and became numbered in the unfit for habitation category. A post-war review of housing need concluded that the problem should not be tackled in isolation, and besides slum clearance there was an urgent need for improvements in education and health provision, as well as in planning and reconstruction services. It was a realistic assessment of the situation, but it made the dimensions of the task even more daunting.

District councils and local authorities had a statutory obligation to provide new houses, but here, too, progress was desperately slow. Finance was obviously an issue. Carrickfergus Borough Council in 1951 accepted a tender of £645,000 for 400 houses, or some £1,600 per dwelling, which was comparatively expensive when compared with the private sector (see page 25). Some authorities were reluctant to build houses for political reasons – they might have to be given to tenants of the wrong political persuasion, and hence upset the delicate voting balance which existed – and some objected to providing homes for people in receipt of National Assistance, on the grounds that such people would be incapable of paying the rent or looking after a proper house. (Such reluctant authorities might have looked with envy at Clones Urban Council in County Monaghan, which in 1953 ruled out building houses on a site popularly believed to be occupied by fairies, and where retaliation was feared.) In the inter-war period Rural and District Councils in Northern Ireland had built over 4,000 workers' cottages which were of a higher standard that most rural dwellings – even if no running water was laid on a dry toilet was provided – but for the most part local councils were reluctant to incur levels of expenditure which would lead to an increase in local rates, and were constantly pestering central government for higher levels of subsidy. Central government, not unnaturally, refused to give more money without having a greater say in how it was spent, and councils everywhere refused to surrender their powers. The Northern Ireland Housing Trust had been created in 1945 to supplement the efforts of the local authorities, and by the early 50s was responsible for some 70 estates in urban and rural areas. It was almost universally regarded as being scrupulously fair in its allocation of homes, and served as a standing reproach to the local authorities. In 1952 the Trust reported with justifiable pride that in a rent collection of £275,000 the previous year only £78 was outstanding as arrears, figures which indicated its reputation as a good landlord.

In Belfast there was insufficient room to build the number of houses required, but there was also strong opposition to the idea of expanding the city boundary to take in greenfield sites which could be used for large-scale development. In 1950 a proposal was made to build 10,000 new houses at Dundonald and Holywood, and 4,000 in west Belfast, but Down and Antrim County Councils refused to give up land, primarily on the grounds that they would derive no rates or revenue from schemes which were for the benefit of Belfast Corporation. Without providing details of its calculations Ballycastle Urban Council claimed that under any such proposal it stood to lose the equivalent of £15,000 in rateable income, and accused Belfast of seeking to become a 'statelet'. Lisburn Rural District Council protested that it had developed the communities of Finaghy and Dunmurry from green field sites to support a population of 10,000 and if Belfast was to encroach, plans for further development would be nullified. A Planning Commission in 1952 recommended the creation of two new townships – one taking in the districts of Glengormley, Carnmoney, Whiteabbey and Jordanstown, the other Finaghy, Dunmurry, Suffolk and upper Falls – and both to be subject to controlled development. Again the two County Councils rallied opposition: Belfast was becoming too big and attracting all the available industry, land was being sacrificed which could be used for food production, there were no proper transport links to get people to and from work, shops or venues for entertainment which would remain in Belfast. One MP felt that if Belfast got any bigger and was made more powerful, Stormont would end up as little more than an elected body rubber-stamping the decisions of the Corporation. It was a classic example of planning decisions being taken in a limited context and subject to objections by vested interests at local level. Nor was the government anxious to prioritise large-scale shifts of population which might have an adverse impact on electoral balances in and around Belfast. Some progress was made however. The Belvoir Park estate, which had been used by the Admiralty as an armaments depot during the war, was acquired by the Housing Trust in 1955, and by agreement with Hillsborough Council (which by an accident of history was the responsible authority) part of it was made available for large-scale development. By 1958 a number of other experiments in dispersed housing in south Antrim led to the merging of seven villages and new housing estates to form Newtownabbey, which with one bound acquired a population of around 35,000 and became the third largest town in Northern Ireland.

(The name chosen was a combination of 'new town' and Whiteabbey, but the alternatives which had been debated included Dalriada, Queenstown, Coole, Edenmore and even Parkerstown after Dame Dehra Parker, the Health Minister who was responsible for housing.) Everyone understood, even if they did not approve of, the importance of managing electoral support and voting registers, so it was taken for granted that the allocation of housing on the new estates would for the most part be organised along sectarian lines. Although there were some signs of mixing in middle class housing developments, it was generally assumed – and not incorrectly – that people in working class areas strongly preferred living among their co-religionists. Religious leaders complained that these new housing developments often neglected to provide places of worship, and with an increasingly paganised population "all kinds of godless and Communistic propaganda will be given a free field."

The alternative to dispersed housing was inner city redevelopment, building smaller dwellings in order to maximise the use of available space. As the post-war Labour government began introducing its ideas of a controlled economy and state regulation, so the planners warmed to the idea that they would decide where people ought to live. Le Corbusier, urging the creation of machines for living in, rather than homes, became the architectural god, and developers in devastated cities throughout Britain saw high-rise flats as the logical way of rehousing the maximum number of people in the minimum amount of scarce inner-city space. Unfortunately from the planners' point of view people throughout Britain hated being displaced and objected to moving into multi-storey flats, seen as tenements, and Belfast was no exception. City Councillors were happy to insist that their electors wanted separate houses with a small garden facing onto the street and in close proximity to their neighbours, and that this was an ideal which could be realised. Multi-storey flats would lead to the occupants leading an institutionalised way of life, contrary to "the homes of their dreams with a little patch of grass." The fact that even by the late 1950s there were still Blitz sites in Belfast which had not been developed suggested that the City fathers had their own idea of what priority should be given to re-housing the least fortunate citizens. One irate Councillor claimed that "if a blackbird sang in a Belfast park on Sunday there would be a deputation to the City Hall next day to have the bird destroyed for desecrating the Sabbath, but no one seems to bother about the poor homeless families." Belfast Corporation had its own views about where responsibility lay for providing new housing and was never averse to developing a case that central government should take a more active role in financing the venture. The government refused to accept responsibility for what it saw as Belfast's problems or indeed to assume overall responsibility for housing, but was equally unwilling to direct local authorities to deal with the issue. Political *amour-propre* was preserved, but the homeless suffered.

A few tentative efforts were made. In 1952 a development of flats at Skegoneill and Parkmount in north Belfast was opened as what was admitted to be an experiment, with even the Minister of Health acknowledging that Belfast people were not accustomed to flats and viewed them with misgiving. Other cautious and piecemeal efforts were made – the estate of low-rise flats along Annadale Embankment, and a tower block on the Castlereagh Road – but it was 1960 before large-scale redevelopment was undertaken. A public inquiry was held into Belfast Corporation's proposals for clearing the area around Upper Library Street/Carrick Hill, where it was suggested that the 1,300 existing houses in the area should be replaced with 426 multi-storey blocks of flats, some of 15 floors, many of five and six storeys, accommodating 65% of the original inhabitants. Given the extent of overcrowding which existed, 100% replacement was not an option, but protests were inevitable and 15 barristers and 30 firms of solicitors were engaged to make representations on behalf of the existing residents against the proposals. At the end of the inquiry it was reported that the main ground of objection was not the replacement levels, but the fact that many people simply did not want to live in flats.

Whether the outcome was satisfactory or not, the fact that public consultation on the proposals had been undertaken was in itself evidence that at last there was some recognition of the need to tackle the housing problem in a more holistic manner. Approving the Corporation's plans in April 1960 the Minister of Health stated that adjustments would be made in the light of developments, that more low-rise blocks might be built to accommodate large families and older people, and that provision would be made for pubs and other social amenities to be located where they would be best utilised. At best it represented a genuflection towards social partnership, and it represented state intervention to an extent that would have been unthinkable before the War, but it embodied the belief that drastic problems required drastic solutions. It was not accidental that 1960 also saw proposals being made for a Belfast Area Development Plan, and the arrival from Edinburgh University of Professor Robert Matthew to make a strategic survey of housing need in Northern Ireland. In his interim report, published in 1961, Matthew warned of the serious consequences which would result if the countryside around Belfast continued to be developed in a haphazard manner. He was confronted with the situation where, in an unprecedented flurry of activity sites for more than 5,000 houses had already been selected by local authorities at Dundonald, Monkstown and Dunmurry, while the Housing Trust in quiet continuance of its remit had earmarked six areas for another 3,000 homes, and around 2,000 new houses a year were being privately built on the fringes of the city. As developers seized the reins, it looked as if the mistakes made in the replacement of rural cottages were about to be replicated on a massive scale.

Matthew's plea for a Regional Plan was based on the belief that Belfast's natural amenities and valuable agricultural land were at serious risk unless there was an agreed approach to future development. It would take time for such ideas to become accepted, and grievous architectural and environmental horrors would be perpetrated in the meantime, but by the early 60s it was becoming clear that to meet the wider needs of society, the needs of the individual (or at least his wish for a small patch of garden at the front of his house) would have to be set aside. But there might also have been the glimmerings of the realisation that elimination of slums and old, decayed communities, unless handled properly could also lead to the loss of desirable, if largely intangible aspects of city life.

One of the objectives of those providing public housing was to make it affordable. In 1950 the Housing Trust announced its intention to charge a maximum rent of 14s (70p) a week, on the grounds that no one should be asked to spend more than a fifth of his total income on rent and rates. Private housing by our standards would seem to have been even more affordable. In 1951 the most expensive house sold in Belfast was a two-bedroom, four reception house on the Malone Road built in 1935 and now costing £9,000; but around the same time a terrace house in Bangor could be had for £200 down and monthly repayments of just under £5. The following year a nine-bedroom house in a 'select' but unidentified area of Belfast was selling for £4,250, but it was pointed out that if only four bedrooms had been on offer the cost would have been nearer £5,000, because larger houses were not selling well in 1952. Indeed, it was noted that larger houses which had been on the market in 1951 at £1,900 were now fetching only £1,200 to £1,300 because the demand now was for two reception and three bedrooms. New houses in a development off the Cregagh Road – two reception, three bedrooms with 15 amp electric plugs in some rooms – were available for £155 down and repayments of just over £2 a month. Later in the decade, a 'smaller villa' in one of the new suburbs cost £1,500 – a deposit of £150, £80 for Stamp Duty, and repayments of less than £12 a month over 25 years. By the late 50s loans of more than three times the borrower's income were available, which suggests that large numbers of people were getting their feet on the housing ladder. That, if true, would seem to represent a change from the beginning of the decade when expectations were distinctly modest. In 1950 the Halifax Building Society was encouraging savings towards home deposit by pointing out that 2s (10p) saved per month would, with interest, yield £21 over 14 years; or for the comparatively well-off £5 a month would generate almost £1,100 over the same period.

There were also bargains to be had outside Belfast. A three-bedroom semi-detached villa in Glengormley with luxury fittings which included polished oak floors, chrome door fittings, a plug for an electric clock in both lounge and dining room, and a Bakelite seat on the WC was on the market for £1,500. In 1956 a three-reception, four-bedroom house with a double garage set in almost two acres of ground and close to Ballynahinch golf club could be had for around £3,500; and in the same price bracket was a detached villa in Cultra with three reception and five bedrooms overlooking Belfast Lough. For expenditure of just over £4,000 a purchaser could pick up a five-bedroom mansion in its own grounds at Warrenpoint; or an architect-designed bungalow in 30 acres at Ballinamallard, six miles from Enniskillen; or a Georgian residence with five principal bedrooms plus outbuildings and 130 rolling acres at Dervock. Affordability, of course, is relative and as will be noted later, Northern Ireland in the 50s was not awash with people who could afford £4–5,000 for a country residence, no matter how desirable.

Desirability, too, is a flexible concept. New houses on offer in 1950 in Notting Hill off Belfast's Malone Road had central heating, a combined kitchen and dining room, and large floor to ceiling windows. This for the time was rather *avant-garde* and was relatively unpopular – it appeared that most people preferred a 'good room' (to be referred to either as 'the parlour' or 'the drawing room') with a separate kitchen and dining room, all furnished with traditional solid three-piece suites and imposing sideboards. Again questions of affordability arose. Gilpin's in Belfast could provide a three-piece Chesterfield suite at prices from £19 to £69, a walnut bedroom suite from £57 to £73, and an eight-piece dining room suite, including sideboard for just under £80. Tughan's offered to fit out drawing room, dining room and bedroom for £216 for first quality furnishings, or £119 for less expensive appointments, plus pianos from £45 to £65. For purposes of Sunday afternoon entertaining in 'the good room' a 21-piece tea-set cost just over £2, and was likely to be patterned with roses, while a china display cabinet to show it off could be obtained for just over £10. In the kitchen, built-in units had yet to evolve and a respectable kitchen cabinet cost £16; but Formica was beginning to make its bow as the wonder material that was scratch resistant, heat resistant, non-fading and easy to clean on kitchen work surfaces.

The modern home could be kept clean with a Hoover, confidently advertised as "the world's best vacuum cleaner" at £33, aided by a Hoover floor and furniture polisher for £30. A washing machine with super-efficient wringer on top was £42, but a fridge was £78. Such figures help explain why throughout the UK in the mid-50s over 50% of homes had vacuum cleaners, 18% had washing machines but only 8% had fridges. In 1952 it was noted with approval that it now looked as if a standardised three-pin plug would soon be available for fitting to all appliances. The trend for 'do-it-yourself' or DIY was beginning to catch on – Dulux white paint was introduced in 1953 and soon replaced brown or dark green, the former favourites to cover grubby surfaces. Distemper, the chalk-based paint which dried to a powdery finish and adhered to the clothing of anyone brushing against it, gave way to oil-based emulsions in an ever-increasing range of colours. *Practical Householder* was launched in 1955, with bright front covers which almost invariably featured a pipe-smoking man showing his wife or son and daughter-in-law how to disguise a disused fireplace, or convert an old treadle-powered sewing machine into an attractive work table with built-in drawers. There was no comparable magazine with step-by-step instructions to show what should be done when, as must have been the case in thousands of instances, nails were accidentally hammered through water pipes and plaster was stripped off walls along with the wallpaper of former decades. Countless gallons of paint were used to cover wooden wainscoting, door frames, mantelpieces, bannisters and any other articles of domestic architecture which seemed at odds with the bright new world of plastic and electricity. By 1959 it was noted that central heating was now being installed in some homes and it could be expected that many new houses would incorporate it during construction. Claims were modest – an oil-fired boiler and three or four small radiators to provide background heating in the bedrooms would cost around £280 and cost about £1 a week to run; but in 1960 an enthusiastic female MP declared, without irony, that central heating was "man's gift to women in the 20th century."

It is difficult to make an estimate of the state of health enjoyed by the people who lived in these houses. A new Ministry of Health and Local Government was created in 1944, and a series of Acts, culminating in the Health Service Act of 1948, went a long way towards restructuring health care and dealing with the decades of neglect which had gone before. The proposals published in 1947 envisaged that all services should be free of charge, at a cost of £5,510,000 a year, or around £4 per head of population.

That sum was to be met through the UK Exchequer contribution of £4,380,000, plus local contributions to National Health Insurance amounting to £930,000, and the remainder coming from local rates. For the poorer members of society, for whom medical care had been a luxury only to be contemplated as a last resort, this was a transformation. But there were also reservations. Within the Protestant community there was a deeply-ingrained belief that 'the Ulsterman' was a hard-working, self-reliant individual, instinctively distrustful of centralised authority, and the idea that, in what soon became known as 'the welfare state' he would be looked after from the cradle to the grave, offended his sense of sturdy independence. In this view, state control and centralised planning would stifle the energy and native genius of the people, and diminish the qualities that had made Northern Ireland strong and successful. On the Catholic side was an unquestioning belief that the role of the state and that of the Church should each be kept within defined boundaries, and that unto Caesar should be rendered only what was rightly Caesar's. If the secular powers were given authority in all matters of health care they would intrude into sensitive areas such as childbirth, where the Church had moral and spiritual dominion. There were even fears that comprehensive welfare provision would deprive Catholics of opportunities to exercise Christian charity and earn rewards in the afterlife. Within a few years the moral reservations of both communities were set aside as the practical benefits of state welfare became impossible to ignore or reject, and the lives of countless thousands of citizens became immeasurably better as a result; but in retrospect it is possible to see that the price which was paid was a diminution in the sense of self-reliance which had existed both individually and collectively, and a further erosion of the community spirit which hitherto had sustained people through difficult times.

Of course, Northern Ireland being what it was, even health care could not be allowed to escape from denominational blight. The Mater Infirmorum on Belfast's Crumlin Road had been run as a semi-religious foundation for many years, depending on financial support from well-wishers on both sides of the religious divide. In 1948 its Board of Trustees decided that the hospital could not come within the new arrangements required by the Health Services Act and still be run on Catholic ethical principles. The consequence was that the hospital, despite being non-denominational in the care it provided, was refused access to state funding, and for many years thereafter depended in a large part on the money raised by the YP (Young Philanthropists) football pools. It was acknowledged that the Mater made an invaluable contribution to the provision of health care for a substantial number of the citizens of Belfast, but, as was also the case with schools, the issue of voluntary status outside the state system was one of political sensitivity, and in the interests of avoiding confrontation with some of its supporters, the government preferred to ignore the unfairness of the situation. It did not redress the balance by any means, but the government also ignored claims made by the National Union of Protestants that the numbers of Catholics entering hospitals as either patients or staff was making it more difficult for the Union to carry out its work of evangelising, because hymn singing in mixed wards was not being permitted.

The official causes of death in Northern Ireland recorded in 1952 included 5,000 dying from heart diseases, 2,000 from cancer and 1,600 from diseases of the nervous system. Although an epidemic of flu and pneumonia in early 1951 was briefly responsible for almost 100 deaths a week, the figures showed that TB, bronchitis and typhoid were all in decline. There were still deaths from what would now be regarded as comparatively minor ailments like whooping cough, appendicitis and measles, and there was something chilling about the lists published in the daily newspapers by the Northern Ireland Fever Hospital. Patients on entry to the hospital were assigned a number and their progress could be tracked through the daily lists as (and if) they moved from Category 1 (dangerously ill) down to Category 4 (convalescent). Visiting was allowed to patients in Categories 3 and 4 but only inquiries by phone for Categories 1 and 2 at specified hours during the morning and evening.

Figures for three main causes of death quoted above had increased by the end of the decade, but the impression of worsening health could easily be misleading. At the beginning of the 50s the Health Service was still new and people's attitude towards it still cautious, and many refrained from coming forward for treatment. Different methods of diagnosis, or classification of diseases, or even improved means of recording statistics could all have helped to make an exact comparison with earlier years difficult. Certainly a drive was on to make better provision for public health. In 1951 plans were announced for seven new or expanded hospitals including Dundonald, Altnagelvin, Gransha, Erne, and Coleraine in the period up to 1965, with a view to providing 5,350 new beds at cost of £14 million. In terms of scope and expense it was remarkably ambitious, and it perhaps deserves to be contrasted with the lesser emphasis being placed on housing, but it was putting in place the beginnings of a legacy. In 1951 there were 100,000 admissions to hospital, and 900,000 out-patient attendances, but with growing numbers of x-ray examinations, laboratory tests and physiotherapy treatments it would not be long before waiting lists would have to be implemented. By way of comparison in 2006–2007 there were 518,000 admissions and 1.5 million attendances, figures far in excess of anything the original planners could have anticipated.

Irrespective of the mortality figures, smoking was not a major health worry. A British survey in 1949 found that 79% of men and 38% of women smoked, with 15 a day average for men, and seven for women, with Woodbines the most popular working-class brand. Another survey in 1958 indicated that the figures for smoking among men were slightly down, those for women slightly up, and there is no reason to suspect that the figures for Northern Ireland were significantly different. Indeed, far from being regarded as a health hazard, smoking was promoted as being positively beneficial. Coaches were happy to go on the record claiming that a cigarette before an important race was helpful in settling an athlete's nerves. It was noted that one of the teams in the FA Cup semi-finals in 1952 had introduced a special training regime which involved early nights, nutritious meals "and not overdoing the smoking." Stanley Matthews, the hero of the 1954 FA Cup Final and a near-teetotal vegetarian, and Stirling Moss the Grand Prix racing driver, were both happy to personally endorse the Craven A brand, which they claimed "gives me all I want of a smoke, and nothing I don't".

Personalities like Matthews and Moss may have been helping to mould popular opinion, but they were also reflecting it. A medical officer at Carrickfergus hospital deplored the fact that when he did his rounds he often came across four or five visitors sitting round a patient's bed and smoking "as if they were in a concert hall". A Stormont MP complained that going to the cinema in Belfast was comparable to sitting in the middle of a London peasouper fog; but when the cinemas in Derry had their ventilation systems overhauled to ensure better smoke extraction system and improved clarity they had to reassure nervous customers that the temperature would not be reduced or comfort impaired. In 1956 when British Health Minister Robin Turton acknowledged a possible link between smoking and cancer, Harold Macmillan as Chancellor of the Exchequer was reported as exclaiming "I only hope it won't stop people smoking", because of the revenue which would be lost. The British Medical Association annual conference that year reluctantly agreed to a smoking ban, but on condition that it applied only to part of the proceedings, and was not permanent. Some so-called experts claimed that being a stone overweight represented more of a risk of premature death than 25 cigarettes a day, while others stated with confidence that more damage was caused by a single day's exposure to fog and urban pollution than 20 cigarettes a day for a year. Every young person who took up smoking had probably passed through a phase when replica cigarettes had been a desirable item of confectionery, particularly when consumed on a cold day when breath produced a realistic impression of smoke.

It was 1957 before the Medical Research Council decided that since one in eight lifelong smokers was likely to die of lung cancer (as opposed to one in 300 non-smokers) there was probably a link. The *Belfast Telegraph* however rejected the proposal that smoking should be banned in public places, seeing this as unwarranted intervention by the state and an infringement of individual liberty. In Stormont Professor Lloyd-Dodd claimed that pipe-smoking was positively beneficial, and warned that, since the debate on the link between smoking and lung cancer was still unresolved, the Ministry of Health should remain neutral and not get drawn into the issue of supporting smoking bans. Before the end of the decade cigarettes were being presented in more attractive ways in crush-resistant packets with flip tops, and gift vouchers began a new craze. Brands like Kensitas and Ardath led the voucher charge which was soon to be followed by other brands, the manufacturers calculating, rightly, that the prospect of a free gift was a short-time inducement to smoking far more alluring than any thoughts of long-term consequences. In any case, the negative effects of smoking were being conquered it seemed. By 1957 the Professor of Pathology at Queen's was predicting that, with 50,000 new drugs now being tested each year it was only a matter of time before a cure for cancer was found.

Smokers in Northern Ireland seemed undeterred by possible health risks, and local tobacconists dispensed Four Square, Park Drive, Woodbine, Gallaher's Blues, Craven A, Bristol, Airman, Dunhill, Senior Service, Players, du Maurier, Baron's, Churchman's No 1 and Olivier among others at prices ranging from 3–4s (15–20p) for 20. Cigarettes with filter tips had been re-introduced after the War to cut down on the amount of tobacco which had to be imported, and although these were at the cheaper end of the spectrum they were, at least initially, disliked by smokers accustomed to getting an undiluted inhalation of nicotine and tar. In terms of advertising no holds were barred. Craven A, for instance, was portrayed as the cigarette for young lovers: "When two young people share the same taste, their hearts are one. When that taste is Craven A … their preference is based on rich, fine tobacco, so cool to smoke, so kind to the throat … with a natural cork tip that protects the lips and keeps the end firm …" By implication un-tipped cigarettes were for old people who relished throat problems and soggy, bedraggled ends with wisps of tobacco hanging out. The filter tip battle was soon won however, and before the end of the decade Philip Morris was being promoted as the premium cigarette with real American flavour, which was presented as evidence that smokers' palates were becoming more discerning. An irate representative of the Grocers' Association who complained that a housewife would rather spend money on a packet of cigarettes than on a pound of butter to feed her family rather missed the point. Butter was never advertised as sexy and sophisticated, and the desirable adjunct of a lifestyle. For those who did worry about health, cigar smoke was held to be less harmful to the mouth and throat than cigarettes. Pipes were also popular and, at least in the advertisements, were felt to lend an air of authority and rugged reliability to the chap who gripped the straight stem between his manly teeth while driving an open-topped sports car, gardening, fixing bicycle punctures, wallpapering or carrying out any domestic chores which did not make him look as if he would ever don an apron and enter the kitchen. In 1956 an ounce of Gallaher's Condor Flake cost the equivalent of 18d, and in 1960 a similar quantity of Wills Handy Cut Flake 22d. Even the acquisition of authority and rugged reliability, it seemed, was becoming more expensive.

In terms of daily health non-prescription medicines were plentiful. Bile Beans – "enjoy the radiant health that makes life worth living" – were a curiously-named laxative that promised to cure everything from blackheads to 'women's complaints'. Aspro not only fought off the symptoms of cold and flu but was also an essential weapon in the war against modern high pressure living: "You'll shed the load of all that depression, and ther'll be no harmful side effects either – just a feeling of peace and wellbeing which has to be experienced to be believed." Andrews Liver Salts cleansed, freshened, soothed and toned the body "and happily is not habit-forming." Milk of Magnesia was promoted as a cold remedy, as a laxative called Mil-Par to "leave the system sweet and cleansed", and in Phillips toothpaste as a protection against mouth acid, which, as was well known, was the reason why half the population lost their teeth before the age of 40. Advice on dentures, incidentally, recommended that boiling water and sharp instruments should not be used to clean them. Since a full set cost over £4 there was an incentive to treat them as a valuable commodity. They were also essential for gripping the stem of a pipe.

In a trial, the details of which were not disclosed, the manufacturers of Sanatogen claimed that their product boosted energy levels from 8% to 66% after two weeks, Sloan's Liniment expanded veins to allow poisons and waste matter to be flushed away, and De Witt's Pills did same by treating the bloodstream. Enos Fruit Salt promised "to overcome the ill effects of lack of exercise, stuffy rooms, warm crowded shops and cinemas – not to mention overcrowded trams, trains and buses." Virol was a wonder food for children, listing among its ingredients egg, malt extract, glucose and fruit sugars, orange juice, iron, calcium, pure beef fat and essential vitamins. It was also claimed as a well-known fact that "restless, irritating, annoying children are invariably worm infested. Beeline Worm Powders clear the system and rectify the problem" – the implication being that any residual displays of annoying behaviour were merely the manifestation of original sin. Beecham's Pills were "worth a guinea a box" because it was recognised by doctors that – ahem – 'regularity' was not enough and that a reliable laxative was needed from time to time. Beecham's Pills assisted in the three essential functions of digestion, absorption and elimination, and taken at bedtime guaranteed that "the sparkle will come back into your eyes. Your system will begin to glow with health. And you'll have lots of energy all day long."

To us this all sounds wonderfully quaint and innocent – a healthy, stress-free and energetic lifestyle could be obtained by popping a few Beecham's Pills at night, swigging down a glass of Sanatogen at lunchtime and chewing a few Aspro throughout the day in the intervals between lighting up another Craven A. Its worth reflecting however that the modern equivalent is a fixation with vitamin supplements and organic food. Holland and Barrett, the purveyors of vitamins and health supplements, currently offer hundreds of products from Aloe Vera through to Zinc precisely because they are holding out the same promises that were once made by Enos Fruit Salt and De Witt's Pills. It was written by a Family Doctor in 1951 but it has a contemporary ring: "So headlong is the rush of life today that we are all of us … steadily becoming more tense and anxious. Nothing less than a slowing up of this Gadarene stampede will give us back the tranquillity so essential to mental normality."

One new and significant cause of stress discovered by the 50s was the threat of nuclear war. An early article in the *Telegraph* in 1953 was reassuring – the heat and blast of atomic bombs were not as difficult to deal with as people imagined: for those living more than two miles from the impact point the burns wouldn't be particularly severe, and reasonably thick masonry with a few feet of soil banked against it would stop gamma ray penetration. The government's private assessment was considerably less optimistic. A Cabinet memorandum of October 1954 postulated an air-burst explosion from a 20 megaton device over Belfast. Total destruction would take place within a five mile radius, Lisburn would be damaged beyond repair, and severe damage caused to Carrickfergus and Newtownards. Significant structural damage would be caused to Portadown, Downpatrick and Ballymena. Serious fires could be expected to occur up to 20 miles from the explosion's epicentre, so towns such as Holywood, Comber, Ballynahinch, and Saintfield could be burned to the ground. An estimated 165,000 houses would be destroyed, along with 18 hospitals, and in terms of casualties it was anticipated that 500,000 people could be killed with another 120,000 seriously injured, and 100,000 left homeless. A bomb exploded at ground level would create less widespread damage, but would leave a crater a mile wide and 170 feet deep where Belfast had been. With only a two-minute warning likely in advance, evacuation was impossible, so dispersal of the population before an attack was considered to be the only hope. Derry was likely to also be bombed, so dispersal of the population would be tricky, and although the memorandum did not spell it out it seemed that parts of Tyrone and all of Fermanagh were likely to become more populous than at any time in their previous history. It soon became clear that radiation posed higher levels of long-term risk than had been thought, so even the above scenario was liable to understate the gravity of the situation.

There was little or no public debate on this, because the government felt, probably correctly, that if such horrifying facts became known panic and hopelessness would set in to an extent which was liable to cause permanent damage to the fabric of society. Planning, which involved the creation of Priority Classes and Additional Classes, proceeded on the assumption that Belfast and Derry would be hit only by some of the less powerful hydrogen bombs. In 1957 it was reported that plans had been drawn up to move 300,000 people out of Belfast in three days, but no details emerged as to how this was to be done, where they would go, and who would be left behind. Three years later it was proposed to purchase Gough Barracks in Armagh as a future HQ for Civil Defence. It was now assumed that there would be a warning period of up to a week before bombs or missiles were deployed, which would give sufficient time for the new quarters to be occupied by the Cabinet and selected senior officials. Other officials would be dispersed to other locations to ensure the discharge of essential services during 'the survival period'. Emergency planning has to take place on the basis that arrangements for the continuity of government are necessary, but such arrangements always prompt questions about what exactly the Minister of Education or the Minister of Labour would be doing in the bunker as nuclear explosions decimated the population.

It is difficult to recapture the sense of threat which existed in a generation which had experienced the practical consequences of war only a few years previously. In 1951 an international conference of astronomers in London listened to a paper by Dr Wernher von Braun predicting that it would soon be possible to place satellite rockets in stable orbit round the earth and that these would act as fuelling stations for a 50 man team which would commence the colonisation of Mars. This was not taken seriously at the time, but by the middle years of the decade rocket science had advanced to the stage where Russia and the US were competing in the development of ICBMs (Inter-Continental Ballistic Missiles) which could deliver nuclear warheads at speeds and over distances which meant that nowhere in the world was safe. Early in 1956 it was reported that at Woomera in south Australia British scientists were working on a top secret project which had the objective of developing a rocket system which was designed to transport mail across the Atlantic in three hours. It says a great deal about public credulity in the 50s that the authorities should have thought it was worthwhile to make so fatuous an announcement. The postal delivery service in due course was revealed to be the Blue Streak missile system, the components of which were each 60 feet long and capable of carrying two tons of nuclear warheads. It sounded so impressive that some people were surprised when, after a hideously expensive development period, the project was cancelled in 1960.

By 1957 newspapers in Northern Ireland were carrying numerous articles on the technicalities and capacities of nuclear weapons, the inability of defence systems to cope with them, the possibility of Britain buying missiles from America (with related issues of who then controlled their deployment), and British H-bomb tests in the Pacific. In an unusual display of internationalism, the Portadown Synod of the Methodist Church in April 1957 took account of all such developments and called for the nuclear powers to agree to a limitation on their testing programmes. The terms of debate changed abruptly in late 1957 when Russia launched the first Sputnik – 180 pounds weight and capable of orbiting the earth every 96 minutes. Thousands of people left their homes on the nights when the satellite was visible as a star moving slowly across the sky and wondered what it all portended. It was February 1958 before the US launched its first satellite, and by then it was clear that, even if there were few signs of von Braun's more advanced predictions coming true, the nuclear threat had assumed new dimensions. Dr EJ Opik, a research associate at Armagh Observatory, tried to settle nerves by claiming that to place in orbit a space vehicle the size of a car would require a launch rocket the size of an ocean liner: such launch capabilities did not yet exist, and a nuclear weapons launcher would have to be considerably bigger than any car currently on the road. People appeared to react to the enhanced threat either by ignoring or by trivialising it. In November 1957 the Christmas season kicked off with the arrival at a Belfast shopping centre of 'Santa and the Satellites', and shortly afterwards the well-known confectionery Rolo was advertising itself as "the perfect fuel for the inner man in outer space".

The Space Age had begun. By 1958 the Director of Armagh Observatory was speculating that the two moons of Mars could be either observatories or artificial satellites built by Martians even more advanced than mankind. Within a few years however, 100,000 people were in Trafalgar Square at a 'Ban the Bomb' rally to welcome the arrival of a group which had marched the 54 miles from the Atomic Weapons Research Establishment at Aldermaston in what was to become a regular event. International tension was high in 1960 as the Russians shot down a US spy plane and paraded the pilot, Lieutenant Gary Powers, making it clear that they were prepared to contemplate a nuclear war with America if necessary.

By then there were only 10,000 horses left on the farms of Northern Ireland, and almost 50,000 workers had left the land. Although it was noticed that lung cancer was on the rise, it was pointed out that cancer of the stomach was more common, and it would be 1962 before the link with smoking was firmly established. More and more green space was being devoured by vast new housing estates around Belfast, but virtually every town was beginning to develop its outer fringe of new dwellings, and the connecting roads were becoming increasingly cluttered with bungalows looking awkward and out of place in a rural landscape. These and other changes meant that the old distinction between city dwellers and their country cousins was becoming eroded as everyone came to town.

There were of course also signs that change was on the way in the wider world. In 1951 it was reported that an 'electronic brain' at Manchester University could undertake three million mathematical calculations in an hour – but it was 50 feet long, seven feet high and contained over 3,000 radio valves. In 1950, and again in 54, 58 and 59 there were warnings that Polar icecaps were melting. It was predicted that by 2000 the Arctic Ocean would be navigable all year round and with sea levels rising cities like London and New York would be vulnerable to severe flooding. In early 1953, in a dispute which was then 120 years old, a party of Argentinians were expelled from the Falkland Islands. There were reports that a short-sighted policy of over-fishing by certain nations was seriously depleting fish stock in the oceans, while the 'assassination' of forests and pillaging of fertile areas of the earth were bound to result in shortages. In 1954 an advertisement for *Picture Post* promised the dramatic story of Robert Cowell, a 23 year old Spitfire pilot and racing driver who disappeared in 1948 leaving two children, but who had now reappeared as Roberta Cowell, 'a modern young woman and potential wife', having undergone a change considered to be unique in human history. In 1960 the British Association for the Advancement of Science recommended a decimal system of coinage, arguing at the same time that decimalisation of weights and measures would be less beneficial. Had they but known it, people in the 50s were being offered a glimpse of the future.

CHAPTER 2

THE BARE NECESSITIES

IN THE PREVIOUS chapter the way was outlined in which Northern Ireland changed from being primarily rural and agricultural in character and became more urbanised, better housed and more prosperous, and how by the early 60s the atomic age and space travel might have been making people aware that the pace of change was liable to increase rather than the reverse. Such awareness is more perceptible in hindsight than it seemed to contemporaries, and for most people most of the time, life seemed to progress very much as it had always done. A preoccupation with the necessities of everyday life is a constant that links humanity across eons, never mind decades.

If the newspaper advertisements are a reliable guide, Northern Ireland in the 50s had a collective urge to stay healthy, which primarily involved avoiding the horrors of constipation, while getting on with a life of cigarette smoking. Part of the fixation with medicines of course can be attributed to a comparatively restricted diet, and although free welfare food like orange juice, cod liver oil and vitamin tablets were still available, only around a quarter of those entitled to them availed of these benefits. In the early 50s something of the wartime situation still remained. In Belfast the undeveloped sites of bombed buildings still paid testimony to the effects of the Blitz in 1941, reports continued to come in of war criminals being tried (850 of them were executed in the course of the 1950s) and above all, rationing was still in place.

The rationing regime was an extraordinary bureaucratic and administrative achievement. Every man, woman and child throughout the UK was given an Identity Card and entered on the National Register, and on 1 January 1947 there were 1,335,823 of them in Northern Ireland. Each holder of a Card became eligible to own a book of coupons issued on behalf of the Ministry of Food and renewed periodically. The coupons were traded in for specified quantities of food, adjusted from time to time as circumstances and supplies dictated. The Ministry's Regional Office was in Belfast, and District Offices and sub-offices administered the scheme elsewhere. Different regimes applied to different products, but

March 1947 was not untypical. 'Straight-rationed foods' were regarded as essential and were dispensed by quantity, for instance, eight ounces of sugar per week for an adult, three ounces of butter, three of margarine, two of cheese, two of bacon, and whatever meat could be purchased for 1s 4d (about 6½p). Bread, flour and 'bread confectionery' were rationed on a system of Bread Units, where one Unit was equivalent to seven ounces of bread per adult per week, or eight ounces of confectionery, or five and a half ounces of flour. Each adult received nine Bread Units a week, adolescents up to the age of 18 were considered to have growing appetites and received 13, and children under the age of four got five Units. 'Points-rationed food' consisted of produce outside the range of essentials, like tinned meat, fish or fruit, dried fruit, cereals and syrup. Each food was allocated a points quota, and each person was given 32 points for a four-week period to be spent as required. 'Personal points-rationed food' was controlled in much the same way, but applied specifically to chocolate and sugar confectionery or sweets. Everything within the regime was rated at 16 points to the pound weight, and each person was allocated 16 personal points for a four-week period. An entire generation of children regarded a visit to the sweet shop as the highlight of the week, as the selected quarter pound of clove rock, bull's eyes, caramel creams or aniseed balls was weighed and measured into a small paper bag, with possibly an extra one added if the shopkeeper was in a good mood. Finally, there were controlled foodstuffs like eggs, oranges and bananas and other perishable goods where a fixed ration could not be guaranteed, and these were distributed equitably as the available supplies allowed. Although not a foodstuff, soap and soap powder used fats in their manufacture and were subject to their own rationing regime, as were clothes and the supply of petrol. It seemed complicated, and there were ceaseless complaints, but overall the system was recognised as being as fair as possible for all concerned.

Various reasons were advanced for the maintenance of rationing several years after the War had ended. It was said that food and supplies were necessary to help feed those parts of Europe under British control. There were economic restraints imposed by the British government to help limit imports and thus minimise the amount of sterling leaving the economy. That same Labour government was dedicated to a planned economy, and decisions were taken that resources should be directed elsewhere than expanding food production. Whatever the reasons most people accepted continued rationing as a necessary evil, but the Conservatives fought the 1950 General Election promising to end the restrictions as soon as possible. Clothes rationing in fact ended in March

1949, and petrol rationing May 1950. The rationing of sweets was lifted in April 1949 but re-imposed in August as demand outstripped supply, and the restrictions lasted until early 1953. There was great excitement in 1952 when the restrictions on soap were lifted and Daz, Tide, Surf and Persil were released onto the market with advertising which suggested that henceforth washing would be undertaken using scientific principles appropriate to the atomic age.

Food rationing was impossible to escape however. Restrictions on bacon, butter, sugar, lard and even eggs and cream were difficult to accept in Northern Ireland given the amount of foodstuffs being shipped to Britain on a daily basis, or indeed available in the countryside where the writ of the Ministry of Food scarcely ran. Supplies were also plentiful in the Republic where rationing did not apply, and the smuggling of butter and other scarce goods by middle-class ladies became almost a respectable pastime. The rule was relaxed in 1950 that no restaurant could serve a meal costing more than 5s (25p), although the size of the portions served remained subject to rationing. Smoked salmon and steak were reported to be very popular in Belfast. In the same year however it was also acknowledged that many families would be sitting down to corned beef for Christmas dinner, and a box of Oxo cubes was regarded as an acceptable present for the festive season. It was also, perhaps, an indication of the prevailing culture that the *Belfast Telegraph* should publish a photograph of two RAF officers from Northern Ireland sitting at a pavement café somewhere in Germany having a cup of coffee. It was such a strange sight that the caption pointed out that such alfresco consumption was "an everyday occurrence" in parts of Europe.

The newspapers were full of recipes, many of them from the Ministry of Food, designed to make scarce items go as far as possible. Rabbit, which was de-rationed in 1950 was recommended as a delicious meal for four to six if enough vegetables were used in a stew or pie, although a sixth share of a rabbit could scarcely have satisfied the average carnivore. Galantine of rabbit, which involved boning, spicing, trussing, boiling, cooling and slicing the creature, must have seemed like a disproportionate amount of work for little reward. Prune Shape consisted of prunes boiled and sieved into a bowl of water and gelatine with a dash of lemon juice, which when set could be served by the proud hostess with whipped cream. Savoury fish loaf consisted of fish and breadcrumbs with a dash of vinegar and anchovy essence, bound together with reconstituted egg and either baked or steamed: it was supposed to be particularly tasty when eaten cold with a salad. Sausages had such a high bread content in relation to meat that careful cooking was required to ensure they did not end up as sticks of vaguely meat-flavoured toast. Late in 1951 when the Conservatives had regained power in Westminster Churchill asked to see what rationing meant in practice, and commented on the food displayed "Not bad, not a bad meal", and had to be informed that it represented a week's ration for an adult. It was clear that, even in Opposition, the wolf had not approached too closely to Winston's door. A survey by the National Federation of Wholesale Grocers in 1953 noted that in Northern Ireland there was an insatiable demand for biscuits; that porridge was by far the most favoured breakfast cereal and levels of consumption were on a par with those of Scotland; that cheese remained unpopular, and overall, that people in Northern Ireland seemed to require less variety in their groceries than in other parts of the UK.

At Stewart's Cash Stores, with its 62 branches throughout Northern Ireland, two pan loaves (baked with white, refined flour) could be bought for 1s (5p) or national loaves using inferior flour for slightly less. Biscuits were so popular that on one occasion in 1951 the Northern Ireland Biscuit Manufacturers had to appeal to housewives for tins to be returned so that full production could be resumed. Fresh-ground coffee came at the equivalent of 27d a pound, while a similar quantity of Nescafé instant coffee was almost twice as expensive, but being new and convenient was obviously well worth it. The consumption of tea increased enormously when it was de-rationed towards the end of 1952, but home baking was declining and likely to decline further as more pre-packed and tinned food became available. Representatives of the jam and preserves industry which was important in Armagh complained at the decline of the white bread 'piece', or the traditional jam sandwich which had filled the lunchboxes of schoolchildren and workmen before the war. In 1953 Kellogg's Corn Flakes were praised for having a high calorific content, which was not considered to be a threat to the waistline but rather an essential component of keeping warm and looking attractive. According to the Kellogg's advertisements cooked breakfasts were a nuisance in terms of preparation and washing up, but tea, bread and butter, and a bowl of cornflakes in the morning would provide 340 of the 2,500 calories which were needed each day. "Watch the girl who makes heads turn when she comes into the office. She's full of sparkle and energy. Her eyes are bright, her hair full of dancing lights, her complexion clear, her whole body brimming over with vitality." It was astonishing that the government did not make a breakfast of Corn Flakes compulsory, but many girls looking at the advertisements must have wondered why the soggy mass at the bottom of their morning cereal bowl failed to deliver the promised miracle. A few years later Kellogg's Rice Crispies with their 'snap, crackle and pop' were being advertised as the perfect cereal for adults who did not like breakfast. Or Corn Flakes.

Various commodities were de-rationed from time to time – eggs in March 1953 for instance – but 1954 saw the final phasing out of rationing and food controls, nine years after the end of the War, and when meat rationing was ended in July 1954 it was the first time since March 1940 that supplies were freely available. A few weeks later a doctor wrote advising people about the dangers of what he rather quaintly referred to as 'over-nourishment', claiming that anyone who was 10 pounds overweight had an 8% higher chance of an early death. A new slimming industry was about to be born. A Dungannon grocer promised housewives a revolution in the kitchen: "You will be surprised and attracted by the many delicious and hitherto untasted novelties with which our shelves are stocked …Shopping at Davidsons is not a fatiguing task, something from which you trudge home wearily to prepare the dinner. No, you will arrive home equipped with best quality goods and stimulated with ideas for varying the menu, so that the art of cooking instead of being a dreary routine will become a real pleasure." Among the delicious and untasted novelties were sardines, which became available for first time since 1938. Cream of Tomato Soup appeared in 1954: "Frankly, it's a luxury soup but (astonishing to tell) well within the reach of all. Packed with the goodness of plump, sun-ripened tomatoes, exotic spices, heavenly flavourings, blended and creamily thickened in the old-fashioned way…" Fish fingers (which barely escaped the ignominy of being marketed as Cod Pieces) were introduced in 1955, and Knorr packet soups in 1956, the latter offering exotic varieties such as Veloute´ aux Asperges, Lyonnais Onion, and Florida Spring Vegetable. Pizza, described as "a savoury cheese and tomato tart, served piping hot" was introduced in 1954 and predicted to become a family favourite, although perhaps with wartime experiences still fresh, no attempt was made to promote its Italian ancestry. On the other hand the supposedly ethnic origins were stressed in regard to Bachelor's Beef Curry and rice: "a dish they'd be proud of in India, yet you can make it at home in minutes." For some reason instant tea – "all the flavour, none of the leaves" – did not win widespread appeal, possibly because, unlike coffee, making tea was such a ceremonial act that housewives were reluctant to abandon it.

If there was delight in the kitchens of Northern Ireland at being introduced, or in some cases re-introduced, to these departures from the rabbit stew regime, there was also some atavistic suspicion about convenience and frozen foods. When Bachelor's Chicken Noodle Soup was launched in 1951 it was described as "the most thrilling food news for years", and was promoted as an inexpensive luxury that could enhance meals for guests while also providing a regular family dinner. Demonstrations of how to prepare the treat were held in grocery stores in Belfast in order to demonstrate how in seven minutes four big helpings could be prepared at the cost of 1s. Whether or not the public ignored the delights of noodle soup, or whether (and perhaps more likely) it just tasted too artificial, a few years later the big attraction of Bachelors Soup Mix was that, mixed and simmered for 20 minutes, it could be presented as a freshly cooked meal. It was no coincidence that the first TV chefs made their appearance after rationing had ended. 1955 saw Phyllis and John Craddock, soon to be Fanny and Johnny, along with Phillip Harbin and Marguerite Patten, entering on their collective mission to educate a nation's taste buds and create a generation of gourmets.

One of the big hits of de-rationing was margarine. Stork was "unbelievably creamy – creamier than you ever thought possible", while Kraft was "a luxurious, mouth-melting margarine with the wonderful sunny country taste", Echo was "all that a good margarine should be" (whatever that was), and Sunbrite was extolled "for the health that sunshine brings", but they were all overshadowed by Summer County which boasted a 10% butter content and was presented as a gastronomic experience in its own right. Even the humble Cookeen was proudly presented as "real fat, good and rich". These branded margarines were sold at around 10d a pound, slightly less than half the price of butter, but with Northern Ireland producing so much butter for export to Britain, and unrationed butter freely available across the Border, one has to wonder if the advertising was not overdone. Only the importance of fat in the daily diet, and the lack of it during wartime can explain the enthusiasm with which margarine in its myriad forms was welcomed back into the kitchen.

A greater variety of confectionery was also making its way back onto the shelves, including such enduring classics as Crunchie, Milky Way, Maltesers, Mars and Spangles all costing 3–4d, but also until 1954 requiring coupons and points. Bounty was launched in 1952, and Toblerone returned in 1956 with the slightly smug inquiry: "How good can chocolate be?" 7-Up appeared in 1959 as a refreshing and wholesome drink for adolescents and very young children. Wall's ice cream was promoted as a nourishing food in its own right, and purchasers were reminded that if a block was wrapped in newspaper it could stay firm for up to three hours.

The perishable nature of ice cream was recognition that domestic refrigeration was minimal, and keeping food like milk and butter cool in summer involved arcane arrangements of damp cloths and basins of water, plus an appreciation of the physics involved in evaporation. One practical consequence was that shopping was undertaken three or four times a week, or sometimes daily. Kitchen design in the 50s did not pay a great deal of attention to storage space, because most comestibles were consumed shortly after leaving the shop. It was 1958 before the first self-service branch of Stewart's opened. The concept of simply choosing goods off the shelf was decidedly *avant garde*, and came with dire warnings of shoplifting, but shoppers were also introduced to the further high-flown ideas of placing their goods in wire baskets and having the cost totalled at a checkout. It was borrowed from America of course, and soon became popular with young housewives, but the older generation of shoppers preferred the traditional mode of handing in a list to a shop assistant, and seeing their purchases tied up with string in a neat parcel. They liked seeing their bacon and cheese freshly sliced rather than pre-packed, and they enjoyed the opportunity to exchange gossip while their bill was totted up and payment was dispatched to the cashier's office either by pneumatic tube or by a spring-loaded device which whizzed across the ceiling. Progress could not be halted however and by 1957 'laundered' or pre-packed food (particularly vegetables) began appearing in the better shops. In a superlative example of misreading the signs the head of Londonderry and District Grocers' Association in 1960 predicted that the new-fangled 'multiple stores' wouldn't last, because ultimately customers valued personal service rather than cheap prices. There might have been some measure of agreement from "the lady who wants to shop in style and comfort", because she would use a BSA bicycle with chain guard and protective mudguards to prevent her dress being caught in the spokes of the back wheel, carrying a detachable basket big enough to hold a week's groceries.

One area where the idea of self-service was not put to the test was in the sale of alcohol. If not purchased over the bar, booze for the most part was bought from the small and simply stocked off-licence operated by the more forward-looking pubs. Although drunken men were occasionally seen in the streets – and in rural towns and villages on days when farmers brought their stock to market it was almost obligatory – protracted over-indulgence in alcohol was not that common. Cost was the most obvious limiting factor. Early in the decade whiskey or gin cost the equivalent of £1.68 a bottle, which was almost two days' wages for a working man. Across the bar a small whiskey ('a halfun') cost 2s 6d (12½p), rum slightly less, brandy slightly more. At the beginning of the decade Guinness was 1s a pint. Blue Star porter from the Ulster Brewery cost a few pennies less, but lacked the marketing muscle of Guinness, and it was widely believed that pubs which dared to stock alternative beers or stout faced a ruinous boycott. During the War the supply of Guinness was discussed by the Cabinet, on the grounds that the drink was essential to maintaining morale in the workforce of the major employers. In early 1951 when a transport strike in the Republic prevented supplies being brought north arrangements were made to ship in emergency rations of Guinness from London; while desperate publicans in Derry ran their own rationing scheme and hired lorries to drive to Dublin through snowstorms, a round trip which took one unfortunate driver a week. And in case there was a perception that Guinness was a drink for the working man only, the firm ran a series of advertisements emphasising the medicinal benefits of the brew, quoting a doctor's endorsement: "Guinness is a very pleasant, safe and stimulating restorative, and I find that many people, especially women, find it a great help, when taken in mid-morning, to get them through the various house duties thrust upon them by the absence of domestic help." Those were the days when Guinness really was good for you. As periodic increases in price took place throughout the decade by the end of 1959 the goodness cost 2s 2d (almost 11p) a pint.

For those with a more discerning palate there was always the wine merchant, willing to provide discreet advice and guidance in the mysteries of bottles with incomprehensible labels and unpronounceable names. From the Christmas 1952 list of a Belfast wine merchant there were offers at prices (in decimal equivalents) that twenty-first century oenophiles can only envy: 1947 Chateau Margaux at £1.37 a bottle; 1945 Gevrey Chambertain for 67p; 1934 St Emilion for 60p; 1927 vintage port at £1.60. But, as already noted, affordability is relative. The Chateaux Margaux cost the equivalent of 27 pints of Guinness, which gives some idea of relative values. Smirnoff vodka was introduced in 1954, promoted as being smooth and palatable, particularly with savoury foods, and no stronger than gin or whiskey. How long it lasted is unknown, but in 1957 an Australian food and wine fair was held in Belfast and a permanent food promotion officer appointed. Besides Australian tinned and dried fruits, there was Keystone burgundy at 57p a flagon, Keystone Rich Ruby at 72p, and something called Manique liqueur, which was made from brandy and quinces, and at £2.25 a bottle was obviously a much more sophisticated tipple than Chateau Margaux. The Presbyterian General Assembly in 1956 reported that gin had been "elevated to the peerage" of drinks, while wine "had invaded the kitchen". Nevertheless, a survey undertaken in 1957 found that people in Northern Ireland spent less on alcohol than did other parts of the UK, averaging just over 5s a week. The figure seems low, but perhaps the strong temperance tradition in some areas had a moderating effect. Certainly when the Milk Marketing Board ran a competition in 1957 to better promote its product the winner was a Lisburn housewife who won a refrigerator and two pounds of butter every week for a year with the slogan "Be wise. Be gay. Drink milk today." The Wimpy burger, wittily described as "the square meal in the round bun" was first offered for sale at Wimbledon in 1953 and the first Wimpy Bar opened in Northern Ireland a few years later. Possibly because of a feeling that they could only be enjoyed as holiday food, Tayto crisps (produced by 20 workers in the kitchen of Tandragee Castle) in 1956 were sold mostly to seaside resorts, although the manufacturers hoped that the American idea of eating them anywhere would catch on. It did, and by 1959 some 30 tons, or approximately 537,600 packets a week were being produced. Coca Cola had been available since 1939 but it was not until mid-50s that selling the bottles from chilling dispensers caught on, thus moving the local consumer a further step along the road to Americanisation. It was entirely in keeping with this trend that the Inglis bakery in the late 50s should begin producing "genuine American" glazed doughnuts. By that time there were 350 chip shops in Northern Ireland, 200 of them in Belfast alone. A fish supper, heavily salted and doused with vinegar before being wrapped in newspaper, cost around 1s 6d (7½p), and tasted infinitely better eaten while walking, rather than seated in the confines of a booth using a knife and fork. The threat to such uncomplicated delights was appearing on the horizon however, because in 1960 Belfast Corporation granted its first license for a Chinese restaurant. Cosmopolitan cuisine was just around the corner, and while the culture of junk food and takeaway meals hadn't arrived in all its horror, it was certainly beckoning.

The proportion of the family budget which went towards the purchase of food and drink is difficult to assess, and was obviously subject to wide variations depending on individual circumstances. The President of the Northern Ireland Grocers' Association in 1954 claimed that 40% of the average family income was spent on necessities like food, rent, heat and light, but the greater amount went to providing 'pleasures' like drink, tobacco, sport and TV. A survey by Queen's University showed that in 1953 £86 million had been spent on food; £28 million on clothes; fuel and light £18 million; alcohol £14 million; tobacco £13 million; private motoring £8 million; other travelling £7 million; and entertainment £4 million. Different terms of reference obviously applied in the two surveys – in which category should clothes be placed, for instance? – and each gave a different interpretation of the balance being struck by consumers between expenditure on necessities as opposed to 'pleasures'. What they both illustrated, however, was the extent to which society as a whole was at last beginning to escape from post-war privation.

Early in the decade the women's pages in the newspapers were filled with articles by housewives claiming it was possible to feed two adults and three children for £2.50 or less per week, although providing for a family of four for £4.50 was probably more realistic. In the later 50s as more and more varied food became available, such costs were beginning to rise. By October 1959 the *Belfast Telegraph* was printing recipes for filet de boeuf a l'amiral, escalope of veal alla zincara [sic], and supreme de volaille a la bonne femme as if the ill-favoured spectre of Prune Shape had never darkened the table. Those who devoted themselves to such culinary delights were obviously a small and elite minority, but how many people could have afforded them had they wanted to do so?

Wages are difficult to generalise about. Differentials applied between what was paid for work in towns and cities, and what applied in the country. Additional variations were observed in the rates offered to men and women, and those available to youth and experience. In the early 1950s around £200–250 a year was probably the minimum for a working man to obtain the basic necessities of life for a small family. In some counties agricultural workers got £5 a week in summer, as well as food and board, but could be laid off for the winter months and receive no pay. A rural postman might earn £3 a week, a creamery worker slightly more, a road sweeper with one of the local Councils slightly less, but many such employees also had the capacity to reduce their food bills by growing their own vegetables or producing eggs. A grave-digger in one of the Belfast cemeteries earned just under £4 a week. In Harland & Wolff and in the engineering industry skilled workers could expect around £350 a year, and members of the RUC up to £400 depending on rank and length of service. A male teacher with an honours degree might find himself on a scale of £450–850; a female £385–680. The Town Clerk of Carrickfergus was well up the pecking order with a salary of £850–1,000, and presumably other Clerks were paid greater or lesser figures depending on the size of their fiefdom.

Remaining with the early 50s civil service salaries ranged from £200 to £2,750. Cabinet Ministers earned £1,700, although the Prime Minister was given £2,850 plus £1,500 in expenses. Doctors, depending on the number of assistants they employed, could command from £1,000 to £4,000 although most were towards the lower end of this scale of earnings. Supreme Court Judges pulled down £3,500, with the Lord Chief Justice netting an extra £1,000, salaries which reflected the linkages with the scales enjoyed by the judiciary in Britain. (In 1953 the 79 judges in the

Northern Ireland judiciary turned down an offer of an increase of £1,000 tax free in favour of availing of the level of increases agreed in Britain. This latter arrangement was implemented at a cost of £235,000 a year.) The Chairman of the Ulster Transport Authority on £6,000 was thought to be the recipient of the highest public sector salary. Private incomes by their nature remained undisclosed but the Northern Ireland Labour Party claimed in 1953 that figures from the Inland Revenue showed that 90% of those in receipt of income earned less than £500 a year, and that no one had an income in excess of £20,000. Such claims are impossible to verify, but in very broad terms do not seem incompatible with the examples of incomes quoted in the preceding paragraphs.

What can be said is that comparative affluence built throughout the decade. In 1960 the average wage had risen to around £9 a week, or £400–450 a year. Sixteen people were now reported to have incomes of more than £20,000; 26 were in the £15–20,000 bracket; 32 earned £10–15,000 ... and so by decreasing steps to 1051 people getting £2–3,000. To put those figures in context, it was stated in 1956 that the earnings per head of population in Northern Ireland were now 70% of the GB average, but that was an increase on the 60% which had applied before the war. There was more food in the shops, more electrical gadgets to buy for the kitchen, and more opportunities to purchase the occasional bottle of Chateaux Margaux. Of course, those of a nostalgic disposition purported to be shocked at late 50s prices, and could not help remembering how, before the War, a dozen eggs cost less than 1s, coffee was 2s 6d (12½p) per pound, and a six-room villa could be purchased for £750. Despite such negativity, it could be predicted with some confidence that a return to serving savoury fish loaf was unlikely, and that consumerism was about to take off.

In any reference to domestic affairs it was clear that men were the breadwinners, women the homebuilders. The stereotypes were deeply embedded. The *Woman's Weekly* in 1951: "Home making is the most useful of all the talents. To make a man feel happy and comfortable and to make a child feel cherished. No woman's work is more important than these." *Woman's Own* in 1951: the woman's place is in the kitchen "for it [the kitchen] is the heart and centre of the meaning of home. The place where, day after day, you make with your hands the gifts of love." Councillor Mrs A Wilson, speaking to Carrickfergus Unionist Association in 1952 on the place of women in public life felt that there was a certain prejudice against women participating in public affairs, but for herself "she believed that the finest job a woman could do was to run her home efficiently and bring up her children to be good citizens." She might well have drawn her inspiration from a report of a conference that same year near San Francisco, where the principal speaker, described as an outstanding career woman and editor, advised her audience that "no matter how efficient a woman may be as a teacher, politician or nurse, her education is incomplete unless she can look with undaunted eye at the kitchen stove and after-dinner dishes." Equal pay was not regarded as a major issue in Northern Ireland. One female civil servant in 1954 claimed after a conference vote in favour of equal pay that women did not deserve equality since by the time they had visited the washroom on numerous occasions, and engaged in frequent gossip sessions, on average they had worked three hours less per day than their male colleagues. Her comments might have been exaggerated but the fact that she was not torn limb from limb was entirely in line with prevailing social attitudes. Marriage, home and family were the trinity of female aspirations.

But such attitudes were just beginning to come under question. The increasing prosperity noted earlier was trickling down and the beginnings of youth culture can be discerned as 'teen-agers' made their appearance. There is still academic debate about when the term 'teenager' first appeared – either in the late 40s or the early 50s – and what exactly it meant. One definition offered was "those who have reached the age of 15 but are not yet 25 and unmarried". Alternatively teenagers could be "those casting off the dependence of childhood without having assumed the responsibilities of adulthood." Or even "those whose distinctive behavioural characteristic is to spend a lot of money on clothes, records, concerts, makeup, magazines – all things that give immediate pleasure and are of little lasting use." One trend was noticed: younger wage-earners gave all their money to mother and received pocket money, while older ones made a donation to household expenses and kept the rest. There were significant regional variations in earning power but by the late 50s it was estimated that UK teenagers collectively had £900 million of disposable income. With young people acquiring a degree of financial independence rebellion against the old order became inevitable.

How much of that disposable income was available in Northern Ireland is impossible to say, but by the early 50s it was noted that the milk bars and snack bars which had been established as a temporary courtesy for American forces during the War were now a permanent feature, and young people had enough money to go to them straight from work rather than eating at home. By 1955 juke boxes in cafes and coffee bars were providing an additional reason not to eat at home. 3d (just over 1p) was enough to play a record, which was cheap compared to the £1.75–£2 it cost to buy one of the revolutionary Decca long-playing discs, "eight full-length tunes on one ten-inch record". (When the Gramophone Shop in Belfast opened in 1952 as "the most up-to-date and luxurious musical rendezvous in the British Isles", it boasted a stock of more than 400 of these new marvels.) As the BBC refused to play the latest American rock n' roll records, and the signal from Radio Luxembourg was capricious, the juke box became the medium for spreading the new message, built around music that parents would misunderstand and intensely dislike. It was noted in November 1955 that 50 juke boxes had been installed, in the previous three months, mostly in Belfast. Since they cost over £600 each, the proprietors evidently calculated that the youth revolution was here to stay.

In Belfast Teddy Boys wore the uniform of velvet collared drape jacket, tight trousers, bootlace tie, yellow socks and crepe-soled shoes, the last being known as brothel creepers on account of their prototypes being favoured by British soldiers stationed in north Africa during the war. It might have been a nod in the direction of Edwardian garb, but when even partly tailor-made a full outfit cost around £70. Styling for the elaborate but compulsory 'duck's arse' hairstyle cost extra, so the Ted's was not a cheap look to acquire. It all seems to have started in London in 1952 or 53 and migrated to provinces, arriving in Belfast in 1955, probably encouraging the juke box craze. In June a Resident Magistrate in Belfast was handing out fines to those involved in turf wars between rival gangs and asking the classic question: "what is the idea of dressing up in this silly and childish way?" The wife of the Governor, Lord Wakehurst, expressed the view that one reason for delinquency among Teddy Boys was they had not experienced enough love in their lives. By early 1956 the Moderator of the Presbyterian Church was also deploring gang culture and expressing his astonishment that anyone should want to dress "in the garb of fifty years ago". Quite apart from the fact that both magistrates and moderators were seldom cited as sartorial role models, such questions missed the point – dressing as a Ted was done to annoy, and to create a separate gang identity. Belfast dancehalls responded by measuring the clothes of male customers, and trousers less than 18 inches wide were banned, as were jackets deemed to be long. By mid-56 some Belfast Teds had been banned from so many dancehalls that they announced their wish to form an 'Edwardian Club', motivated, so they said, by a desire to take up handicrafts, carpentry and other useful activities. It conjured up a rather touching image of the Club members retiring, after a rousing bout of basket weaving, to discuss over port and cigars the burning issues of votes for women and reform of the House of Lords.

There was no comparable style for teenage girls, and certainly nothing that constituted a recognised uniform of rebellion. Girls or their mothers had dressmaking skills to create clothes and copy the dresses they had admired in the movies, or in magazines like *Woman's Weekly* and *Woman's Realm* where patterns were plentiful. In the national finals of the 'Sew, Save and be Smart' competition in 1950 the contestants from Northern Ireland were considered to have performed with great credit. Later in the 50s stars like Audrey Hepburn and Leslie Caron provided a look which was based on a black polo sweater and duffel coat, and it was imitated by the girls who hung around in coffee bars pretending to like jazz, but there seemed to be no dominant style that every girl had to follow. In Northern Ireland the slacks and duffel coat look was deplored – it might be all right in London but here, parents agreed "we don't want our daughters looking older than they really are, or trying to act sophisticated." The 'Woman's View' column in the *Belfast Newsletter* urged young ladies to consider that they were liable to cause outrage to parents if they came down to breakfast wearing slacks and scarlet nail varnish.

Adult society maintained an almost anthropological interest in this new species which rejected their parents' values and instead drew their inspiration from rock n' roll. It was solemnly reported that those really devoted to the new music were known as 'hepcats' while those who missed the point of it all were 'squares'. Kids who became deeply involved in the intricacies of jiving were said to be 'gone' and 'in the groove'. When the film *Rock Around the Clock* was released on 1956 there were riots by teenagers who insisted on jiving in the cinema aisles and tearing up the seats. Responding to the lead taken by several British cities, Belfast Corporation Police Committee issued its ban; and a complicit BBC duly cancelled a scheduled 10-minute live broadcast of a rock concert lest the beast of youth culture should be unleashed and the cameras "might show something that viewers would not like."

Elvis entered the UK charts in 1956 with *Heartbreak Hotel* and *Blue Suede Shoes* and soon acquired the reputation as the only singer who wore out his trousers from the inside. Inevitably the BBC refused to play his records. No such danger was threatened by Tommy Steele who became the first British rock star with *Rock with the Caveman,* where lyrics such as "Rock with the caveman, Roll with the caveman, Shake with the caveman, Make with the caveman" were regarded as unlikely to provoke frenzies of trouser abuse. But the audience response to a Bill Hayley concert in Dublin in March 1957 rapidly escalated into riots and Garda baton charges; and although in Belfast the corresponding concert in the Hippodrome was two-thirds empty, 2,000 teenagers gathered outside the venue and had little difficulty in provoking their own riot with the 'squares' in RUC uniform.

The *Belfast Telegraph* in 1958 deplored the fact that young people now had disposable income, and recorded with distaste that in some shops there were eight people under 21 for every adult customer, while "idol-worshipping teenagers" were content to spend two-thirds of their pocket money (pocket money!) of 15s (75p) on a single record. But records were already in danger of being overtaken by the magic of 'the magnetic tape recorder', which even in 1950 raised the possibility of young people being able to share music in ways previously impossible. Before the end of the decade Elvis was expected to make £250,000 a year, while lesser idols like Paul Anka were making £2,000 a week and talking of retirement at 18. To the post-war generation of adults such developments were proof that the barbarians were at the gate.

Apart from the excesses of rock music, even incipient signs of defying authority were seen as symptoms of a wider malaise. Northern Ireland was still a strongly church-going society and there were notices for over 200 church services of various denominations in Belfast and district on Sundays in 1950. An *Irish News* editorial of 1952 cited "the gangster film, the dance hall, the lack of parental control" as contributory factors in the growth of delinquency, but regarded as the root cause a "loss of anchorage" which was prevalent in society as a whole. The Northern Ireland Housewives League favoured physical chastisement for children, and less reliance on child psychology: "A child of 7 or 8 brought to a psychologist learned to make excuses for himself, and could soon find an excuse for anything he might do." The Lord Chief Justice and his colleagues on the bench were in favour of granting less probation, and handing down more custodial sentences, but the *Belfast Telegraph* ran an editorial claiming that 'parental delinquency' was the real crime, and it was up to parents, teachers and ministers of religion to create a better spirit of social responsibility. A judge in Ballymena recommended that parents taking a sally rod to delinquent kids would be far more effective in preventing unlawful behaviour than any judicial punishment he could hand down. The periodical *Unionist* in 1953 editorialised that "since flogging was abolished and blood-lusted bullies treated as lost souls ... crimes of assault have increased ... Children and teen-agers have too much money and too little to occupy their minds, with the result that they are prone to be influenced by the shocking gangster films and literature of the day."

In fact juvenile crime figures show little significant change over the decade. According to Ministry of Home Affairs statistics 142 young offenders were sentenced in 1950 and 173 in 1959. Over the same period the number of young people accommodated in the various training schools rose from 367 to 518. Incidents of breaking and entering involving young people grew in number, as did crimes of violence against the person, but in neither case was the increase significant – indeed in the latter category they rose from four cases to 24 at the end of the decade. None of these figures give much indication of a society in the grip of a youth-inspired crime wave. Offences involving bicycles trebled from 243 up to 720, but – perhaps an indicator of the extent to which motorised traffic was taking over the townscape – those based on games in the street fell from 336 to 282. An advertisement in 1950 for Milo, a chocolate flavoured drink based on malted barley, claimed that 'difficult' teenagers threatening to cause mayhem could be soothed back to tranquillity by having their over-stretched nerves comforted by a hot night-time drink. In 1953 the Minister of Home Affairs in Stormont deprecated what he saw as the rise in juvenile crime, claiming that women and young girls in Belfast were now carrying hat-pins and even hammers to protect themselves from assault. He refused, however to believe that, despite demands, new legislation was the answer: "The tendency in the present day to shift responsibility from the home to the state can only end in disaster … In many cases, honest discipline in the home is regarded as out of date, and until some of the old Ulster family discipline takes the place of the present day sloppy thought there is little that can be done by the state."

The role of the state *versus* the role of the family was an issue which was to provoke discussion for many years to come. The Northern Ireland Cabinet in 1957 debated whether to seek agreement from Westminster to amend the Children and Young Persons Act, because it was feared that if the degree of protection from punitive action that it afforded to young people were to become public knowledge, the IRA would recruit more juveniles to carry out acts of terrorism. During the discussion the Attorney General made the point that very few judges would see any merit in handing down a jail sentence to a 14 year old, irrespective of his crime, and a more effective way forward might be to seek a power allowing the imposition of punitive fines on the parents of miscreant youngsters. In the event the law remained unchanged, but in early 1960 a slightly feverish correspondence was carried on in the letters columns of the *Belfast Telegraph* after a mother wrote that she had made her 17 year old daughter put on her gym slip preparatory to the administration of a spanking with a hairbrush. Debate took place between those who regarded chastisement of grown-up daughters as a colossal failure of parenting, and those who felt it to represent a long-overdue return to necessary values in the home. (Reading between the lines there was evidence of a third school of thought which held that, irrespective of any considerations of family discipline, spanking 17 year old girls in gym slips was a good idea in itself.) No clear conclusion was reached, but if the number of letters published was an accurate indicator it looked as if the traditionalists lost the day.

In terms of law and order in the wider sense it is difficult to get a clear picture. There is something nostalgic about the list of offences given in the Ministry of Home Affairs report for 1950: 2,920 breaches of the Gaming and Betting laws, 2,450 under the Liquor laws, 1,178 misdemeanours under the Education Acts, 158 under the Railway laws, 60 under the Game laws, 60 offences by prostitutes, 10 under the Wireless Telegraphy laws, 80 cases of being drunk in charge of a bicycle, and 17 of being drunk while driving a horse-drawn vehicle. In 1952 there were 736 cells available in Northern Irish prisons, but the average daily occupancy was only 303, and by the middle of the decade it was only slightly higher. In the later 50s the figures for prison occupancy were distorted by the introduction of internment and detention for those suspected of being involved in subversive activity, but the number of indictable offences rose only from just under 7,500 to just over 7,600, and within those figures the average of 1,500 sentences handed down for larceny each year provided reassuring evidence that one of the most popular categories of wrongdoing largely avoided violence.

In Britain the debate about capital punishment was in full swing in the early 50s. Giving evidence to the Royal Commission on the subject the British Lord Chief Justice was opposed to the idea of exempting women from hanging, because they were seeking equality in every other way; while a group of doctors was somewhat hesitant about recommending to the Commission that gassing should be used as an alternative to hanging, recognising that there were "highly unpleasant historical associations" involved. In a proposal which prefigured future developments in Northern Ireland, the Scottish Police Federation suggested scrapping jury trials and having capital cases heard by a bench of three judges charged with reaching a unanimous decision. Opinion in Northern Ireland was broadly in favour of making the punishment fit the crime. In 1953 the Northern Ireland Lord Chief Justice called for corporal punishment to be retained as a deterrent to be used when all else failed. His report noted that "crimes of dishonesty" had risen from 2,400 in 1938 to 6,800 in 1952. It was not thought that the increase was caused by poverty or lack of essential commodities, or even political or industrial unrest, and a number of alternative explanations were offered: 1) a general fall in respect for the law; 2) literature and entertainment "where a great deal goes without censure"; 3) a desire to live at a higher social standard; 4) the stress of modern life; 5) decay in family life and lack of parental control; 6) poor housing; 7) a growing spirit of social irresponsibility; 8) freedom from fear of being caught and convicted; and 9) a lowering of moral standards. That it had been thought worthwhile to compile a list of such subtle variations – there seems little operative difference between causes 1 and 8, or 2 and 9 – was a fascinating social commentary in its own right.

As noted, public opinion in Northern Ireland tended to favour capital punishment, and among Unionists, ever-nervous of IRA attacks, there was virtual unanimity. A diplomatic row between Belfast and London ensued in 1956 when a Labour MP, Sidney Silverman, supported by former Home Secretary Chuter Ede and by one of the Northern Ireland Members, Montgomery Hyde, brought on a Private Member's Bill to abolish the death penalty. As drafted, the Bill had UK-wide application, and would apply, if passed, to Northern Ireland. The government in London, it became clear, regarded this not just as a matter of law and order, but as an issue of 'enlightenment and morality' which it was prepared to assist on to the statute book. A free vote would be allowed, and the government was very reluctant to provoke a row with the abolitionist lobby over the fact that Northern Ireland wished to be excluded. The Home Office let it be known that, if the Northern Ireland government wished to see the scope of the Bill limited to the mainland, it would be extremely helpful if the Home Secretary could say that Belfast was prepared to bring forward its own Bill. When these subtle hints were ignored in Belfast, a senior Home Office figure threatened to use the nuclear option, citing the provision in the Government of Ireland Act of 1920 which reserved to Westminster the ultimate power to over-ride the decisions of the Northern Ireland Parliament. The power undoubtedly existed, but even to suggest its use was against all constitutional convention, and would constitute a disaster in terms of inter-governmental relations. It was recognised in London that any such outcome could not be contemplated, and the threat was withdrawn. Shortly afterwards, in March 1956, the Minister of Home Affairs announced in Stormont that the death penalty would not be abolished in Northern Ireland. What emerged in Britain as the Homicide Act in 1957 did not abolish capital punishment, but reduced to six the instances of murder (such as killing a policeman, or killing during the course of a robbery) which were punishable by death. In Britain abolition was brought in on an interim basis in 1965, and was made permanent in 1969. In Northern Ireland the provisions for capital punishment were not repealed until 1973. The death penalty had not been applied since the early 1940s, and most people assumed it had been abolished, and many were surprised and shocked when in July and December 1961 first Sam McLaughlin and then Robert McGladdery were hanged in Crumlin Road prison.

The themes of moral laxity and a disintegration of standards were given various iterations by establishment figures. The Catholic Bishop of Derry in 1950 complained that Sunday had now become "a day of sin, of entertainment and intoxication" – an admonition which must have aroused interest among young Protestants – and warned that "those who ran dances at present, no matter in what hall, took on themselves a grave responsibility, especially if they allowed people from all parts of the country to come, people very often of doubtful character or easy virtue, who come, not to enjoy the dance but very often from questionable motives." Such comments were doubtless intended to act as a warning to good Catholic parents to lock up their daughters, but the concerns were inter-denominational. A Protestant clergyman in 1952 also complained: "Bound up with this increasing desire to squander money on non-essentials there were the attendant evils of sexual laxity, loosening of the marriage bonds and increasing crimes of sordid violence." For good measure he berated girls for appearing in fine weather in dresses "so scanty that they offend Christian modesty and the honour of womanhood." A *Belfast Telegraph* editorial concurred: "In matters of personal behaviour there is a laxity that is certainly more widespread than it was. The spirit of something for nothing seems to have caught hold of many young people, and it is impossible to disregard reports of a loss of pride in honest work for its own sake." A *Derry Journal* editorial echoed the theme, protesting that "indelicacies, improprieties and moral risks which were considered exceptions 20 years ago are now being accepted as the normal pattern of so-called teen-age behaviour." British Sunday papers were held up for particular criticism, but imported comics did not escape either: besides glorifying violence, "many of their illustrations are indecent, certainly unfit for a place in Christian homes, or for reading by Christian children." (It might be noted in passing that the sense of outrage in the same editorial extended to Radio Éireann, for its policy of playing jazz and "other such abominations" while ignoring Irish music.)

There was also outrage when the *Belfast Telegraph's* Woman's Page in 1954 suggested that sixth-form girls should be taught how to apply make-up properly. "It is shocking ... there is time enough for dolling–up in later years. At 16, one should be unconscious of self, busy concentrating on tennis and Tennyson" was a typical reaction. The headmistress of Richmond Lodge girls' school in 1952 appeared to have no problems with sixth-form lipstick, but without implying that her charges were guilty of such a lapse in taste warned of the dangers inherent in imported American comics: "they provided physical and emotional stimulus which excited the immature mind and personality, and set a standard of speech, behaviour, thinking and feeling which could, in one generation, debase the culture [which] centuries of Christian tradition, humane ethics and a lettered education had so painfully, and so imperfectly, created." Against that benchmark it could be regarded as an advance in liberal values that, six years later, the subject of debate was whether school caps and berets need always be worn in public.

It is probably safe to say that those who made the most stentorian denunciations of Teddy Boys and moral laxity were themselves models of propriety, because in adult circles non-conformity with the accepted norms was the ultimate horror. The advertisement for Vaseline Hair Tonic was typical: "Do people whisper behind your back?" because of unruly and un-groomed hair. The advertisements for Jackson the Tailor ruthlessly played on social insecurity and snobbery. A new suit earns a young manager the promotion he has been denied for so long, and the avuncular Mr Jackson points up the moral of the story: "Show me a man who has ceased to take an interest in his clothes and I'll show you someone who no longer has any ambition." A middle manager refuses invitations to parties and receptions because his only suit is shabby. Again Mr Jackson offers considered advice: "What you need to put you on good terms with yourself and at ease in company is a suit with good cut and a certain individuality". A young woman described by her husband as "a loveable little snob" is unapologetic about forcing him to buy a new suit. "When you go for a continental holiday with a party, as we did this year, its natural to want to get to know the nicest looking people", which meant, of course, the best-dressed people.

Jackson supplied two-piece suits from the equivalent of £7.75 to £10.75, while Weaver to Wearer on Belfast's North Street could do the same for £6.30 and throw in a gabardine raincoat for an extra £4.45. If one lived in Derry which, in terms of newspaper advertising appeared to be a shoe fetishist's heaven, the outfit could be completed with high-class brogues at just under 50s (£2.50). Presumably to act as a deterrent against becoming a Teddy Boy, pork pie hats were advertised as being particularly suitable for "the young man just out of school". In 1954 the next big thing predicted in men's leisure wear was the 'Sun-toga', a piece of terry-towelling with a hole in the middle, a belt and a large waterproof pocket in front, which could be adapted for any form of activity, on or off the beach. It was agreed that in the best circles, a man's braces (or 'galluses' in the vernacular), should not be displayed in public, and should be worn under the shirt if necessary.

In 1952 an apoplectic observer at Wimbledon directed his wrath at the shorts worn by the tennis players, querying whether "there was a single male contestant who could play tennis dressed otherwise than as a prize fighter. This male semi-nudity may be all right in the boxing ring, but it doesn't fit in with the fashionable and sunny Wimbledon scene. It is stark and unsightly." Obviously immaculate white flannel trousers had a secret appeal for the writer. A man wrote to one of the Belfast newspapers in 1960 to boast that he was still wearing an overcoat that he had purchased in Lisburn in 1908 for less than three pounds. Complaints were made in 1951 about the aberration of men using women's shampoo to wash their hair; and it would be years before men's toiletries were acceptable. Brylcreem and red Lifebuoy toilet soap was all a chap needed to face the world, and a whiff of body odour was merely a sign that honest labour had been undertaken. At every level the same message was reinforced – fit in, be respectable and don't challenge authority.

Female fashion deserves a lengthy study in its own right, and is not a task to be entered upon here. Wartime utility clothing was on the market until 1952, with restrictions on length, decoration, pockets and trimmings to save on material. It was perfectly adequate, but definitely unglamorous. Dior's New Look of 1947 rebelled against that with luxurious and voluminous skirts, wasp-waisted jackets and rich fabrics. The King forbade Princesses Elizabeth and Margaret to wear such clothes when rationing was in force, but Holywood and high society had no such scruples, and throughout the 50s the A-line, the Sack, the Trapeze, the Tent, the Swoop and the Empire line defined what rich and successful women wore.

How much of this was actually worn in Northern Ireland is difficult to say, though Swears and Wells in Belfast in 1952 were advertising Snow Leopard coats at 95gn (just under £100), Blue Frost Mink at 80 and squirrel at 55gn, suggesting that a fairly prosperous, if limited clientele existed. In Ballymena as late as 1958 fur-trimmed coats in the swagger style were on sale for £28, or in mohair at prices ranging from £3–6, with handbags reduced to 12s 6d (62½p), but presumably it was the bargains at Goorwiches or C&A at more modest prices which found their way into most wardrobes. Certainly in the provincial newspapers references to Dior or Balenciaga, or to mink coats were conspicuous by their absence. "If you have a figure at all appropriate to wearing slacks" the Gor-Ray brand offered a choice of 23 different combinations of hip, waist and height measurements. Early in 1952 the Family Doctor writing in the *Belfast Telegraph* was despairing of women "who think it is glamorous to trudge through the snow and pound the icy pavements in paper-thin shoes, invisible stockings, thin two-piece costumes, and cotton or equally unprotective gloves..." There is a sense that here was a man only just preventing himself from purple-faced spluttering that women should forget about fashion and only go out in sturdy shoes and sensible knickers. The price was said to be coming down but in 1957 the "invisible stockings" still cost around 6s a pair. In 1951 news was received that in Cheltenham a new American-style of dress shop was arranging clothes in clearly-marked sizes and allowing potential purchasers to try on garments in a private cubicle before purchasing. It was noted in 1956 that the black shawl, once a universal female garment in Belfast, had now disappeared from the shops. It could be read as part of the same trend that in the January sales in 1960 black sealskin coats were reduced from £595 to £525, but in the course of a newspaper competition that year it also emerged that many women were still wearing outfits purchased in the 1930s, with the practice of converting wedding dresses into ballgowns apparently widespread. Advertisements for Tampax were carried from 1950 but in such elliptical terms than no male reader (and perhaps even some females) could have been expected to know what was being referred to.

The theme of young girls attempting to look sophisticated was recurrent, although in one example from 1953 the scope of attack broadened: "If a young girl wears such sophisticated clothes that she passes for her mother's sister, that's wrong. And if mother (even with a well-preserved figure) wears little-girl dresses, that's wrong as well." It was an interesting argument – clothes were not just an indicator of social status, but also of age. There was an assumed progression from garments appropriate for children, which were in due course replaced by those appropriate to a young woman, which in turn yielded to those deemed suitable for a married woman, and finally the garb of the middle-aged or elderly, with each transition marking a rite of passage. There was little prospect in the 1950s of confronting the spectacle of grannies in low-cut tops and miniskirts but the pressure for women to look like goddesses was ever-present. It was reported in 1950 that women in London could easily spend £20 a year on cosmetics – lipstick at the equivalent of 37p, face powder at 27p and a new product called mascara being the main sources of temptation. And permed hair. In Derry in the late 40s a Parmalette Machineless Perm could be had for 30s (£1.50) "because a Smart Hair Style is just as important as a Well-fitting Garment". A salon in Belfast in 1952 was offering the 'Schoolgirl Special' at 15s (75p), the 'Teenage Glamour' at 17s 6d (87½p), up to the 'Falcon Royal' at £2 10s (£2.50), and America's latest sensation, the 'Magic Fhix Zoto Fluid' at £1 more.

The cheap alternative was a Toni perm pack bought from the chemist and applied at home if the smell could be tolerated. Anecdotal evidence suggests that home perms were like any form of DIY – good results could be achieved, but were not inevitable. By the end of the decade nature had supplanted artifice, and the 'Vitamin Perm' at just over £3 was available to women who wanted to look as if their hair had not been permed at all.

It falls into the category of It Couldn't Happen Now but 16–21 March 1953 was designated National Corset Week, and there is an entire thesis to be written on the reasons why in newspapers throughout the 1950s advertisements for corsets were so ubiquitous. Brands like Maidenform, Berlei, Playtex and Triumph competed to give the most natural look with the most extreme degree of technical assistance. A device marketed in 1953 called the Coronation Controlette gives the general idea. An article in 1951 claimed that a woman's character could be deduced from the corset she wore: "With a short girdle the long back curve is missing. Consequently the girdle rides up at the back, tearing the stockings and tipping the pelvis forward. The tummy muscles sag, the girdle corrugates around the waist, and the wretched owner asks 'Why oh why am I so difficult to fit?'" Things began to get better in the 1960s, but freedom and comfort in women's clothing were not the primary consideration in the preceding decade.

Despite these handicaps it was apparent that Northern Ireland had discovered sex by the 50s. Complaints were made about the contents of the student magazine *PTQ*, suggesting that it should drop vulgarity and innuendo in favour of good clean fun. "What is a saxophone? Its an ill wind that nobody blows good" was recommended as the standard to aim for. In 1956 following a raid on premises in Gresham Street in Belfast, the local Head Constable explained the categories of material lifted: 1) "romantic fiction varying from the suggestive to the pornographic but aimed at the creation of sexual excitement"; 2) "books on the psychology of love, harmless in themselves but when displayed with books in the first category were likely to exhibit or generate erotic tendencies"; 3) photographic studies of semi-nude figures in suggestive poses "published with a view to the creation of sexual impulses"; and 4) "sadistic books … definitely erotic in appeal." Those reading at the time of the raid were middle-aged or elderly men "not of a high standard intellectually". Shortly afterwards a Resident Magistrate ordered the material to be destroyed on the grounds that it was liable to deprave or corrupt the minds of those open to immoral influences. "As well as corrupting the hitherto uncorrupted minds of youths, the books would also open to the already corrupted fresh vistas of perversion …" For generations of youth Gresham Street had been famous for the pet shops which flourished there – a rabbit for 1s was a deal much favoured by uncorrupted minds – and this must have seemed like another example of the wish to move with, or even ahead of, the times. In the Republic, meanwhile, a dispute arose when Customs officials impounded a consignment of *The Observer* on the instructions of the Censorship Board, on the grounds that the paper contained an article on family planning. There was a question whether the Board had any authority to impound newspapers, but the view seemed to be taken that on such a dangerous topic as limiting childbirth, moral authority more than made up for any legal deficiencies.

A raid on the same Gresham Street premises in 1960 saw 6,500 magazines removed, but on examination only 757 of these were found to be obscene. It conjures up a vision of earnest young constables conscientiously wading through page after page of this literature and debating whether it was romantic fiction aimed at the creation of sexual excitement, or whether it was merely dealing with the psychology of love. During the subsequent court proceedings a psychiatrist argued that none of the books was likely to corrupt a healthy mind, even among adolescents, thereby opening up an entire new field of debate about what counted as 'healthy' when it came to minds. A week later Derry Corporation ignored such philosophical niceties and banned a film about Oscar Wilde, largely on the grounds of Wilde's reputation rather than on the content of the film itself. Derry Councillors tended to take their line from the list of banned or censored publications circulated in the Republic, but the levels of judgement displayed is indicated by the fact that the same Councillors also banned the 1959 film *Expresso Bongo* – the only time in his entire career that Cliff Richard contrived to attract a suspicion of sexual depravity. In 1958 the *Irish News* felt the need to issue its own classification for films, distrusting the liberal tendencies of the British Film censor. In this new arrangement category C films were held to be suitable for families; category B for adults and adolescents; category A for adults only, sub-divided into A1 (partly objectionable, even for adults, as in *I was a Teenage Werewolf*); and A2 (held to be completely objectionable, for example *Dragship Girl*). The law of unintended consequences probably ensured that many corruptible youths were grateful to have a reliable guide to the films which had the highest explicit content.

The debate on public morality reached a climax (if one can use the word) with the prosecution in the Old Bailey in October 1960 of Pan Books for the publication of *Lady Chatterley's Lover*. Until 1959 the standard test for obscenity was said to be anything that would be unacceptable to a 14 year old schoolgirl, but under the Obscene Publications Act of that year expert witnesses were for the first time allowed to be called in order to determine on one side or the other, the question of whether, "taken as a whole", the book's character was of a nature which was in the interests of "science, art, literature, or other objects of general concern". Prosecuting Counsel ignored these tiresome restrictions and early in the proceedings gave his own memorable assessment of what constituted acceptability in the field of literature: "Is this a book you would even wish your wife or your servants to read?" The fact that Penguin published the book at the price of 3s 6d (17½p) meant that it could easily stray into the hands of wives and servants, and even those without servants, who would be unable to comprehend the scale of the social threat represented by condoning a sexual affair between a titled lady and a mere gamekeeper. The fact that Lady Chatterley appeared to enjoy sex with her gamekeeper, and that DH Lawrence did nothing to suggest that he condemned such enjoyment was held to be conclusive evidence that the book could not possibly possess literary merit. In the House of Lords debate on the book Lord Hailsham introduced his own criteria for determining literary worth: "Before I accepted as valid or valuable, or even excusable, the relationship between Lady Chatterley and Mellors, I should like to know what sort of parents they became to the child … I should have liked to have seen the kind of house they proposed to set up together; I should have liked to know how Mellors would have survived living on Connie's … income of six hundred pounds … and I should have liked to know whether they acquired a circle of friends, or, if not, how their relationship survived social isolation." The jury – none of whose members were 14 year old schoolgirls – acquitted Penguin of issuing an obscene publication, and three million copies of the novel were sold in the next three months.

In Northern Ireland the 1959 Act did not apply and the relevant law was the legislation of 1857. In November 1960 a Nationalist Motion was debated in Stormont, not referring to *Lady Chatterley* by name, but calling on the government to take effective action against the objectionable and immoral literature which, it was claimed, was freely available for purchase throughout Northern Ireland. The Motion had been tabled in March but the *Lady Chatterley* decision in London now made it important to establish whether the book would be permitted to be sold in the province. Several hares were started. Cahir Healy read extensive extracts from *The News of the World* and *The People* in such detail that a Unionist MP predicted that the day's Hansard would sell as many copies as *Lady Chatterley*. Other Members pleaded for a distinction to be made between works which were intended to be obscene, and those where words and incidents in isolation might be held to be obscene, but which in the context of the overall work contributed to its reputation as literature. Reference was made to the works of Boccaccio, Shakespeare, Joyce, Fielding, Flaubert and Twain as well as Lawrence. It was a serious and orderly debate and there was general agreement that "filth for filth's sake" ought to be condemned, but rallied by Brian Faulkner as Minister of Home Affairs, the Unionist Members voted against the Motion on the grounds that effective action against harmful material already existed and was being implemented. It was not stated overtly, but it was clear that the government and its supporters were wary of endorsing a line of action which resembled the state censorship they had so frequently condemned in the Republic. Towards the end of November Brian Maginess as Attorney General ruled that, while he had not enjoyed reading *Lady Chatterley* and hoped that those who bought it would not leave it lying around where young people might read it, he did not regard the overall work as being obscene, and he did not intend to prohibit its sale. He refused to divulge the source of the copy of *Lady Chatterley* on which he had based his judgement.

The *Lady Chatterley* trial constituted a watershed, because it heralded the arrival of what came to be called the permissive society, the society which is so different from the age of Victorian morality which preceded it. It was just one of the ways in which the Northern Ireland of the late 50s was beginning to look more like the society we know today, and less like the country which lay on the far side of the gulf opened up by the War. Speaking to the Institute of Directors in 1959 Terence O'Neill, then the Minister of Finance, outlined the progress which had been made since the beginning of the decade. Among the figures he quoted were average wages in manufacturing industry up to £380 in 1957, one family in four now in possession of a TV, and the same proportion of car ownership. Before Christmas the wine merchants were offering Martell Cordon Bleu brandy for the equivalent of £3.25, Remy Martin for less than £3, and Charles Heidsiek champagne for just over £1.50. Not just in Britain but in Northern Ireland there were many who, in MacMillan's phrase of that year "had never had it so good". Also in 1959 a man stated that he had dropped off at Nutt's Corner airport two friends, who bought tickets at more than £20. All three then had a meal together at a cost of another £1. The motorist complained that in light of such expenditure he should not have been charged 1s for parking. In the same year RT ('Buster') McShane, Irish weight-lifting champion, opened Belfast's first gym aimed at those interested in keeping fit rather than becoming champions. Besides a coffee bar, novel features included classes for businessmen and for women. In 1960 cat and dog food – Cattomeat and Kennomeat respectively – began to be advertised, because "gone are the days when kitchen scraps alone were thought to be good enough for the family pet." As an example of what constitutes the bare necessities it was an apt summation of the developments which had taken place during the decade.

The flax harvest
Pulling the flax by hand was one of the most laborious tasks of the farming year.
(Courtesy of the Belfast Telegraph)

A ploughing competition in 1953
The Ferguson tractor could cultivate land which was difficult or impossible for horses.
The marquees indicate that the spectators intended to linger.
(Photographer: Arthur Campbell, Public Record Office in Northern Ireland, document
number D4122/B/39693)

The potato harvest
Gathering the Comber crop for the tables of Belfast.
(Public Record Office in Northern Ireland, document number INF/7A/11/6/1692)

When farming was child's play
With increasing mechanisation on the farm, the efforts of family members and
neighbours became steadily less important.
(BELUM.Y5326, © National Museums Northern Ireland, Collection Ulster Museum)

Glynn, Country Antrim
Picturesque thatched cottages, but water carried in, one white enamel pail at a time.
(Official UTA photo; Colourpoint Collection)

All the fun of the fair at Ballyclare in 1959
The town's traditional May Fair was one of many such gatherings whose time was passing,
as was the role of the donkey as a working farm animal.
(Courtesy of the Belfast Telegraph)

Sandy Row in Belfast in the mid-1950s
Cobbled streets, little shops and a delivery boy on a bicycle were typical features of
inner-city working class communities whilst living standards rose throughout the 50s.
*(Photographer: Arthur Campbell, Public Record Office in Northern Ireland, document
number D4122/B/55690)*

The lure of the silver screen
People queuing up for the opening of the thousand-seat Tivoli cinema in Finaghy, in 1955.
(Courtesy of the Belfast Telegraph)

The Picture House, Royal Avenue in Belfast
Known as The Avenue at the time of its closure in the early 1980s, this was one of a small handful of cinemas that did not feel the need for a glamorous name.
(HOYFM.BT.742, © Belfast Telegraph, Collection Ulster Folk & Transport Museum)

The circus comes to town
Seen here at Portadown Fair Green in 1959, Chipperfields was one of the biggest touring circuses in Europe in the post-war years. In an era when animal rights were given low priority, this circus even included a zoo.
(Official UTA photo; Colourpoint Collection)

The Festival of Britain in 1951
The farm and factory building on the exhibition site gave Castlereagh a (temporarily)
futuristic appearance.
(Public Record Office in Northern Ireland, document number COM/F4/8695)

The Festival Express running between Belfast and Derry
The Festival of Britain celebrates excellence, and a steam train in its glory has caught the mood.
(Official UTA photo; Colourpoint Collection)

The 1958 Northern Ireland World Cup team
They returned as heroic in defeat and set a standard never again matched.
(Courtesy of the Belfast Telegraph)

A selection of newspaper advertisements
from the 1950s

CHAPTER 3

A GOOD NIGHT OUT

ONE OF THE more insoluble problems presented in history is whether the things that made people laugh in earlier civilisations than our own are in any way similar to what we understand as constituting a recognisable sense of humour. Although the word 'comedy' is applied to the works of Sophocles and Shakespeare, neither of them bears a striking resemblance to *Only Fools and Horses*. We can presume that certain constants apply in every age – people have always wanted food, drink, warmth and a bit of social interaction with the opposite sex, but what amused or entertained them when these needs had been fulfilled? In previous centuries the nobility had minstrels and bards, hunting and jousting, while the lower orders had dancing, fighting and the odd public execution to stimulate their cultural appetites; but what did a chap do on a wet Monday night when the fire was smoking, the meat was burned, the beer had gone sour, the minstrel had laryngitis and the girls had all decided they wanted to wash their hair? They must have wished that somebody would hurry up and invent smoking.

To update and particularise that question, how did people in Northern Ireland spend wet nights in the early 50s? There were a number of options, but none was without its drawbacks. It was not a telephone-rich society, so social engagements were negotiated well in advance. At the beginning of the decade there were around 60,000 phones in Northern Ireland, but a high proportion of them were for official and business use rather than domestic chit-chat, and there were 11,000 on the waiting list, so communication still required face-to-face contact. Another 5,000 phones were installed in 1952, but the demand was still twice as great as the supply. It was rumoured that in Lurgan in 1950 it was quicker to walk than to make phonecall to anywhere within a mile of the town. An investigative reporter noted that there were 479 subscribers in Lurgan, 85 in Moira, 68 in Waringstown, and that the seven operators at the Lurgan switchboard were able to establish a connection to any of them within an average of four seconds. Outside the towns and cities the vast majority of the population believed that the most effective means of communication was to write a letter, address the envelope with delivery instructions which sometimes relied on the local knowledge of the postman at the other end to sort out the fine details, and apply a stamp to the envelope before walking to the nearest red-painted pillar box. For anything more urgent a call could be put through at one of the Gilbert Scott-designed public phone boxes which stood at relatively convenient public access points, sometimes outside the local Post Office. Inside the kiosk a complex ritual was undertaken of lifting the receiver, inserting four penny coins into the appropriate slot in a metal box below, and dialling the required number. Button A on the box was pressed when the call was connected, and Button B, located conveniently below Button A, was pressed when the call was not answered and the pennies were returned. 'Pips' were sounded when more coinage had to be inserted to prevent the call being terminated. Particularly in rural areas an un-technological race of people regarded the 'phone-box' with suspicion, terror and loathing, to an extent incomprehensible to a generation raised in a world of instant communication. But because of their status as a means of communication in an emergency, kiosks were rarely vandalised and (if the absence of reportage is true) never used as public toilets. Even by the early 60s telegrams were still being delivered (around 390,000 of them) but that was down from the 1.6 million which had been received in 1946, and the General Post Office was aware that, like the small boy carrying a message in a cleft stick beloved of Victorian novelists portraying life in the bush, this was a means of communication which was becoming surplus to modern needs.

Eating out was comparatively expensive and the choice of food limited, although with the ending of rationing the menus on offer became slightly more adventurous. Pubs were popular but again drinking was expensive relative to what most people earned. For most of the 50s in smaller towns (those with less than 5,000 inhabitants) pubs were required to close at 9.00 pm, although in country areas some unofficial leeway was usually negotiated with friendly local policemen. In larger towns closure took place at 10.00 pm and in theory without drinking-up time. The practice was widespread of men drinking until 9.00 pm, then driving at speed to the nearest large town to continue quaffing. It was acknowledged as unfortunate that in rural areas where in summertime people tended to work until dusk there was no opportunity to slake a thirst after 9.00 pm, whereas in the towns where work ceased at 6.00 pm the opportunities for drinking lasted until 10.00 pm; but this was Northern Ireland and such incidental anomalies were felt to be less important than preserving society from the perils of increased access to alcohol.

A survey published in 1949 claimed that in the UK as a whole, 79% of men and 49% of women went to the pub on a regular or semi-regular basis, although it was acknowledged that there were regional variations, such as in Wales where the temperance movement was strong. One suspects that the figures for Northern Ireland would have been significantly different, too. Although in many Northern Irish pubs the snug was situated just inside the front door, and drinks could be ordered with discretion, in rural areas women simply did not enter licensed premises, and even in the larger towns a certain stigma attached itself to women who frequented such venues. The pub in Northern Ireland was a male preserve, dedicated to the serious business of getting drunk, and with few concessions to female sensibilities. Squalor was accepted as an appropriate concomitant to an activity which still lacked full social acceptability, and lounge bars with carpets, soft seats and higher prices were a revolution in the vintner's trade which was happening only slowly. An informal *modus vivendi* seemed to be in place under which police would raid premises and fine the owner £2 or £3 for serving drink outside licensed hours, and the drinkers themselves 5s. One owner in County Armagh was aggrieved to be fined £5, the additional sum being imposed because the police complained of the inordinate delay which had taken place before they were admitted to the premises.

There was a continuing suspicion in certain quarters that moves were afoot to make alcohol respectable. Churches, particularly Protestant ones, by the mid-50s were complaining about increasing numbers of lounge bars attracting women and young people, and seemed almost regretful that "the day of the squalid public house is fast disappearing". Temperance societies monitored BBC programmes, even on radio, to detect references to booze, while the absence of a license at Nutt's Corner airport caused despair among those promoting tourism. But the government was very wary about changing the licensing laws in case opposition by the churches would spread to the backbenches. A fierce debate took place in Belfast Corporation about allowing alcohol to be advertised on the side of buses. The advertising agency concerned offered £65,000 but would increase that to £78,000 if drinks could be promoted. Despite transport services operating at an annual loss of £45,000, the temperance lobby contested the issue and the higher figure was only agreed by 20 votes to 17. This was not a society which regarded alcohol as the acceptable middle-class drug.

In terms of access to alcohol the picture was confused by the presence of numerous clubs which operated under a more relaxed regime than that applied to pubs, primarily because the police found it almost impossible to enforce the law. It was difficult in practice to distinguish between clubs which existed primarily for professional or recreational purposes, and those which were little more than drinking dens, often open until the early hours of the morning, and on Sundays. By the mid-50s there were around 135 licensed clubs in Northern Ireland, and it was recognised that both membership and the amount of money spent on alcohol within them had increased significantly since the end of the War. The Ulster Transport Club had over 1,800 members and Shorts almost as many. All sorts of figures could be, and were, quoted about the ratio of drink-generated revenues to membership. During a debate in Stormont in 1955 it was claimed that one unnamed club with 160 members had spent almost £12,000, or £74 a head on alcohol during the previous year. At the other end of the scale the example often quoted was the Down Hunt Club in Downpatrick, where the 42 members collectively disbursed a mere £81 over the year. By the late 50s there were 147 registered clubs, with a membership well in excess of 50,000, and they were recognised as being impossible to regulate with any degree of consistency.

Hotels were the third member of the so-called alcoholic trinity, and endless debate took place about the minimum number of rooms which had to be available for occupation for an establishment to hang onto its liquor license. It was argued that a paying guest was treating the hotel as a temporary home, and was therefore entitled to a similar degree of access to alcohol as would be the case in domestic circumstances; but how far should that dispensation extend in practical terms? In practice, not very far. In accordance with the law, drinks were supposed to be removed from tables at 9.00 pm or 10.00 pm, even if a wedding reception was in progress, and in some cases even residents were denied wine with their meals on Sundays. It would be easy to dismiss such restrictions as the application of outmoded puritan principles, but they represented an element in society which was genuinely concerned with these matters. Changing attitudes towards alcohol were another example of the shift in post-war values, and the process was not universally welcomed in an essentially conservative society. There was general acceptance of the fact that the overall levels of public drunkenness had declined significantly since the War, which in turn prompted the further debate about whether extending drinking hours would lead to increased or diminished levels of consumption. The debaters can perhaps be forgiven for not reaching any firm conclusions on that particular issue. Concern for the health of drinkers was not a consideration. To an extent which is creditable, concern for the moral wellbeing of society was a far more significant preoccupation.

Proposals to try and regularise the drinking laws were politically fraught. On the one hand it was recognised that it was necessary that order should be imposed on the drinks trade, but it was also acknowledged that any attempt to do so would probably result in a liberalisation of the regime, which would attract the opposition of temperance societies and the Protestant churches. A White Paper was published in 1955 but it was three years later before the government plucked up the courage to set out its proposals for legislation. A delegation from the United Christian Temperance Conference, representing 29 Protestant churches and organisations, who met the Minister of Home Affairs towards the end of 1958 was fairly typical. It opposed a uniform closing time of 10.00 pm, opposed the idea of a 15-minute drinking-up period, opposed the idea of a liquor license for Nutt's Corner airport, advocated the closure of all clubs on Sundays, and was strongly in favour of swingeing penalties being imposed for any breach of the licensing laws. It was not an approach which facilitated much compromise.

After a protracted period for consideration the government decided that a uniform closing time of 10.00 pm should apply to pubs, but the idea was rejected of them closing for three hours in the afternoon on the lines of the English model. Among the arguments advanced against this last proposal were those that the Oul Lammas Fair would cease to exist if visitors couldn't get a drink in the afternoon, that farmers would have to change their way of doing business on market days if they had to sell their animals before the pubs closed in the early afternoon, and that football supporters could not be expected to wait until 5.30 pm on Saturday before being able to discuss the afternoon's game over a drink. The ban on Sunday opening was maintained, the hours during which alcohol could be sold to hotel residents on Sundays and Christmas Day were shortened, no licenses were granted in respect of bus terminals, restrictions were placed on the extent to which restaurants could provide wine, and no dispensation was granted for pubs to open for business on Sundays or Christmas Day. On the other hand scope was provided for the more extended issue of licenses in rural areas, and one for Nutt's Corner, greater use of occasional licenses, and no significant proposals to deal with the nuisance presented by the less respectable clubs. Convictions for drunkenness were in decline – 1,830 in 1951 down to 1,238 in 1957 – and this was cited as evidence that more alcohol was unlikely to be consumed under the new proposals, but overall it was difficult to argue that opportunities for drinking had not been increased. Convictions for drunkenness rose slightly in the wake of the new law (1,731 in 1964) but thereafter diminished dramatically (29 in 2003) as police procedures changed, and in fact it is impossible to draw a meaningful comparison with the earlier figures. The Presbyterian churches in particular were incensed at what they saw as the government breaking an understanding which had been reached in 1955, and 70 congregations in Belfast were read an address that the government had acted in bad faith and forfeited its claim to the confidence and support of the people. One of the government's own backbenchers agreed: "In recent years the Unionist government in Northern Ireland has made some enemies, has lost the allegiance of a good many friends and has not made any considerable number of new ones. It would be more than unfortunate – it would be a disaster – if even the least feeling of antagonism should develop between the churches and the government." The government held its nerve however and introduced the reforms, obliging the churches to swallow their scruples; but in many eyes it represented a further crumbling of society's moral framework, and decades were to pass before any further liberalisation was attempted. When the new laws became operative in January 1959, there were no reports of rural pubs being swamped with customers wanting to take advantage of the additional hour of serving time, and the publicans interviewed felt that it was an extra hour's work for little extra profit.

As an alternative to the pub, club or hotel – or perhaps following on from them – there was dancing. In 1955 there were over 100 venues listed in the Belfast papers, around half of them used only on Saturday nights and festive occasions, but a good number used for mid-week relaxation or for corporate and business functions. During the summer months the ballrooms in the seaside resorts had dancing every night except Sunday, usually from 9.00 pm until 1.00 am. Every town with social pretensions had its ballroom, with names like the Golden Slipper, the Orpheus, the Starlite, the Pallidrome, Romano's, the Trocadero, the Arcadia – Portstewart even had its Palais-de-Dance – designed to suggest a world of sophistication and disciplined flirtation in an ambience of *fin de siècle* Vienna. There were novelty nights, Scottish nights, fancy dress nights, old time nights and countless variations which seemed to owe little to terpsichorean abilities. Nevertheless, the capacity to move gracefully around the floor in a foxtrot, waltz or quickstep was an essential social skill, and dancing classes were ruthlessly favoured by middle class parents determined to ensure that their offspring would learn how to move, physically and metaphorically, in the right circles.

In rural areas in every village there was a hotel, a parish hall, a parochial hall, an Orange, Foresters' or Hibernian hall or similar venue (a farmer's barn in good weather) where a small group of local musicians with varying degrees of skill could provide the necessary accompaniment to the collective gaiety. In many of these gatherings the parish priest would be on hand to ensure that high moral standards were observed, and that alcohol was not openly consumed. Complaints were made about young people jiving and colliding with those who wanted to display more traditional skills. Limavady Council prohibited jiving and jitterbugging in 1956 in the Town Hall on the grounds, justified or not, that such activity was causing ceilings in the building to crack. Despite such strictures, the *Coleraine Chronicle* in April that year was advertising no less than 14 dances in the area. In 1947, long before anyone had acquired the habit of being bored by television, the Ranfurley Arms in Dungannon had a dance from 3.00 pm to 6.00 pm on Christmas Day. Every provincial paper advertised dances every week and they formed part of social life to an extent which today seems beyond comprehension.

In the early 50s dancing in the larger ballrooms took place to the strains of a resident or semi-resident orchestra, with perhaps 15 to 20 musicians in tuxedos sitting behind stands reading sheet music and playing big band sounds, film scores and other favourites that the dancers had heard on the radio. Brylcreemed men and poised young women danced in a manner indistinguishable from that of their parents. Credit for breaking this worthy but unadventurous mould has been attributed to two iconoclastic bands from Northern Ireland – Clipper Carlton and Dave Glover – who initially began by introducing an interlude in the dancing when the band members would put on an informal show which the dancers could watch. Gradually the show came to dominate the entire performance with the musicians coming out from behind the sheet music to demonstrate their versatility, and by the late 50s that unique cultural hybrid, the Irish showband, had been born.

It did not prefigure a rush to Sodom and Gomorrah, but dancing to the showbands was regarded by authority figures as further evidence of moral laxity. In an age when opportunities for physical contact with the opposite sex were comparatively rare, a slow waltz could represent an erotic Odyssey. The Bishop of Derry's Lenten pastoral of 1959 referred to increasing numbers of marriages at too young an age, a trend "which is to be attributed to the abuse of the dancehall … Lent is a fitting time for breaking dangerous habits and getting a grip on oneself in this matter of amusement." His views were echoed by the Bishop of Raphoe who warned of dangers to the physical and moral health of young people who allowed themselves "excessive indulgence" in dancing, although what he would have considered an appropriate level of indulgence remained unclear. It is not difficult to see why Bill Hayley, Elvis and the American rock 'n roll invasion was regarded with such fear and loathing by the guardians of public morality.

But in the late 40s and for most of the 50s cinemas represented the main attraction. There were 46 cinemas operating in Belfast and its suburbs during the early 50s with evocative names like Gaumont, Alhambra, Gaiety, Lyceum, Coliseum, and Astoria. Derry had the Palace, the Strand, the Rialto and the City; Dungannon had the Astor, the Castle and the Viceroy; Enniskillen favoured the Ritz and the Regal; Ballymena the Towers and the State; Strabane the Commodore; Markethill the Olympic; Coleraine the Palladium and the Picture Palace; Irvinestown the Adelphi; Rathfriland boasted the Rath; and Kilkeel the Mourne. As with ballrooms, the names were meant to convey a certain sense of style. Of course, some proprietors prided themselves on a less romantic approach and Lisburn, Portadown and Cookstown were among the towns where viewing films took place in the pragmatic surroundings of The Picture House; but Dromore in County Tyrone made its own gallant stab at metropolitan sophistication by naming its cinema The Montague. An electricity strike in 1956 closed 128 cinemas throughout Northern Ireland, apart from the other 12 which had their own generators.

It is hard to recall the thrill of movies in what is now regarded as the golden age of cinema, but with so many cinemas to choose from and programmes changing frequently, usually on Monday and Thursday, it was unsurprising that some people went to 'the pictures' two or three times a week. We know more about the cinemas in Belfast than anywhere else, but it is reasonable to assume that what obtained in the city was replicated on a smaller scale elsewhere. The cinemas themselves were mostly designed to be opulent and impressive, and while some of the smallest ones could accommodate only around 500 (the Picturedrome on the Shankill Road, or the Diamond on the Falls), many could accommodate up to 1,500, a few 1,800, and the Ritz in Fisherwick Place could seat 2,200. Once inside a typical programme would include the main feature, a supporting film, a newsreel, a cartoon and a trailer for the forthcoming attractions. Cigarettes could be smoked, ice cream gnawed from a stick and sweets eaten in warmth and comfort at affordable prices. Depending on the degree of swankiness required, seats could cost less than 1s or as much as 5s, while the West End cinema on the Shankill Road kept its prices pegged at 1d, 3d or 6d between 1934 and its closure in 1960. The Gaumont in Castle Lane and the Ritz both had large and flamboyant organs until they were removed to make way for the new Cinemascope screens. Some people in Northern Ireland took the view that the cinema was, in modified form, the devil's playground, and irrespective of the content of the films shown objected on moral grounds to the screening of movies; but for most people a visit to the cinema was a form of affordable escapism which could not be found anywhere else.

Some of the films shown in the 50s are still regarded as classics – *White Christmas; Singin' in the Rain; Ben Hur; Psycho; High Noon; Bridge on the River Kwai* – and feature in the collection of anyone with aspirations to be a cineaste. There was also one which was described in advance as "The Supreme Human Drama of All Time … The Greatest Motion Picture ever made" – otherwise known to posterity as *The Ten Commandments*, shown in May 1958. But alongside the handful of classics there were hundreds of forgettable and forgotten screen-fillers, whose content can be deduced from titles like *Marshmallow Moon, Secret of Convict Lake; Canadian Mounties versus Atomic Invaders; Bride of the Gorilla; the Great Rupert;* and *Beast from 20,000 Fathoms* – many of them part of a sub-culture of American movies reflecting the national paranoia about atomic mutations and/or Communist plots. The Castle cinema on the Castlereagh Road showed so many westerns that for a time it was known colloquially, and more or less affectionately, as 'John Wayne's Stable'. The Rex on the Woodstock Road was owned by Willowfield Unionist Club. The Gaiety in North Street was reported to have evolved a protocol whereby its customers came from the Falls Road on three nights a week and from the Shankill on the other three. Many of these cinemas became targets for arsonists in the late 60s and early 70s, while others were forced to close by economic forces and changing tastes. Once attendances began to decline the trend became self-reinforcing – no one wanted to sit in a 1,000 seat cinema which is less than a quarter full – and more and more became converted into carpet warehouses and furniture showrooms. The Grand Opera House, now one of the jewels in Belfast's cultural crown, was almost converted into a bowling alley in the 50s and survived only because it showed films as well as staging live acts.

There was virtually no Sunday cinema. A dispensation had been granted during the war years which allowed films to be shown for members of the armed forces, and a few individual managers were able to hang on to this exemption, but generally speaking the screens were dark on Sunday. In 1956 Unionist MP Nat Minford, who was not renowned for his liberal views, suggested that at least some cinemas might be opened on Sundays, showing films which had been approved by religious bodies, since with everything else closed, including parks, children had nowhere to go but the roads and streets. No action resulted however. Indeed consideration was given to implementing restrictions on the hours during which young people should be permitted to go to the cinema, there being some fear that those keeping late hours at the movies were contributing in some way to juvenile delinquency. The content of the films shown was also carefully controlled and the X certificate was introduced in 1951. The duties expected of the censor were illustrated by a review of *The Lavender Hill Mob*, released in 1951, and now regarded as one of the minor classics of British cinema. A respectable bank clerk (Alec Guinness) teams up with the owner of a factory making tourist souvenirs (Stanley Holloway) to steal a delivery of bullion and smuggle it out of the country disguised as miniature Eiffel Tower paperweights. Until the last minute it looked as if the scheme would succeed, and the *Belfast Telegraph* reviewer wondered if censor had done his job properly because for most of the film it looked as if crime was going to pay: "We know, of course, that the censor would never pass it, but it is a definite surprise when the finale shows us that retribution has overtaken the wily criminal."

As already noted, on Derry Corporation Nationalist Councillors upheld the principles of the Catholic Church 'blacklist', using private late-night viewings of films to determine where the prohibition should apply. Since each Councillor was allowed to bring up to six guests, these viewings became immensely popular, but high standards applied and at one stage seven out of eight films were being turned down. Anything suggestive of teen culture was suspect, so titles like *Blue Jeans,* or *Teenager Lovers* aroused disapproval. That the Belfast Corporation Police Committee carried out the same function was indicative of the city's approach to its moral guardianship. Just occasionally however, a surprising result emerged. In 1955 *The Wild One*, starring Marlon Brando was held to be acceptable in Belfast. This was not intended, nor would the Police Committee have regarded any such attribution as a compliment, to represent a liberal approach; but it was felt that the excesses of a Californian motorcycle gang depicted in the film could never take place in Northern Ireland because the RUC would never permit such behaviour. In an interesting example of censorship in reverse, Central Armagh Unionist Association resolved in 1955 to request all three cinemas in Portadown to show the film *Martin Luther* at the same time, arguing that the moral content of the film was uplifting in itself, and suggesting that such an arrangement would not affect attendances because there was nothing in the film that any Catholic viewer should find offensive. The managers of the Portadown cinemas failed to appreciate the point. When the film was released towards the end of 1954 a review in the *Irish News* regretted that some of the more disreputable aspects of Luther's life had not been brought out, and in particular the anti-Semitism and rabble rousing which, the critic alleged, had led some scholars to insist that he was the forerunner of Hitler. It is doubtful whether the Armagh Unionists had access to such scholarship.

In Britain the official Committee on Children and the Cinema concluded in 1950 that movies did not bear sole responsibility for moral laxity and delinquency, but concern was expressed at kids being exposed to films with the message that "the highest values in life are riches, power, luxury and public adulation." That warning had little impact on the makers of films in the 1950s, and far from heeding it, it seems fair to say that the entertainment industry thereafter adopted what was meant as a criticism and enshrined it as the credo of its artistic ambition.

There were concerns in Belfast in 1956 when the film *Rock Around the Clock* was banned in towns and cities throughout Britain because the music incited youngsters to scream, jive in the aisles and rip up the seats. Jeremy Thorpe, later to acquire fame for, among other reasons, being leader of the Liberal Party, but then bidding to become an MP expressed the disquiet gripping society at large: "what worries me is that a fourth-rate film with fifth-rate music can pierce the thin shell of civilisation and turn people into wild dervishes." Or as a writer to the *News Chronicle* put it: "A cinema, sir, is a place where people go to enjoy films, and not a centre for tribal dancing and the relief of sexual neuroses..." Derry Corporation and Belfast Corporation Police Committee would certainly have agreed, but so too would most other people. But no industry ever became bankrupt by giving people what they wanted, and for a period in the mid and late 50s new cinemas were being built and old ones refurbished in Northern Ireland, an expression of confidence that the magic of the movies was here to stay.

For those nervous about the moral dangers of the dancehall and cinema, a night at the theatre held some attraction. Here again, while drama groups flourished in a number of towns, it is Belfast about which most information is available, and even that is far from being comprehensive. In the early 50s recognised international stars like Vera Lynn, Bob Hope, Laurel and Hardy all appeared on Belfast stages – the latter two confined to their hotel room on Royal Avenue for fear of being mobbed by fans. Such acts would appear at the Grand Opera House where boxes cost up to 30s (£1.50), the grand circle 3s 6d (17½p), and an unreserved seat in the gallery less than 1s. In other words, prices were for the most part comparable with those for the cinema. Over Christmas pantomimes ran in the Opera House and the Empire Theatre in Victoria Square, and a circus could usually be found in the King's Hall at Balmoral.

In Derry in 1952 the Christmas pantomime was *Christopher Columbus* and around 18,000 spectators were attracted during its three-week run. There was nothing parochial about these entertainments – in Derry in 1951 Noel Coward's *Blythe Spirit* was playing to packed houses at the Convent of Mercy Past Pupil's Drama Club, at the same time as the Derry Drama Club were mounting Rattigan's *The Browning Version* and St Patrick's Operatic Society was offering *The Mikado*. By 1953 Newry's annual music festival was celebrating its twenty-fifth year and flourishing, and the provincial newspapers were full of notices for the productions of drama circles and amateur players. Portadown Drama Society fortnight attracted such interest that some nights saw more than one play being staged. Portstewart Drama Festival was equally well supported, attracting drama groups from as far away as Belfast, while the Ballymoney festival in 1953 featured players from Armagh, Larne, Bangor and Queen's University. References to other, smaller 'drama weeks' throughout Northern Ireland were frequent. In 1956 Coleraine Music Festival attracted over 1,000 entries and ran for a week, while the same year Portstewart Festival had over 1,800, a sizeable number of them in Irish dancing. Such towns would have been affronted at any suggestion that Belfast was the cultural centre of Northern Ireland. Of course those with less discerning tastes might have visited Lisburn to see the largest living rat in the world, reportedly two feet long, plus the celebrated two-headed calf, as well as Minnie the Mischievous Monkey. Coward and Rattigan might have appreciated the competition.

The state of health of the theatre in Belfast during the 50s is not easy to assess because some of the traditional venues had converted or were in the process of converting to use as cinemas. In terms of straight theatre the Lyric was just beginning in the O'Malleys' house in Derryvolgie Avenue, and the Arts was still a small studio theatre in Little Donegall Street. In the late 40s and early 50s the big beast in the jungle was the Group Theatre where JG Devlin, Joe Tomelty, Harold Goldblatt, Elizabeth Begley and their colleagues held sway with a mix of classical drama and the ever-popular Ulster play featuring local accents and situations. Of those who won their spurs in the Group Billy Millar from Glengormley left to become Stephen Boyd in Hollywood, James Ellis and Colin Blakely took a less spectacular path towards developing their own screen personae, while James Young ('our Jimmie') made his reputation out of appearing not to act at all. A rumpus developed when the board of the Group, nervous of staging anything with a significant political content, cancelled a production of Sam Thompson's *Over the Bridge*. Reviewed in the *Belfast Telegraph* in 1960 as "a sincere but wordy play", it dealt with trade unionists confronting sectarianism in the shipyards, and was in effect a plea against bigotry, but the board felt that it was contrary to the theatre's policy of avoiding political controversy. Public rows and resignations followed. Thompson sued the Group for breach of contract and the whole affair descended into a debate about whether Northern Ireland was sufficiently self-confident to allow a degree of artistic controversy. Then, as was the case on subsequent occasions, no convincing answer was forthcoming. Although the Group continued in existence it never regained the prominence it had once enjoyed, in terms either of popularity or of artistic excellence. It was a positive development however, that building work was taking place on the new Arts Theatre in Botanic Avenue, designed to seat 400 people, twice the capacity of the old theatre in Little Donegall Street.

What produced such a rush of blood to the head is impossible to say but in 1956 the Minister of Finance, George Hanna, made a formal proposal that the government should purchase a disused theatre in Belfast, the Coliseum, and gift it, with continuing funding, to the newly-formed Ulster Theatre Trust. Only £50,000, he maintained, would be required for purchasing and refurbishing the building, and for the first year's running costs of what would be known as the Ulster Theatre. It was argued that the Empire theatre was sufficiently well-established to be untroubled by new competition, the Arts theatre group had a policy of *avant garde* productions and a clientele unlikely to be attracted to anything mainstream, and the Group was by then expected to go out of business in the near future, so the new theatre would be a natural fit on the cultural scene. For a Minister of Finance it was a remarkably insouciant approach to funding any organisation and his colleagues were not persuaded to back Hanna's whim, whereupon he came back with a proposal that a historic house and around 80 acres of land should be purchased as the site for an Ulster Folk Park. This too was rejected, but the idea surfaced again in 1957 when it was suggested that £80,000 should be spent on buying part of Belvoir Park for this purpose, with the additional benefit of preventing the encroachment of buildings along the banks of the Lagan below Shaw's Bridge.

Classical concerts featuring the City of Belfast Orchestra were held regularly in the Ulster Hall and Grosvenor Hall. The WEA (Workers' Educational Association) ran lecture series at the university. A fairly typical example from the early 50s was 10 talks on *An Introduction to Philosophy*, or six on *The Aesthetics of Architecture*. Whether such evenings counted as entertainment is difficult to say, but for those who liked intellectual uplift with more visual aids, in December 1954 a lecture in the Ulster Museum was given by Professor Anthony Blunt, then Surveyor of the Queen's Pictures and later to acquire prominence in quite a different capacity as the companion in espionage to the Russian agents Burgess and Maclean. In 1955 the Education Minister, Harry Midgley, proposed the foundation of a College of Music, claiming that for an initial outlay of £90,000 and running costs of £11,000 a year 200 students could be accommodated.

The idea was rejected by Midgley's colleagues as inappropriate at a time of financial restraint, with the result that when Hanna brought forward his proposal for an Ulster Theatre the following year, Midgley led the charge against it, arguing that if his idea was not going to be supported, he saw no reason why Hanna's should be favoured. A College of Music was another idea whose birth would be delayed for further years.

What seemed like an ideal opportunity for the spreading of cultural wings arose with the Festival of Britain in 1951. One of the declared aims of the Festival was "to provide a holiday celebration and a stimulus to the people of Britain after years of war and austerity"; another was "to show the world at large the strength of the British achievement in the Arts, Science and Industry" – both commendable objectives, but not exactly in tune with the views of a significant section of the population in Northern Ireland. Harry Diamond, the Nationalist MP for the Falls division of Belfast stated bluntly in Stormont towards the end of 1950 that for Nationalists to welcome the Festival was tantamount to recognising the partition of Ireland. A separate festival celebrating Northern Ireland might just have been acceptable in Diamond's view, but as it was, he doubted whether there was a multitude of people who felt they had anything much to celebrate.

While Nationalist MPs at Stormont invariably viewed public affairs through the prism of partition, there was some validity in Diamond's assessment that the public, irrespective of political affiliation, had little appetite for scarce funds to be expended on a celebration which, however valid from a British perspective, had a more restricted resonance elsewhere. Even in Britain the Beaverbrook press was determined to accentuate the negative, claiming that the Festival was unaffordable at a time of national belt-tightening, and would in any event prove to be both bureaucratic and dull.

There were grounds for such an assessment. The pillars of the Festival were the Central Exhibition on London's South Bank; a Science and Technology exhibition at one of the museums in Kensington; and an architectural exhibition in Poplar in east London. Apart from that there would be a shipbuilding and engineering exhibition in Kelvin Hall in Glasgow; and a travelling exhibition of amorphous character which would tour on board the converted aircraft carrier HMS *Campania*. Early on in the planning process it was made clear that there would be no dedicated space in any of these events in which to particularise the contribution of Northern Ireland or any other region of the UK – the idea was to celebrate Britishness in the widest sense. Northern Ireland was to devise events which would best celebrate local achievements. These would be submitted for approval by the local Festival committee, then by the overarching Festival Council in London, and finally by the Ministry of Finance which was the source of local funding.

It was not a formula which was likely to produce spontaneous jollity on a large scale in the best of circumstances, and in Northern Ireland it gave birth to a Festival programme in which three main events were regarded as part of the overall UK effort, and everything else was delegated to local authorities, drama societies, sports clubs, agricultural organisations and the like. The three principal events were a Farm and Factory exhibition on the Castlereagh industrial estate, then on the outskirts of Belfast. This was to focus on the development of the linen industry and agriculture in its past, present and future incarnations. The other two events were an extensive programme of arts and culture directed by Tyrone Guthrie, then working as a freelance director; and a visit by the floating Festival on the *Campania*.

By late 1950 it was apparent that local enthusiasm for the Festival was muted. Out of 60 local authorities contacted (the other 13 seemingly regarded as nugatory prospects) only 27 had anything planned, and of those 18 were in Antrim and Down, the areas which arguably took most pride in their loyalty to Britain. Councils in Fermanagh had one event planned, in Tyrone two and in Armagh three. Pre-arranged events like the Balmoral Show and an international ploughing match were co-opted to form part of the programme, and local groups were urged to organise their own arts festivals, sports events, tree planting schemes, or even just painting and clearing up unsightly premises. As the Chair of the Northern Ireland Festival Committee, Sir Roland Nugent said, with what was either enthusiasm or desperation, "Anything which displays the life of the country at its best, with all the richness of local colour and character, is a legitimate Festival activity." The Festival was planned to run from the beginning of May to the end of September 1951, and before the end Nugent was urging local committees to organise library exhibitions, shop window display competitions, or shopping weeks. His message was that, although the Festival was being driven by the British government, it was not itself a political affair, and in Northern Ireland was intended to be fully inclusive of local interests.

This balancing act seemed to drain much of the creative energy from the project, and by March 1951, two months before the scheduled start of proceedings, even the *Belfast Telegraph* acknowledged that there was no widespread demand for the Festival, and it had been progressed because no one wanted to be labelled as a killjoy, but in reality people felt they had been talked into something, almost against their wishes. To initiate proceedings Dame Dehra Parker, the Minister of Health, formally opened a Sir John Lavery exhibition in the Ulster Museum. Bonfires were lit and church bells rung, and the Lord Mayor of Belfast sent telegrams to 11 Belfasts in the USA, plus one each in South Africa and New Zealand. Even Sir Basil Brooke, who had a vested interest in striking a celebratory note, could only suggest that the Festival offered the opportunity for people to show the superiority of human will over pessimism and hostile circumstances.

Inevitably, therefore, the Festival became the victim of partisan politics. In Bangor everything from a collection of photographs of old Bangor, to a shopping week, to an exhibition of postage stamps, to the annual regatta was billed as part of Festival; but in Newry, while it was intended that the local music festival and the agricultural show should be brought under the Festival banner, in the event neither well-established event saw any advantage in changing its livery. Eventually a variety concert, a whist drive and an Empire Day parade followed by a tree-planting ceremony, running on consecutive nights in late May, made up the town's Festival contribution. The fact that proceedings took place in Orange halls and concluded with the singing of the National Anthem indicated that there may have been an absence of cross-community support. In Dungannon it was unclear whether Festival events took place, but the *Dungannon Observer* directed attention to Cookstown where a Festival week took place in late July featuring, among other attractions, a parade of 'non-Catholic' youth organisations, a fancy dress parade, a football tournament and a Fire Brigade demonstration. Proceedings were opened by a religious service for 'non-Catholics' and subsequent events took place under a large number of Union Jacks. Sir Basil Brooke opened the *Derry on Show* exhibition with the hope that "Derrymen would always be generous enough to allow Ulstermen everywhere to share their pride in the story of Londonderry" – an aspiration the *Derry Journal* refused to encourage, claiming that the event in Northern Ireland could be written off as "simply and solely a Unionist Party stunt ... a political and partisan demonstration in indecently thin disguise." The editor of the *Irish News*, speaking at a *feis* in July, saw in the limited success of the Festival the ultimate failure of the British efforts begun in 1690 to eliminate Gaelic culture, and congratulated his audience on the fact that they were not presently being forced to look happy at a Festival of Britain funfair.

Given the political climate of the time, a festival celebrating British achievements in the world was never going to play well in Northern Ireland. Nationalists were still smarting from the provisions of the Ireland Act of 1949, which reaffirmed the constitutional basis of the state as an integral part of the UK, and was seen as the British government copper-fastening Partition. In the circumstances, and irrespective of whatever personal feelings they may have held, Nationalists could not be seen to support a celebration of Britishness, and once that boycott was in place, allegations of a Unionist Party extravaganza became a self-fulfilling prophesy.

There were, of course, numerous successful events held under the Festival banner, although there was a sense of contrivance about claims that the Apprentice Boys' demonstration in Derry in late August had attracted record crowds because it had been 'associated' with the Festival. Although ill-health prevented King George VI from visiting the Farm and Factory exhibition at Montgomery Road, Castlereagh, his place alongside the Queen was taken by Princess Margaret, and it was described later by Sir Roland Nugent in suitably reverential terms: "It must surely have been one of the most delightful days in the history of Northern Ireland." It was claimed that the total of 150,000 people who visited the Farm and Factory site was far in excess of what had been predicted, but it was difficult to measure success or failure of the event overall. In Britain tourism rose by 15% and was estimated to have generated £19 million, which was almost twice the total cost of the Festival. In Northern Ireland, it had cost £72,000 to stage the Festival, but tangible benefits were impossible to identify.

Perhaps the most telling measure of success was the fact that soon afterwards the Irish government began to organise its own celebrations of Irish life and achievements in the yearly event *An Tostal* (roughly translated as 'At Home') which set out to create a "truer conception of the Irish nation and of the progress made in the cultural, social and economic spheres in the relatively short time since we won our national independence" by means of artistic, sporting and cultural events. It became a mirror image of the Northern Irish version of the Festival of Britain, with plaques being unveiled in honour of Wolfe Tone, two-minute silences observed for those who had died in the cause of achieving independence, parades led by veterans of the old IRA, all taking place under displays of Papal flags and Tricolours. In terms of non-Nationalist participation the results were entirely predictable, but this was dismissed by the *Derry Journal* as Unionist jealousy of "a great national festival". If imitation was the sincerest form of flattery it was no doubt unintentional.

Sport played an important, but not a dominant part in 1950s life. The amateur ethic remained fundamental. In line with the ethos of austerity then prevailing the London Olympics of 1948 received modest coverage, with the Unionist press regretting Britain's lack of success in winning medals, but also finding consolation in the fact. As the *Derry Standard* explained, there were two possible explanations. The first was that, unlike the Americans, British sportsmen and women had been deprived for the last nine years of proper food and nourishment; but the second, and more attractive reason was that British athletes refused to become 'pot-hunters', and played the game for its own sake rather than training to win at all costs. It was a thoroughly British mindset which was to cause increasing bewilderment in years to come as a succession of foreign nations refused to recognise the character-building virtues of learning to lose gracefully. The Helsinki Olympics in the summer of 1952 received respectful but limited coverage in the Belfast newspapers, and even less in the provincial press. The USA winning gold in the 3,000 metres received considerably less column inches in the *Irish News* than a report on the Ardoyne Confraternity Football League; while the *Newsletter* saw Britain's share of the medals again being eclipsed by the USA and Russia, and deplored the threat of impending professionalism: "If this [the Olympic Games] becomes a giant competition between two great nations, rich in talent and resources, the spirit of the Olympics will be destroyed." But, the paper added, "happily our sense of proportion, whether in victory or defeat, persists…" Four years later the Melbourne Olympics received slightly more attention, with Thelma Hopkins acquiring the status of home-grown heroine for winning silver in the high jump, but respectful notice was also taken of the achievements of Freddy Gilroy and John Caldwell, two Belfast boys boxing for Ireland, and of Ron Delaney winning gold for Ireland in the 1,500 metres. But again the provincial papers felt that such events would be of no interest to their readers. By 1960 television coverage of the Games in Rome provided a greater sense of immediacy than before, with the BBC in particular realising that extensive coverage of major sporting events was worth the additional expense involved. Increasing opportunities for spectating promoted increasing interest, and the seeds of a celebrity culture were being sown.

Until then however, sport was viewed, as the *Newsletter* indicated, with a sense of proportion. Fred Daly was not lionised for his achievement in winning golf's Open championship at Lytham St Anne's in 1948. Road racing for both cars and motorbikes had been popular since the late 1920s, because Northern Ireland was the only part of the UK with authority to close public roads to allow racing; but when they showed up for the Ulster Tourist Trophy races at Dundrod in the early 50s, Stirling Moss and Juan Fangio, then among the leading drivers in the world, were not hailed as heroes. Moss, indeed, in 1954 accepted the handicapping system which would have required him to lap the slower cars 23 times before he could have a chance of winning. On that occasion the race was won by a driver called Armagnac, who received a substantial advantage because his 750cc Packard was assumed to be capable of only reaching 64 mph, but in fact proved to have a top speed of 72. Nobody seems to have protested. When Roger Bannister broke the four-minute mile barrier in May 1954 it was noted in the *Belfast Telegraph* with no more than polite interest. There was no suggestion that Bannister, a medical student, should forget his career and focus instead on becoming a celebrity, and indeed later in the year he gave up athletics in order to complete his studies. As an irate letter-writer expressed it that same year when the BBC altered its scheduled programmes in order to cover the mixed doubles final at Wimbledon: "I think the BBC is wrong in its assumption that we are a sports crazy nation."

Football, too, had a different set of values. Due to the fact that it was played in both Protestant and Catholic schools, the game had a broadly bipartisan following, although the capacity for friction was never very far away. Crowd trouble at a game on Boxing Day 1948 against local rivals Linfield led Belfast Celtic, one of the Irish League's most successful teams, to withdraw from all competitions at the end of the season. Many of Celtic's players and a reasonable section of its support were Unionists, but the club was regarded as being Nationalist, and despite its undoubted success was allowed to fold. For years to come football fans would debate whether Celtic had been the greatest club side in Ireland, but in 1949 football, although important, was still just a game, and even the demise of a successful club did not become an event of national significance. It could be difficult to distinguish between the tensions generated by inter-club rivalry – crowds on the terraces traditionally granting themselves a certain latitude in verbal expression – and those motivated by sectarianism, but the violence which broke out during a game between Linfield and Derry City in early 1955 when one of the Derry players waved at the crowd what was described as 'a religious emblem' there was little chance of mistaking the character of the subsequent disturbances.

Within football a certain code of honour still applied. In 1950 a player at Middlesbrough was suspended for seven days and fined £15 for disputing a referee's decision, and from contemporary reports the Irish League teams competed on the same basis of respect for the referee's authority. 1950 was also the year when Glentoran sold 18 year old Jimmy McIlroy to Burnley for what was thought to be £5,000 (such details were not made public) a figure which compared reasonably with the £20,000 which was reported to be the very top transfer fee paid in the English First Division. When Burnley came to Grosvenor Park to play a friendly against Distillery at the end of 1952 floodlights were used for what was said to be the first time in Northern Ireland, and although they cost the equivalent of £4.50 to run for the full 90 minutes, the experiment was generally regarded as being successful. Five years later, in 1957, although others had travelled by boat and coach, Glenavon became the first Irish League team to fly to Europe for a match, an event recognised as being so historic that the Mayor of Lurgan travelled on the flight to wish the players good luck on behalf of the people of Armagh.

Players regarded international football as the pinnacle of a professional career. When England lost 3–6 to Hungary at Wembley in November 1953 it triggered what was virtually a period of national mourning, since it was the first time in 90 years that the team had been beaten by a foreign side at home. The agony was compounded the following year when in the return match in Budapest the score was 7–1, and a debate took place within the Foreign Office whether England should play such matches in future, because losing to Iron Curtain nations could be regarded as damaging to British prestige and policy objectives. A few years later when a GB team had been beaten 4–1 by the Rest of Europe at Windsor Park it was suggested that it was the use by foreign players of 'ballet-style boots', as opposed to solid British toecaps, which had given them a decisive advantage. It was another example of Johnny Foreigner refusing to respect tradition, but even if they were better it is difficult to imagine that in the 1950s any man or boy in Northern Ireland would have turned out for a game of football wearing poncey boots, or even, God forbid, Continental-style tight shorts. Football in the 1950s was the embodiment of conservative values: no matter how cold it was, any local player who appeared wearing gloves at Windsor Park would have been taken behind the main stand and beaten to death for being homosexual. The GB against the Rest of Europe was an all-ticket match staged in 1955 to mark the seventy-fifth anniversary of the IFA, and the 58,000 spectators paid an average of 4s 6d (22½p) a head for the privilege. It would not have been an inconsiderable sum for a working man, and it says something about the popularity of football, although on this occasion part of the attraction was the fact that the GB side was captained by local hero Danny Blanchflower. It said something, too, about the class of spectator who favoured rugby, when the following year the price of admission to the covered stand at Lansdowne Road for an international game was raised from 15s (75p) to £1.

In Northern Ireland international football had its own baggage. The administrators of the game in the two parts of Ireland – the Irish Football Association (IFA) in the north and the Football Association of Ireland (FAI) in the south – were locked in permanent disagreement about nomenclature. The IFA insisted that it had been the governing body of the sport in Ireland before partition, and after 1921 it was the southern clubs which had seceded to form their own Association, but that did not alter the fact that the Belfast-based body was the only one which legitimately could claim to have 'Ireland' in its title. The result was that the Northern Ireland football team continued to turn out as 'Ireland' and the southern team as 'the Republic of Ireland'. In 1953 when the International Football Federation ruled that Northern Ireland should play its home games at Windsor Park under the name 'Northern Ireland' the IFA contested the decision on the grounds that the national game of Ireland was Gaelic football, and soccer deserved to be represented in the north under the existing terminology. The appeal was upheld, and as a consequence in 1957 it was England 2 Ireland 3 at Wembley.

This terminology had wider implications. The *Irish News* continually tied itself in linguistic knots to avoid using the term 'Northern Ireland' anywhere in its columns, not just in its reporting of football matches, but this became increasingly difficult to sustain in the build-up to the 1958 World Cup in Sweden. A friendly game against Italy at Windsor Park in December 1957 ended in a 2-all draw, and the 'rough tactics' of the Italian players provoked a near riot, with police using batons to protect the visitors. But the re-match in January at the same venue ended in a 2–1 victory for 'Ireland', and the team qualified to go through to the final rounds of the World Cup. For this latter game the *Irish News* referred to 'the Irishmen', 'the Irish', 'the IFA side' and 'the Six County side', but since the paper had previewed the game and given an extensive report on it there was evidently a reasonable degree of interest among its readers, and shortly afterwards Nationalist readers were able to follow the fortunes of a side named 'Ireland' which came from 'Northern Ireland' without suffering lasting psychological harm.

For Protestant supporters of the side there was an equally delicate moral dilemma. The IFA's Articles of Association prohibited the sanctioning of football on Sundays, and two of Northern Ireland's qualifying games in Sweden were scheduled for Sundays. Despite protest meetings, lobbying from the Protestant churches, MPs and the Loyal Orders, and calls for the team to be withdrawn from the competition the IFA stuck to its decision. The *Belfast Telegraph* pointed out the inconsistency that thousands of men who would not go to Windsor Park on Sunday would be perfectly prepared to watch World Cup games on television on the same day. Thereafter all the Belfast newspapers settled down to reporting events from Sweden. 9 June, Ireland 1, Czechoslovakia 0, "long passes baffle the clever Czechs". 12 June, Ireland 1, Argentina 3, "here was real world class from both teams". 16 June, Ireland 2, West Germany 2, "a great day for Ireland, the also-rans who held the world champions". 18 June, Ireland 2, Czechoslovakia 1 after extra time, "120 minutes of glory and determination". It could not last however. A squad of only 17, plus fatigue and injuries arising from having to play a fifth game in less than two weeks led to a 4–0 defeat by France. On the night of the French game there was some nervousness in political circles that the result of a Belfast Corporation by-election in the Victoria ward might be affected because so many people would be watching or listening to events in Sweden. As was usually the case in Belfast, sport was transitory, politics were permanent.

The Lord Mayor of Belfast, who accompanied the team to Sweden and was reported to be prominent in leading the after-match celebrations, announced that the performance of the team had done more for the image of Northern Ireland than any publicity campaign could have accomplished. But despite this, there were no hysterical receptions for the team returning home, no media interviews, no newspaper columns or ghosted autobiographies. If the Belfast papers were measured in their enthusiasm for the returning heroes, the provincial press barely acknowledged their existence. The *Derry Journal* carried a brief story headlined 'Their World Cup Run Ends' before commenting that the thousands who had watched the World Cup on TV would in future expect something more sophisticated than the normal kick and rush tactics which prevailed in the Irish League. The *Newry Reporter* ignored the competition until almost the end when it was realised that one of the heroes of the Ireland side was a local boy, Peter McParland, whose exploits merited a brief mention. The *Ballymena Observer* reported that the Vice Chairman of Ballymena United, by virtue of being a member of the IFA selection committee had been given a free trip to Sweden for the World Cup. He was stated to have been impressed by the games he saw, and by the beauty of the scenery and the friendliness of the people. The entire report consisted of a single, brief paragraph: football had to be kept in perspective.

Perhaps the excitement was retrospectively exaggerated, because although in October Ireland were ahead three times against England before drawing 3-all in front of a crowd of 58,000 at Windsor Park, no team from Northern Ireland ever again came close to equalling the exploits of 1958 in Sweden. In December 1959 the IFA announced that no team would be entered in the 1962 World Cup in Chile, because qualifying games would be played on Sundays. An informal street poll by the *Belfast Telegraph* found a surprisingly high level of support for the decision. A few days later the Secretary to the IFA announced that there was no truth in the rumour that players like Danny Blanchflower and Jimmy McIlroy might be eligible to play for England because they played for English clubs. In September 1960 the Lord's Day Observance Society was still reminding its members to be vigilant in case the IFA should decide to revisit its decision. It might have been some consolation to know that the Northern Ireland Ploughing Association was also agonising over an invitation to take part in a competition in Rome which might involve competing on a Sunday. After a debate on whether ploughing constituted a sport as such, the Association took the advice of the Orange Order and decided not to enter if Sunday involvement was required.

Such matters were taken seriously. In 1960 the Cabinet took some time to discuss the handling of a football match at Windsor Park involving a team from East Germany. Since East Germany did not have diplomatic recognition in the west, it was felt to be inappropriate that the East German national anthem should be played. And if the visitors' anthem was not played, advice from the Foreign Office was that it would not be appropriate for the home side to play theirs, and this was the procedure being adopted in England where another East German side was to play on the same day. But what would be the consequences of not playing 'God Save the Queen' before a match at Windsor Park? It was eventually decided to pass on the Foreign Office advice to the IFA, but in doing so, it would have to be made absolutely clear "that it must not be interpreted as meaning that the Northern Ireland Government are saying that 'God Save the Queen' should not be played at Windsor Park." In the event, both games were cancelled when the East Germans had difficulty in obtaining visas, and the IFA was spared the agony of making a decision that the government chose to avoid.

Apart from beach volleyball, most of the sports familiar to us today were available in the 1950s, and there were even entertainments like hare-coursing and beagling that are now less well regarded. A demonstration game of American football held at Ravenhill in 1954 was described as "an entertaining match between spacemen" and a form of rugby "without inhibitions" but with overtones of square dancing. A bright future was not predicted. It was inevitable that religion should exercise an influence on the activities undertaken. For Catholics, provided Mass had first been attended, Sunday was a day for recreation, while for Protestants even gardening or washing the car on a Sunday were liable to provoke disapproving frowns. It followed, therefore, that Gaelic sports attracted little support from Protestants, who, quite apart from finding uncongenial the nationalist ethos of the Gaelic Athletic Association, might have objected to paying for any form of entertainment on the

Sabbath. Comments made by the President of Derry GAA Board in 1950 indicated that the gap in cross-community understanding was unlikely to be easily bridged. Re-integration of Ireland as a national unit, he said, was a sincerely desired objective, but it had to be realised that such a development was only the first step to restoring in all its aspects the Gaelic way of life. The Tyrone senior football squad in 1958 presented its old jerseys and a Christmas hamper to the Republican internees in Crumlin Road prison, electing one of them, *in absentia*, to a position on the County Board. The same year at the Derry County Convention complaints were made that at the previous year's All-Ireland final, some of the very scarce tickets had been sold to persons known to be supporters of soccer and "followers of foreign games." Such sentiments were sincerely held by Gaelic enthusiasts, but they indicated a mindset which prided itself on its very absence of inclusivity. Nevertheless both Gaelic football and hurling were among the most popular spectator sports in Ireland, with All-Ireland finals at Croke Park regularly attracting crowds in excess of 80,000. Many Catholics (and a fair number of Protestants too) regarded rugby and cricket as elitist games perpetuating the traditions of the old ascendancy, and although the occasional international rugby match at Ravenhill might attract an influx of Catholic spectators from the south, the fact that no Catholic grammar school in Northern Ireland played rugby limited its appeal. Rugby indeed showed no sign of wishing to shed its elitist image. In 1954 the heads of 19 (Protestant) grammar schools turned down a proposal from the Minister of Education that soccer should be introduced into their sports programme. Although four were in favour, the rest were opposed, arguing that, given the greater size of a rugby team, more boys could gain the benefits of physical exercise. It was also suggested that rugby was less likely to distract boys from their homework, because no games at adult level were played at night, and besides, rugby was preferable to soccer in terms of team-building. What such contrived arguments amounted to was a form of crypto-snobbery, and an unspoken belief that soccer was the proletarian game played in intermediate schools by uncouth ruffians with no knowledge of Latin gerundives.

The GAA ban on playing 'foreign' games, although sometimes more honoured in the breach than the observance, inevitably had the effect of limiting Catholic participation in non-Gaelic sports. In 1954 the GAA authorities refused permission for Radio Éireann to broadcast a commentary on a St Patrick's Day game because the station was also carrying a soccer commentary the same day. Golf and bridge were held up as examples of pursuits in which both communities could meet on terms of friendship, although it was the professional middle classes who enjoyed the camaraderie, and the quantitative effect on wider community relations was small. Many tennis clubs were attached to particular churches, and opportunities for engagement with players from a different background occurred only in the course of competitions. Although popular in the greater Belfast area, the sport lacked widespread appeal in rural areas. Boxing was regarded as a Catholic sport, although the success of local boxers at Olympic Games throughout the 50s was well received in all quarters.

For those who did not participate in sport, there was always the opportunity to bet on the results of sporting encounters. Thousands of people did the weekly football pools, introduced into Northern Ireland in 1948 – the Mater hospital, indeed, received substantial funding (£169,000 in 1954) from the proceeds of one local pools promoter – and laid their wagers on the horses running at courses throughout Britain and Ireland, or on the greyhounds racing round the tracks at Celtic Park and Dunmore Stadium in Belfast or Brandeywell Stadium in Derry. Strictly speaking betting on the outcome of football matches was illegal, but the pools companies got round this inconvenience by extending credit to the punters, so that the money passed across was not a wager on that week's matches, but payment for the previous week's bet. There was widespread criticism when the Minister of Finance in 1951 introduced a tax on betting, because this was regarded as the government giving recognition to what had previously been an unacknowledged activity. As was the case with public houses, the police appeared to have developed an unofficial protocol with their local bookmakers which resulted in raids being made and fines paid on a regular and fairly business-like basis which recognised that betting was not going to go away, but ought not to be seen to be officially tolerated either. A Protestant minister in 1953, after warming up on sexual laxity, crimes of violence and the loosening of marriage bonds, found it astonishing that in "a Protestant country" the government should tolerate the existence of 400 illegal betting offices and refuse to check the craze for betting on football polls, which he claimed was sweeping through society. When the government introduced its proposals for the reform of betting and gambling in the summer of 1957 there was a general feeling that a balance had been struck between bringing the previously unregulated industry under some kind of control without being so draconian as to drive gambling underground. Bookmakers would be licensed at £25 a year, as would their premises at £250, and because this would apply only to businesses which had been in operation before July 1952 it was calculated that the number of bookie's shops would fall to around 100 in Belfast and 30 to 40 elsewhere. As was the case with the licensing laws the Protestant churches objected to the new proposals, but it must be assumed they did so with a feeling of resignation. They had mounted considerable resistance when Premium Bonds were introduced in 1956, on the theological grounds that what a man earned should be a fair reward for work undertaken, and any money not earned by honest endeavour was morally unacceptable. In June 1957 when ERNIE – the deliberately humanising acronym for Electronic Random Number Indicating Equipment, otherwise known as "a green-eyed mathematical genius" – picked the first 96 numbers to qualify for £1,000, the General Assembly of the Presbyterian Church still regarded it as shocking that the girls who worked in Post Offices should be obliged to sell Premium Bonds as part of their duties. When the government was promoting gambling as a national pastime, it was difficult to insist that bookmakers should be denied a living. The Belfast and District Bookmakers' Association took a legal action against the government on grounds of unfair discrimination in that the law's provisions did not recognise businesses commenced after July 1952, but lost in the Court of Appeal in 1960, possibly the only time the industry as a whole had made a mistake in calculating the odds.

If there is a common theme running through this account of leisure activities in the 50s, it is morality. The authority figures who most objected to loose behaviour in dancehalls were likely to be from a different tradition than those who found fault with football being played on a Sunday, and while Catholics were liable to be more concerned with the content of films, Protestants were more queasy about gambling and Sunday drinking. But all of them, from whichever religious tradition, had a view of what constituted appropriate public behaviour which today would be dismissed as almost Victorian. But they also recognised that the glaciers were beginning to melt, and that the assumptions which had governed society were beginning to change. Very few believed that such change would be for the better.

CHAPTER 4

THE BOX IN THE CORNER

IF THE BBC's figures are to be relied upon it seems that on Saturday nights a large section of the population of Northern Ireland avoided dancing, theatre, cinemas or anything to do with sport and stayed at home to listen to the wireless. In 1945 there were 150,000 wireless receiving licenses taken out. Given the fact that in many rural areas people could not afford a wireless, and making due allowance for the quota of persons in society who would have considered it morally reprehensible to buy a license, it seems safe to suppose that the vast majority of people who could listen to the radio, did so. Radios were bulky devices by modern standards, at times resembling pieces of walnut-veneered furniture, full of glowing valves which took time to warm up, and with large tuning dials marked with stations like Hilversum, Luxembourg, Allouis and Warsaw which provided somewhat uncertain signals with remote parts of the wider world. Some were at the leading edge of electronics however, and a model such as a Ferguson "5 valve, 3 waveband superhet with a special 2 watt negative feedback output stage and high sensitivity elliptical PM speaker" at 45gn (just over £47) demonstrated that even in the early 50s there was a clear link between perceptions of excellence and incomprehensibility of technical data. Until transistors came along it was difficult to reduce the size of receivers and even a 1952 Ferranti portable had a 'lightweight' battery which weighed eight pounds and cost just under £16. Radiograms, which combined a radio and a record player, constituted a formidable piece of furniture and occupied pride of place in the sitting room of any family who could afford one. Those with the autochange function which allowed a number of records to be loaded in advance were particularly expensive. None of this radio equipment was particularly cheap however, and it was little wonder that firms like Radio Rentals did a steady trade in hiring and repairing.

On BBC channels there was a choice between the Home Service, the Light Programme and the Third Programme, or alternatively there were the offerings of Radio Éireann, or 'Athlone' in common parlance. To take a snapshot, on a Saturday night in January 1952 the Home Service had local and national news, the weather forecast, a roundup of the day's sport, a play, *The McCooeys* (of which more later), *Letter from America* by Alistair Cook, plus light entertainment. The Light Programme had the *Jazz Club*, an omnibus edition of *The Archers*, recorded music on *Family Favourites*, and a concert by the BBC Midlands Orchestra. The Third Programme had choral and orchestral concerts, plus talks on British Foreign Policy and Three Kinds of Ancient Art. Radio Éireann was popular in the west of the province where the BBC was difficult to receive, and had programmes of recorded music, a Gaelic spot, a concert of traditional Irish songs, a *Farmers' Feature*, and *The Ballad-maker's Saturday Night*. All programmes ceased before midnight. To modern sensibilities all this might seem unspeakably bland, particularly for a night supposedly to be devoted to entertainment, but for many thousands of people on hundreds of Saturday nights, this was entertainment.

At other times and on other nights the thousands laughed at *The Goon Show* and *Hancock's Half-hour* (the latter from time to time featuring Harry Secombe when Hancock's nerves were unable to take the strain of appearing on the programme), and long before it acquired cult status the Third Programme did a 12-part dramatisation of *The Hobbit*. *Children's Hour* introduced a generation of young people to historical drama, music, talks, serial plays and news. *Gardener's Question Time* did (and continues to do) exactly what it said on the tin; three times a week *Workers' Playtime* introduced three lunchtime variety shows from factory canteens throughout Britain; and perhaps most quirky of all *Educating Archie* featured a ventriloquist and his dummy in a medium where the entire point and effect of ventriloquism was lost. But in terms of local output pride of place went to *The McCooeys*, a weekly soap opera about a Belfast working-class family written by Joseph Tomelty. The name of the family was chosen by Tomelty because he wanted it to be neutral in political and religious terms, and the phone book was consulted to ensure that no one would feel they were being singled out for satire. A number of McCooey families without telephones later made their presence known, but apparently without rancour. The programme ran from 1948 to 1957 and was listened to by half a million people in Northern Ireland, or one in three of the entire population.

Because of technical restrictions BBC Northern Ireland had to share a wavelength with BBC North-East and until 1963 programmes were shared between the two regions. It was not an ideal arrangement on either side, but the *Irish News* claimed most complaints came from England because the Northern Irish accent was incomprehensible, or, as the *Derry Journal* put it "the McCooeys are Greek to the Tynesiders". It must have worked the other way round, too, and pronounced Geordie accents are unlikely to have charmed listeners in rural Fermanagh. The *Derry Journal* of course was never averse to political point-scoring, claiming that Northern Ireland was so unimportant to the rest of the UK that it didn't warrant its own wavelength, and the paper insisted on listing the BBC Northern Ireland programmes under the heading 'Northern England and the Six Counties'.

What radio in Northern Ireland didn't have was political content. Throughout the 1940s a series of rows had arisen between BBC programme planners and the guardians of Unionist sensibilities, particularly in regard to the insertion of Irish content in St Patrick's Day broadcasts. An *Irish Half Hour* programme had been much favoured by the Dominions Office, perhaps still nursing a fantasy that Eire could be lured back into the Commonwealth, but this was detested by Unionist leaders who felt that it gave the impression to uninformed listeners in Britain that the two parts of Ireland had made an equal contribution to the war effort. Dismay at the content of broadcasts which were seen as giving undue prominence to the Nationalist perspective on affairs was voiced at a number of Cabinet meetings, but since the BBC was an independent organisation there was a limit to what could be done officially. The Northern Ireland Regional Director, however, seemed to be engagingly open to unofficial persuasion and was accused by some of making editorial decisions on the basis of what was acceptable to the members of the Ulster Club (an institution described by non-members as "a hotbed of Orange fascism") and generally taking the line that nothing should be broadcast which would assail the constitutional position of the province. When Eamon de Valera undertook what was blatantly a propaganda tour in Britain in 1948 Sir Basil Brooke held a meeting with senior BBC staff in Belfast to discuss whether their coverage of the Taoiseach's speeches would be seen as endorsing his views on the partitioning of Ireland. That attitude towards broadcasting persisted throughout the 50s. In Unionist eyes the BBC was a British institution and should not be used in ways which would undermine Northern Ireland's connection with the rest of the UK. News values and claims of objectivity were felt to be secondary considerations. Such differences of outlook were to provide the basis of many misunderstandings throughout the decade.

Despite such deficiencies, the place of radio in the affections of society seemed assured and permanent. Although the BBC had resumed TV transmissions in Britain in June 1946, in 1950 the manager of the radio department in a Belfast store held a demonstration in front of experts to prove that TV was not a viable proposition in Northern Ireland. For 20 minutes the group watched a receiver displaying 'flying particles of light' which stubbornly refused to form any recognisable pattern or picture. This demonstration was intended to persuade people not to hold off buying radio sets in the expectation of TV arriving. An amateur expert in Portadown claimed to be able to pick up signals from Sutton Coldfield near Birmingham, but it was reported that the pictures he received were "usually distinguishable, but not often clear."

Nonetheless the advent of TV was recognised as inevitable and in 1950 the *Belfast Telegraph,* drawing on the English experience, offered guidance on what to expect. It was explained that a TV receiver was "an object like a largish, chunky wireless set, with an oblong glass eye forming the most of one side". The paper warned that what was shown through the oblong glass eye was fundamentally different from the recorded action seen in the cinema, and was reckoned to be so addictive that it was fortunate that the BBC transmitted for only one hour in the afternoon and two in evening.

At the end of 1950 BBC announced plans for eight new transmitters to be erected by 1953, with Belfast sixth on the list of priority areas ahead of Aberdeen and Plymouth. Corrective statements had soon to be issued as the demands of the Cold War re-armament programme drained off manpower and resources, and the government refused to release essential supplies to the BBC, and soon 1954 was spoken of as being the earliest that the people of Belfast could expect to join the community of viewers. Within Northern Ireland there was little sense of disappointment that access was being denied to a cultural feast, but in some circles at least there was a distinct feeling that, once again, the province was not being treated on the same footing as the other parts of the UK.

The door was certainly being cracked open. By 1951 it was reported that there were two local holders of TV licenses, and one of them, a radio dealer, even claimed to be able to watch televised cricket from his home on the Antrim Road. As new transmitters like Sutton Coldfield and Holme Moss became operational reception in parts of Northern Ireland became possible, and although bad weather tended to play havoc with the signal, reports were received of experiments in locations like Kilkeel. Adventurous souls in Bangor were able to receive signals by the summer of 1952, and when the Kirk o' Shotts transmitter in Scotland became operational it was reported that reception was so improved that payment of the £2 license fee became almost palatable. When the Wenvoe transmitter in Wales began operations, also in 1952, it was noted that H-shaped aerials were beginning to be seen on houses all down the east coast of Ireland. 80% of the population of the UK was now, at least in theory, capable of receiving signals, but Northern Ireland was lumped with areas like Tyneside, Aberdeenshire and Devon and Cornwall as the unfortunate outcasts.

For many people in Northern Ireland their first exposure to the new medium would have occurred as TV was given its first public exposure at the Ideal Home Exhibition at Balmoral in September 1952. The initial response was muted, most people remaining unconvinced of the attractions of sitting in a darkened room watching a small flickering screen on a piece of equipment the cost of which was far beyond the normal family budget. A *Belfast Telegraph* editorial admitted that it was inevitable that TV would arrive in Northern Ireland, but wondered gloomily whether all such developments were necessarily beneficial: "Truth to tell, there are times when progress is more than a little disturbing." Certainly when it came to reviewing the highlights of the Exhibition TV was not referred to, and the main attraction was held to be a combined teapot and hot water jug which used only half the quantity of dry tea leaves normally required, and kept warm for three-quarters of an hour. There was no turning back the tide however. Although it was suggested that the typical cost of a TV receiver would be around £75, plus £10–12 for the aerial and a £2 license fee, the first advertisements to appear in the Belfast papers shortly afterwards were for a 17 valve Cossor with a 12 inch screen and a built-in radio costing £96. They were soon followed by inducements to purchase sets like the Regentone with a 15 inch aluminised tube which promised a picture so bright that it allowed the possibility of daytime viewing. From then on the stream of innovations and improvements never slackened.

By the end of 1952 what was causing a real tremor in Unionist hearts was the possibility that the BBC might just possibly be able to begin broadcasting in Northern Ireland in time for the Coronation of Queen Elizabeth in June the following year. Anxious potential viewers were assured that Sir Basil Brooke was using his political contacts in London to ensure that the project was delivered on time. The *Irish News* predictably dismissed the Coronation promise as the equivalent of bread and circuses, but by January 1953 the *Belfast Telegraph* had begun to publishing details of the TV programmes available in Britain, together with advice on the kind of food it was easiest to eat while viewing. Solemn discussions took place about whether the canny Northern Irishman would be prepared to follow his British counterpart and sacrifice the family holiday in the interests of buying a TV. It was pointed out that positioning a TV set in the viewing room was something deserving of serious consideration, because once installed moving a set was "often beyond the power of the average viewer", although it was not explained whether that warning related to the technical difficulties of moving a set, or to its physical bulk and weight. Motorists were asked to fit suppressors to their engines to cut down on interference with reception, and set owners were warned that hairdryers, cake mixers and other items of electrical equipment could also impact on the viewing experience. There was even debate about the ethics of televising the Coronation. On the one hand it was clearly desirable that the ceremony was seen by as many loyal subjects as possible, but on the other it was also important that the coverage was not so intrusive as to convert a sacred ceremony into something resembling a peepshow, as was said to be the trend in America. People contemplating the purchase of a TV set must have felt they were entering into a new and not entirely welcoming territory, where the concept of 'entertainment' was being given a different and slightly disturbing meaning. Going to 'the pictures' suddenly seemed like a very simple pleasure.

The BBC local service was inaugurated 1 May 1953, but it was a decidedly low-key affair since the range of the temporary transmitter, erected on the Glencairn Road in north Belfast, was 12 miles, and BBC London insisted, with a decided lack of fraternal feeling, that all outside broadcast units were being held on the mainland rehearsing for coverage of the Coronation the following month. As broadcasting began there were 600 license holders in Northern Ireland, but on the basis of sales of TV sets it was estimated that there were 5,000 by the date of the Coronation. The *Belfast Telegraph* published helpful advice for those planning Coronation parties: the room to be darkened but one window left open, an adult to supervise the TV set at all times, and the best seats to be reserved for older people. For those without access to TV arrangements were made for newsreel footage of the ceremony to be flown to Belfast for showing in cinemas on the night of Coronation, at late sittings, and special trains were laid on from Dublin to bring in southern viewers.

The local TV service was still very much in its infancy and its limitations were shown during the Royal Visit which took place the following month in early July. Since the new Queen and Prince Philip were undertaking a tour of the entire UK, there was perhaps some reluctance on the part of the BBC to lavish too much attention on the visit to any individual area, but the feeling in Belfast was that the coverage shown on the national network had been very disappointing. A temporary crisis was reported at Government House in Hillsborough, where the Queen and the Duke were staying, when poor reception on the Governor's TV set raised fears that even the meagre footage being broadcast would be difficult to view. Medical equipment in Lagan Valley hospital in Lisburn was suspected of being the source. The sense of disappointment at poor coverage was assuaged by assurances from London that in July the Corporation's best cameraman and his assistant would be sent to Belfast to cover the Twelfth celebrations for the first time. In the event coverage of the celebrations was edited down to two minutes, and those were considered in Unionist circles signally to have failed to capture the colour and pageantry of the spectacle. Demand continued to grow however, and by Christmas 1953 there were around 7,000 sets in Northern Ireland, with no sign of demand diminishing. Until the area was enlarged where programmes could be received, however, and the price of TV sets became more affordable, viewing would remain a minority pastime. If 7,000 sets represented a pool of around 30,000 viewers, it still paled in terms of popularity with the 475,000 who reportedly listened to *The McCooeys* each week.

Disappointment at the BBC's coverage of the Twelfth in 1953 was symptomatic of the uneasy relationship already referred to which existed between the broadcasters and the Unionist establishment. A White Paper in 1952 proposed Broadcasting Councils for Scotland, Wales and Northern Ireland, the membership of each to include representatives of local authorities, religious and cultural groups, and to be possessed of a substantial degree of autonomy in determining the content of local programmes. When this was discussed in the Stormont Cabinet fears were expressed that such control of local content "might result in the exclusion of good features taken from GB programmes to make way for poorer quality local items." These local items, it was delicately hinted, were liable to have a Gaelic colouration. (It was indicative of the sensitivities which existed on this point that it was only in 1948 that a local prohibition on broadcasting the results of Gaelic games had been lifted.) There was some discussion about whether Northern Ireland with its own Parliament and control of local affairs would lose face by shirking a challenge which Scotland and Wales were prepared to accept, but following consultations with local interest groups Sir Basil Brooke reported to his colleagues that the Regional Council proposal would be acceptable only if the government had the power of choosing and dismissing the membership. Since it was highly unlikely that the BBC would agree to such a degree of control, it was felt that the Regional Council in Northern Ireland should be established as an advisory body only.

In the circumstances, it was inevitable that once the dazzling novelty of TV had worn off it would not be exempt from Unionism's sense of what was fit to broadcast. Early in 1954 complaints were made that an edition of the quiz programme *Animal, Vegetable or Mineral* had been based entirely on a selection of objects held by the National Museum in Dublin, a circumstance which was held to amount to the BBC tacitly condoning the fact that thousands of people in the Republic watched TV without paying a license fee. A few weeks later the BBC's St Patrick's Day programme concentrated on events and locations in the Republic, ignoring numerous sites in Northern Ireland strongly associated with the Saint, and this was followed up by a feature from an Irish club in London in the course of which *A Soldier's Song* was aired. Unionist MPs in Stormont objected that only the term 'Ireland' had been used in these programmes, as if Northern Ireland did not exist, and saw in this "some subtle cause at work" which could not be explained by mere ignorance on the part of the BBC.

The reputation of the BBC suffered yet another blow towards the end of March when the religious programme *Lift Up Your Hearts* contained remarks by the Catholic Bishop of Leeds, Bishop Heenan, who offered the view that "we are so used to the toleration of minorities in England that we take it for granted. They don't elsewhere – in Spain for example, and in Northern Ireland – but their intolerance is nothing compared with the savage treatment of believers where active Communists are in control." Having already issued an apology for causing offence with the *Soldier's Song* incident, the BBC hurried to disassociate itself from Bishop Heenan's remarks, attributing the incident to human error, but also pointing out that since programmes involved human beings, it was impossible to offer any guarantees that no similar offence would ever be caused in the future. This was dismissed by Lord Brookeborough (as he had by then become) as "utterly inadequate", but was sufficiently offensive to prompt the Bishop to comment that he had suggested only that there was religious intolerance, not persecution, in Northern Ireland and that Brookeborough himself was "notoriously intolerant". As protests and counter protests were made – the Grand Orange Lodge of Ireland, the National Union of Protestants and the Anti-Partition League were among the first to join in – a Stormont debate did nothing to quell the storm. Strictly speaking broadcasting and the affairs of the BBC were not within the competence of Stormont and should not have been debated, but the occasion was turned into a glorious, full-scale Parliamentary battle where even comments like those of Nat Minford – who expressed a desire personally to cremate Bishop Heenan – were allowed to go unpunished. Shortly afterwards the Director General of the BBC wrote to Brookeborough to express regret at causing offence to the people of Northern Ireland, and offering assurance that there were no dark influences within the Corporation working against the interests of the province. By then dark influences were being detected everywhere. When a Unionist MP warned that the forces behind Senator McCarthy's anti-Communist drive in the US were the same influences as those behind Bishop Heenan, the *Irish News* promptly published an editorial giving strong support to McCarthy.

March 1954 continued to be a bad month for the BBC. The editor of *Panorama* mislaid the pre-arranged item on the St Patrick's celebrations and substituted at short notice a travel film *Ireland – Land of Welcomes* which promoted tourism in the Republic but again made no reference to the North. A propaganda film *The Promise of Barty O'Brien*, a fictional account of how rural electrification was brought to a farming family in an under-developed area in the Republic provoked further complaints. The film was one of a series showing the application of practical aid in various European countries, but Brookeborough objected on the grounds, among others, that it was not made clear that the family portrayed lived in the Republic, and that a misleading impression of agricultural life in Northern Ireland could be created. This was getting into the territory where attempts to counteract misrepresentation was coming dangerously close to censorship. An arrangement was said to have been made thereafter whereby the Regional Director in Belfast was to be consulted about the inclusion in any programme of content dealing with Ireland, north or south. Whether or not that was either practicable or practised, controversy appeared to be avoided for the next few years. Careful monitoring may have been responsible, but it seems equally possible that the result was achieved by the BBC in London deciding that all references to either part of Ireland were to be scrupulously avoided in the station's output.

Concerns about the dangerous effects of TV were not confined to the Unionist community however. A meeting of the Catholic Hierarchy at Maynooth in June 1954 was not encouraged by the prospect of TV spreading to Ireland. The meeting noted that in Britain in 1953 for every 100 licenses issued 71 were for radio and 29 for TV, but by 1954 the comparable figures were becoming more nearly equal, with radio licenses down to 58 per hundred and TV up to 42. The trend was not welcomed: "It is impossible not to be horrified at the thought that, through the medium of television, it might be possible for that atmosphere poisoned by materialism, fatuity and hedonism which is often breathed in so many cinemas to penetrate the very walls of the home." Public morality was back in town, and if anything, this seemed like a threat to the social fabric even more threatening than the dancehalls.

But the genie could not be put back in the bottle. By September 1954, a little over a year from the commencement of broadcasting, there were 14,000 local TV owners, and by April 1955 the figure had risen to 24,000. In mid-1955 the erection of a new transmitter on Divis mountain gave TV access to 80% of the province, and demand for sets in rural areas took off. Even so, it would be some time before parts of Londonderry and a few remote areas in the Mournes were able to receive signals. Freak atmospheric conditions were blamed for the loss of the BBC signal in July 1956, when for a period all that could be received in Northern Ireland were programmes from Germany and Holland. Viewers did not respond positively to the novelty of the situation.

It was a sign of the extent to which TV was becoming accepted as a political medium that in November 1955 Brookeborough took part in a live TV debate with a panel of journalists which included William Hardcastle of the *Daily Mail*, and Jack Sayers of the *Belfast Telegraph*. The subjects for discussion were controversial (gerrymandering, the Ulster Special Constabulary, the IRA, relations with the Republic) but the questioning was not abrasive and Brookeborough was able to put across the government's position without being subject to intensive cross-examination. At the end he even managed to include a rather laboured aphorism, claiming that such was the disposition of Nationalist politicians in Stormont that if there was to be a debate on eggs, they would claim that Nationalist hens were the victims of discrimination. In his private diaries Brookeborough professed himself pleased with the outcome, although he would have preferred fewer political questions and more opportunities to talk about life in Ulster. The idea that a politician should expect that he would be allowed to talk about social rather than political matters was an indication of the limited extent to which the rules of the new medium were understood. It was also the age when political interviewing was in its infancy. Nevertheless one of Brookeborough's fellow Ministers considered that his leader had been roughly handled by interviewers who were prejudiced in their approach and anxious to gain personal publicity. (A few years previously when Anthony Eden was interviewed on TV each question and answer were carefully rehearsed in advance, including the sign-off comment from the interviewer: "May I say thank you very much indeed for letting me question you?" The days were yet to come when the interviewer was the one who deigned to give politicians a platform.)

The BBC's monopoly was coming under challenge. In September 1955 ITV was launched in London. It was favourably received. There was an hour-long wait before the first commercial was aired, which turned out to be for Gibbs SR toothpaste, and at the end of the first night it was generally agreed that the programme content was comparable to that of the BBC. Early in 1956 it was reported that Northern Ireland was thirteenth on a list of possible ITV regions to receive the new service, and a five year delay was expected before the benison would be bestowed.

There were soon complaints in Britain about the deliberate populism of ITV. It introduced imported programmes from America like *I Love Lucy* and quiz shows such as *Double your Money* and *Take your Pick* which gave prizes, often, it was noted, to people with little discernible talent. These were ventures which the BBC regarded as the promotion of anti-intellectualism and refused to imitate. *Sunday Night at the London Palladium* offered unashamed glamour, and even the ITN news was deliberately less stuffy and solemn that BBC version. Within three months of being launched in the areas which could receive it, ITV was attracting around 60% of the viewing audience.

The *Belfast Telegraph* TV columnist spent a night in June 1954 watching ITV from a house on high ground in north Belfast where the signal from a new transmitter near Manchester could be received. He reported that reception was acceptable, the quality of the programmes was well up to the standards of the BBC, and the commercial breaks were not distracting. ITV officialdom paid lip service to the idea of including some intellectual roughage in their overall output, but admitted that building audience share – and hence profitability – was the first objective. Most people displayed little reluctance to being entertained and audiences continued to grow. Once again it seemed that the poor Northern Irish public was destined to be deprived of a treat enjoyed across the water.

In Northern Ireland enthusiasm for ITV was restrained at government level. It was noted in 1955 that the Independent Television Authority in London had appointed a news editor and a number of cameramen whose sympathies might not favour Unionism, and while it was recognised that any government interference with journalistic issues in an independent organisation would be counter-productive, it was felt appropriate to log the concern. Brookeborough set out the dilemma which Unionism faced with both the BBC and the future ITV: "What I should be inclined to fear more than the treatment of, say, some special programme about the IRA would be the more subtle and continuing injection into news items of anti-Ulster ... or pro-Republican sentiments by members of the staff who are not in sympathy with our traditions and outlook. Such things are often hard to pinpoint or challenge, but their cumulative effect can be most damaging." By 1957 it was reported that ITV were preparing to broadcast an interview with the IRA Chief of Staff, and although it turned out to be a hoax – the Chief of Staff proving to be an opportunistic Dublin journalist – the incident prompted fears that, even within ITV "there must be some sinister forces at work." The Reformed Presbyterian Synod voiced different concerns, arguing that ITV's advertisements for alcohol were the cleverest and most effective commercials aired, and that more people would be tempted than ever before.

The viewing public in Northern Ireland was not made privy to the government's concerns, but their sense of being deprived of something worthwhile was heightened by the fact that the BBC remained resolutely opposed to the idea of offering an unrelieved diet of entertainment. On weekdays programmes were interrupted after teatime – the 'toddler's truce' – to allow mothers to get the youngest children to bed before viewing resumed at 7.00 pm or 7.30 pm. The schedule for a Saturday night in April 1956 gives a flavour of what the BBC felt was appropriate for weekend relaxation: 7.00 pm, News, weather; 7.30 pm, *In Town Tonight*; 8.00 pm, *Scotland's Food Exhibition*; 8.20 pm, a play *Opportunity Murder*; 8.50 pm, *The Norman Evans show* (a Manchester comedian); 9.50 pm, *Saturday Night Out*; 10.15 pm, Mary O'Hara with her harp; 10.30 pm, *Sports Special*; 10.50 pm, News; 10.55 pm, Weather and closedown. As with the radio programmes noted earlier it seems startlingly unexciting by today's standards, but thousands appreciated such a mix of information and entertainment, and gazed with rapt attention until the National Anthem was played at the closedown and the picture dissolved into a bright dot in the middle of the screen.

By 1956 the glamour of TV had faded sufficiently to allow value judgements to be made. Complaints were aired in the women's pages of the Belfast papers that the content of programmes for women was inappropriate: "if we are going to have these friendly, girlish sessions, don't let us be sent back to school. We are bored with the tiresome paternal attitude adopted." It went without saying, of course, that when the BBC attempted to abandon paternalism, that too was a mistake, and TV was readily cited as one of the causes for the increase in juvenile delinquency: "This was inevitable with today's encouragement of free expression, and the opportunities young people had for reading bad literature, together with the spread on television of bad plays." Some responsibility was also attached to the growing cult of informality whereby TV interviewers were calling guests by their first name despite having been introduced only a few hours previously. This was regarded as possibly being permissible in sport, but parents and teachers must deplore such daily disregard of fundamental courtesy.

The BBC retained its strict standards, with newsreaders – who for some reason were regarded as being less important than the news they delivered – still not identified by name. In September 1957 BBC Northern Ireland began transmitting home-grown content with a daily five-minute slot for local news and features. This was broadcast from an unadorned studio with an announcing desk and an interview table. It was recognised that for financial reasons locally-produced programmes in Northern Ireland would for some time be confined to the studio and the content would be limited, but it was hoped that where visual images were felt to be necessary to illustrate the items under discussion, such distractions would be kept to a minimum. It was evident that the line between reporting and entertainment was not to be blurred.

But despite such displays of intellectual Puritanism and the absence of ITV the medium continued to flourish. In 1957 the Assistance Board was horrified to learn that a man in receipt of the dole had entered into a hire purchase agreement to purchase a TV, such a financial outlay not being regarded as essential to keeping body and soul together. Never slow to exploit a political opportunity, an *Irish News* editorial, tongue firmly in cheek, argued that the man's so-called extravagance merely fulfilled the objectives of those who for so long had campaigned for generosity in the welfare services – in other words the Unionists. Political point-scoring apart, it was an interesting sociological observation: in the space of a few years TV was on the way to becoming a necessity, not a luxury. It was indicative of the tightrope the BBC had to walk however, that a short time before the above complaint was made an apology had to be issued when the *Radio Times* in publicising a mass to be broadcast from Dungannon referred to the "supposed Corporeal Presence" of Christ in the Sacrament. Even non-Unionists reserved the right to feel offended on occasions.

Issues of public morality continued to snare the attention of the public representatives sitting in Stormont. In December 1957 Nationalist MP James McSparran made a bid to stake out the moral high ground, asking: "Has [the Prime Minister's] attention been directed to the indignation and disgust aroused among decent people of all religious beliefs in the Six Counties by recent television programmes which, under the pretext of discussing matters of public interest, are in reality pandering to the depraved tastes of a small section of the community and to their morbid desire for details about various forms of sexual perversity, prostitution and other crimes of indecency…"

No mention was made of the titles or specific content of the objectionable programmes, but it was agreed that they represented a threat to Christian values. One Member confessed that when television came to Northern Ireland he had hoped it would keep young people away from dancehalls, and encourage families to spend evenings together watching elevating programmes. Brookeborough with a commendably straight face professed that he sympathised with the views offered and would convey them to the BBC, but he was firmly opposed to censorship. Of course no one was going to appear as the champion of depraved tastes and morbid desires, and McSparran's appeal won cross-party support. In the following days the letter columns of the Belfast papers rang with similar complaints: "I find it difficult to see what good was achieved by bringing a homosexual to the studio to discuss his problems" was a typical offering, and fears were expressed that the BBC, frightened of being thought prudish in the face of ITV's surging popularity, had now gone too far in the opposite direction.

In the course of his comments McSparran moved on to an additional and quite different cause for concern: "The whole system of broadcasting whereby Cabinet Ministers are attacked most vigorously and cross-examined fiercely by Press correspondents is absolutely ridiculous and to my mind is becoming more ridiculous. It is all done in the name of democracy, but it is only making a mockery of ordinary public life as well as the status of these responsible Ministers. They should have some status and not be subject to attack by every Tom, Dick and Harry of a Press reporter." It was a fascinating example of parliamentary camaraderie, particularly in Stormont where exchanges across the floor of the Chamber were often of the most intemperate kind, and Ministers subjected to outright vituperation. It also perhaps indicated that TV had not yet earned its spurs. It seemed to be acceptable for a newspaper editorial to call into question not only a Minister's policies but also his political integrity, but not for a TV reporter to present a direct challenge along the same lines. Whether or not he intended them to be interpreted in such a light, McSparran's comments seemed to indicate that, in his eyes, the gentle handling Brookeborough had received at the hands of his TV interviewers two years previously was perfectly appropriate, and not a display of media pandering to the Unionist establishment. Perhaps only in Northern Ireland with its built-in electoral quotas would it have struck a politician as inappropriate that government Ministers should sometimes be questioned on their policies outside Parliament.

The display of political accord on the role of broadcasters which was generated by McSparran's speech was comparatively rare however. As early as the 1949 Stormont election discussions had taken place on the issue of party political broadcasts, but these had broken down in the absence of agreement on the amount of airtime which should be allocated to each party. A similar stalemate occurred in 1953, but by the late 50s it was realised that TV could be a valuable means of getting party messages directly into the homes of the electorate, and the stakes became higher. For the 1958 Stormont election the BBC offered eight slots for party political broadcasts on the radio, to be repeated on TV in sound only. The Unionist negotiators promptly claimed six out of the eight, leaving the Nationalists and the Northern Ireland Labour Party (NILP) with one each. In the subsequent discussions variations of this formula were suggested, including the novel proposal that the Nationalists and the NILP should make one joint broadcast, but eventually the Unionist claim prevailed. In the 1959 Westminster elections the same situation arose in a different form. Because Westminster elections were contested on a UK-wide basis, the BBC calculated that the nexus between the Conservatives and Unionists and between the Labour Party and the NILP, dictated that in the province the Unionists and NILP were entitled to the same amount of airtime. On the basis that they were fielding many more candidates the Unionists demanded four times as much exposure, adding that the NILP were standing only in Belfast. An additional complication was that Sinn Fein had been proscribed as an illegal organisation in Northern Ireland, but not on the mainland. At a series of meetings with senior BBC officials in Belfast it was pointed out by Unionist negotiators that for Sinn Fein to seek or achieve publicity with a view to advancing the party's aims and objectives was an offence in law, and that participating in broadcasts should therefore be forbidden. At that stage the Home Office became alarmed at the thought that if Sinn Fein could not participate in the election on the same basis as all the other parties in the UK it might constitute a breach of parliamentary privilege. In the resulting confusion the BBC's plans to include Northern Ireland in a series of televised regional debates quickly ran into the sand. Given that the format envisaged for each debate was the spokesman for each party facing questions from the audience, which no doubt would have included plenty of his or her opponent's supporters, it was probably not a great loss to democracy when it was decided to omit Northern Ireland from the scheme.

In 1958 ITV announced that it was planning to begin broadcasting in Northern Ireland in May 1959 – the potential to reach 800,000 viewers at last made a commercial service economically viable – but the General Post Office (GPO) proved unable to provide the necessary telecommunications links with the mainland and progress stalled. This became a matter of contention. It was claimed in September 1958 that local owners of TV sets "have long since discovered that an alternative service is an absolute necessity if interest is to be maintained and we are to get value for our money". Even in Stormont there were complaints that viewers in Northern Ireland should not have to pay the same license fee as the rest of the UK, because not only was ITV still unavailable, but BBC Scotland, whose signal was the one received in the north, occasionally imposed its own judgement on what should be transmitted, without consulting Belfast on the matter. If an important event in Britain clashed with an occasion BBC

Scotland considered more important, the Caledonian interest prevailed, the disgruntlement of Unionists in Northern Ireland notwithstanding.

By 1959 the BBC had returned to its place in Unionist demonology. In January a film about Northern Ireland for the *Tonight* programme was presented by Alan Wicker. It was a portrait of gritty realism, featuring interviews with men in a bookmaker's shop, slogans on walls and disreputable back streets. Following its transmission predictable howls of protest were heard that there had been no references to industrial development, to beauty spots, or to the role played by Northern Ireland in helping to win the War. Brian Faulkner in Parliament claimed that the programme had done "lethal harm" to the chances of further industrial investment in the north. Despite his Party leader's professed dislike of censorship Belfast MP Joe Morgan claimed the film was a further example of BBC bias, typical of 40 years of misrepresentation, and called for immediate state intervention, with the government to be placed in overall control of broadcasting. Rather than oppose such a crass proposal, the BBC once more avoided the issue of political interference in broadcasting and hurriedly withdrew subsequent Wicker reports.

The following month saw a row over the panel game *What's my Line?* where the object was for the panel of well-known figures to deduce from a series of "yes" and "no" answers the usually idiosyncratic occupation of the contestant, who mimed the actions associated with his or her job. (The contestant who worked as a saggar maker's bottom knocker – an obscure aspect of pottery manufacturing – represented the standard of exoticism to be aimed for.) In the course of an interrogation one of the panellists, Gilbert Harding, asked a female contestant originally from Northern Ireland, possibly on the basis of her accent, whether she was involved in cross-border cattle smuggling. Huge offence was taken at this in Belfast. Harding was a professional controversialist who was rude and irascible both on and off screen, with a list of prejudices which included the Catholic Hierarchy in Ireland, officialdom, and anything American. By his standards his question was nothing which merited apology. He professed himself to be fed up with the touchiness of viewers in Northern Ireland: "If they go on being as sensitive I shall begin to think they have something to be sensitive about". Had he been made aware of it Harding would have been fascinated by the rhetoric at the Ulster Unionist Council annual conference shortly afterwards, where a motion was debated asserting that the BBC gave too much prominence in its programmes to the position of the Catholic Church, and it was claimed that in the BBC's London headquarters a Roman Catholic Radio Guild had been formed by staff to promote Catholic doctrine and propaganda.

For those on the lookout for offence a minor classic was in the offing. In April the BBC screened the *Small World* discussion programme featuring the distinguished American newsman and broadcaster Ed Murrow, in conversation with guests Noel Coward, James Thurber and Virginia McKenna. It was a BBC/CBS joint production, intended to have an emphasis on wit and interesting conversation rather than in-depth analysis of major issues. Comments by Virginia McKenna to the effect that the IRA were "young idealists" who concentrated on blowing up buildings but avoiding injury to people, caused instant apoplexy in Unionist circles, particularly since a recent IRA ambush in Tyrone had almost succeeded in killing three police officers. As the customary protests rained down on the BBC, Brian Faulkner, the government Chief Whip resigned from the BBC Advisory Board, and the second episode of *Small World* was cancelled forthwith. In Stormont the debate followed predictable lines, with the Unionists' allegations of BBC bias being met by opposition cries of censorship. In similar fashion Miss McKenna's Belfast Nationalist background and her status as a distinguished artist were also searchingly examined, with Nat Minford declaring that hers was the kind of name one would bestow on a greyhound. The defining moment of the debate however, came when Brookeborough declared that he would never normally pay attention to the views of someone like Miss McKenna, but in view of her opinion of the IRA, "if she were put across someone's knee and spanked it would do her a great deal of good." In due course this *bon mot* was picked up in Britain. Michael Foot in the *Daily Herald* stated that the Director General of the BBC should have told Brookeborough to go to Hell, and McKenna invited onto a special programme to repeat with emphasis everything which Unionists had found offensive. As the ripples spread it was subsequently reported that McKenna had been invited to contest the Fermanagh/South Tyrone seat at the next election in the Nationalist interest.

ITV eventually arrived on the local scene at the end of October 1959. Two consortia had been bidding for the franchise, involving the three Belfast Unionist newspapers, and headed by Lord Antrim and Laurence Olivier respectively. Since the aims and objectives of both were not dissimilar the Independent Television Authority persuaded them to merge as Ulster Television Ltd (UTV), and in addition to factor in a greater degree of non-Unionist participation. Given its doubts as to where ITV loyalties lay, the government was wary of the new channel. In June 1959 the Minister of Labour confessed in the Cabinet that he faced a difficulty in granting a work permit to one of the senior personnel UTV wanted to recruit as head of their technical division, but whose background was untrustworthy – that is, suspected of harbouring anti-Unionist views. Yet to refuse a permit in such a case without citing due cause was liable to generate highly unfavourable publicity, and could cause charges of discrimination to be debated in Westminster. On investigation, it was established that the person concerned would be in charge of cameras and lighting, but would have no input to, or influence on the content of programmes, and the Cabinet decided that, on balance, the risks of withholding a permit were greater than those of granting it. But it had been a close run thing.

Channel 9 went live on 31 October 1959. Proceedings were introduced by Laurence Olivier, who had been recruited as a Director of the new company, and who on this occasion was suspected to have lunched well rather than wisely. The Governor of Northern Ireland, Lord Wakehurst made appropriate comments, and viewers settled down to watch *The Adventures of Robin Hood, 77 Sunset Strip* and news bulletins from ITN. It was generally conceded to have been a positive experience.

Inevitably, the UTV honeymoon was short-lived, and by early 1960 complaints were being made that in the commercials which had been broadcast before a five-minute religious affairs programme one had promoted a brand of ale, and the other had advertised a bra! Sensibilities were further outraged in March 1960 when an investigative documentary into youth culture entitled *Living for Kicks* caused outrage by its failure to condemn the moral shortcomings it exposed: "This feature, with its pseudo-clinical probings into the lust-life of various moronic nonentities was morally and artistically indefensible." Armagh Council, not customarily the champion of public virtue, condemned it as an example of "bringing filth to the fireside", while in Parliament Cahir Healy professed himself to be scandalised by the admission of a 17 year old male that of the 13 girls he claimed to have been in contact with "only one was what her mother expected her to be." It seemed not to have occurred to any of the critics that the professions of sexual freedom might have been exaggerated; and that even so, if such behaviour was taking place it was better to know about it than to hope it would go away if ignored. The idea that television had a role to play in informing society, not just entertaining it or supporting its traditional values, was one which would take some time to win acceptance in Northern Ireland.

It seems likely that UTV had a positive impact on the local BBC. Not only was there now a degree of competition in local programme-making, but the commercial station, reliant in reaching the widest possible range of viewers was much less bound to the Unionist establishment than was the BBC, and brought to its programming more of a bridge-building philosophy than the state broadcaster had felt to be necessary. Unashamedly populist, the commercial channel offered programmes which were designed to entertain in ways which the BBC's Reithian culture initially found difficult to emulate. UTV had a management and staff composed largely of local figures, and although the Northern Irish content was limited, the station's mix of programmes was popular from the start. Certainly as the TV industry headed into its second decade in the province there was a general feeling that the viewing public was better served as a result of the competition between the broadcasters.

By the end of the 50s there were a number of signposts to what would soon emerge as couch culture. In 1957 as part of a trial of the new schools programmes which were about to be launched, a boys' intermediate in Belfast took possession of a 27 inch TV, then the biggest screen in Northern Ireland. It was described as "a tremendous thing", but that may have been less of an expression of admiration for its ability to bring culture to the classroom as a wry acknowledgement that it had required the efforts of six people to carry it into place. The TV critic of the *Belfast Telegraph* suggested in 1959 that non-stop programming was encouraging people to slump in front of the screen for entire evenings, and that 10-minute breaks between programmes should be introduced. This, he claimed, would force the production of better programme content because audiences would not be allowed to remain in a semi-hypnotised trance, and would exercise greater critical judgement. Even then, it was a wonderfully romantic view, displaying a rather touching lack of insight into behavioural science. Shortly after, in 1960, a remote control gadget was advertised. This was a simple device which, when plugged in to the TV set allowed volume and brightness to be adjusted from the comfort of the armchair. Remote switching of channels was less important when there were only two to choose from, but the idea clearly had potential. A pay-as-you-view set was advertised in 1960. Known as 'slot TV' the idea was that viewing time was purchased by inserting coins into the set, and any money over and above the rental payment was returned. By the end of 1960 it was reported that the government was considering allocating the proposed third channel to the BBC, and in addition colour transmissions might soon be possible. Even in terms of domestic architecture television had now exercised a decisive influence. Where once the 'good room' had been used once a week or reserved for formal occasions, it now became the space where people consumed meals while watching TV, sitting on more comfortable furniture and surrounded by far less clutter than formerly. Although the advent of more TV sets within the house would dilute the effect, for a while in the early 60s what in many homes had been akin to a mausoleum was now on the way to becoming a living space.

But that was in the future. Where TV had a more immediate impact was on cinema attendance, particularly after ITV began broadcasting. Initially it looked as if cinemas in Northern Ireland were escaping the malaise afflicting Britain, and in the mid-50s, even as closures were taking place on the mainland, new picture palaces were opening here. The phenomenon was not to last however. In his Budgets in 1957 and 1958 Terence O'Neill as Minister of Finance lowered the tax on cinema admissions, and exempted from tax altogether the smaller cinemas in rural areas, specifically acknowledging that attendances were falling. By 1959 audience numbers were down by more than 20% compared to 1956. The news was not all bad – although seven cinemas had closed over the same period, five new ones had opened and three existing ones had been modernised – but the writing was on the wall. It was noted that there were numbers of people in Northern Ireland of a Puritan bent who regarded cinemas as dens of vice and who would shudder at the thought of entering one, but who were perfectly happy to sit at home and watch a movie on the TV. As TV became the dominant medium of entertainment cinema attendances were bound to slide. By the late 50s there were around 140 cinemas in Northern Ireland, employing some 1,200 people. Projectionists earned an average of £8–16 a week, and were held to be underpaid for the level of skill involved, while male ushers on £6–13 were reasonably recompensed for working indoors in less than arduous conditions. Regrettable though it was, there seemed to be no way of saving employment in a sphere which only a short time ago had appeared to be fulfilling a permanent need.

Even by 1960 TV reception was still poor or non-existent in the peripheral regions of Northern Ireland and towns like Larne, Warrenpoint, Enniskillen and Strabane would continue to suffer until the necessary booster masts had been built. But booster masts did not come without strings, so to speak. ITV was aware that its programmes were received in the southern border counties, and was attracted to the idea of including those viewers in its audience figures, and hence boosting the price it could charge for advertising. At the same time it was clear that the Republic would soon be establishing its own TV service, and might possibly beam its programmes into Northern Ireland, a course many Nationalists were known to favour – the President of the GAA indeed publicly insisting on it – and if ITV attempted penetration in the south, it would almost certainly encourage retaliatory action. In the event both the BBC and ITV were persuaded to forego seeking cross-border audience enhancement, and the fledgling southern TV company was only too glad not to have its appeal undermined by programmes beamed from the north. The broadcasters showed a disinclination to become embroiled in a political squabble, and an unofficial truce seems to have obtained. Within a few more years the Telstar satellite was being used to beam images from America, and multi-channel television was moving from concept to reality. In the years since television was introduced to the province, Northern Ireland had made the transition from a radio-focussed society into the beginnings of the multi-media circus of today. The Palais-de-Dance, the McCooeys, the Picturedrome and even two-headed calves were among the victims left in the dust when the juggernaut had passed.

The social impact of television is a field of study in its own right, but it is arguable that in an essentially rural society such as Northern Ireland the effects were more profound than in the more industrialised and less conservative areas of the UK. Society in post-war Northern Ireland was already undergoing a process of change, but the advent of television, bringing the world into the living rooms of the people, inculcating new ideas and challenging traditional attitudes with unprecedented immediacy, was one of the most significant factors in accelerating the transformation. And of course it would not be many years before the same medium of television brought the realities of life in Northern Ireland into the living rooms of the world.

CHAPTER 5

UP, UP AND AWAY

ONE OF THE other major promoters of social change in the 1950s was the huge growth in private transport. Trains, boats and planes existed for purposes of transportation, but for most ordinary people it was trains, buses (trams in Belfast) and bicycles – or walking. It was reported that textile magnate Sir Milne Barbour had registered one of the first cars in Ulster – indeed in Ireland – in 1904, bearing the letters IA1 in white on a red background. When the new Northern Ireland Parliament opened in 1921 Sir James Craig was the only Cabinet Minister to own a car, even though by then he shared the road with an estimated 3,300 other drivers. By the early 30s there were around 36,000 vehicles of all kinds being driven in Northern Ireland, which worked out at around three for every mile of roadway; and given that the majority of these vehicles were to be found in and around Belfast, it can be assumed that the rural roads were not exactly congested with machinery. Even by 1950 it was calculated that the traffic density was less than eight vehicles per mile but rising steadily, if slowly. Nevertheless, in the immediate post-war years Northern Ireland was still a society where personal mobility was not regarded as an entitlement. Particularly in rural areas, the distance which could be covered by bicycle defined the extent of most people's travel ambitions, while walking was still regarded as a perfectly reasonable means of meeting the requirements of the daily round. City life was of course lived at a more hectic pace, but overall, for most people expectations of travel remained broadly similar to those which had been entertained by previous generations.

Change was occurring however. The Holidays with Pay Act of 1948 introduced the concept of two weeks paid holiday for those in employment. Although modest in scope by our own contemporary standards, this created a more widespread concept of affordable leisure time than had previously existed, and new aspirations for travel blossomed as the austerity of the war years slowly receded.

For some people that meant foreign travel. The parlous state of the

British economy in the early 1950s led to restrictions being imposed on the amount of sterling which was allowed to leave the UK, and an upper limit of £50 was set for what could be taken abroad. If the figure seems to us to be unduly parsimonious, it must be viewed in the context of 14 day holidays in Europe being available for around £30 for travel and accommodation, thus leaving £20 for spending. In Belfast in 1951 Thomas Cook was offering 17 days in Montreux in Switzerland for under £29, 17 days in the Austrian Tyrol for just over £26, and five days Paris for under £14. Switzerland was highly rated by Northern Irish travellers, followed in terms of popularity by France, Norway and Sweden, with Italy favoured for religious festivals. Spain was advertised as "a glory of blazing sunshine, brilliant colour, richly ornamented buildings, music and dancing, gay nightlife and dreamy siestas, orange groves ..." (the phrase "gay nightlife" still being regarded as a synonym for carefree but wholesome heterosexual fun). Benidorm was still a little fishing village, the cult of 24 hour drinking was unknown, and it could reasonably be assumed that whatever hotels had been booked were probably fully built. Photographs of travel in such exotic locations could be taken with a Kodak Brownie camera costing less than 36s (£1.80), a sophisticated device which, provided bright sunlight was available, could take eight coloured pictures on a single roll of film. Many potential travellers must have been influenced by such considerations, because early in 1953 Thomas Cook moved to bigger Belfast offices. It was not until 1960 that the first direct flights from Belfast to Majorca and Benidorm became available – 14 nights full board plus all transport from under £60 – but after that the entire concept of foreign travel as an affordable luxury underwent a fundamental change. Almost literally, horizons were made wider.

Of course, travel by air was not only the quickest, but was also the most glamorous and expensive way to travel. In 1950 Air France was offering return flights from Belfast to Rome for £61, and to Madrid for £57. The British Overseas Airways Corporation, or BOAC, flew from Prestwick (about 30 miles outside Glasgow) to New York for a return fare of £228, although off-peak and 15 day returns were £60 to £90 cheaper, with the promise of on-board meals at "reasonable prices". Trans World Airlines (TWA) and Pan Am caught on to using Shannon as a more westerly departure point and their return fares were £130, or just under £200 for a seat in Presidential class. There was ample time for on-board meals to be purchased: in 1955 it was cause of celebration that the flight time from London to New York had been reduced from 13 to slightly less than 12 hours. That, however, compared very favourably with the advertisements for Pan Am's flights to Australia and New Zealand in 1951, when included in the five day package (no price quoted) was hotel accommodation in New York and San Francisco, and a free berth for the trans-Pacific leg of the journey.

It went without saying that passengers dressed at the height of fashion, because they were members of a decidedly elite club. Advertisements showed air stewardesses fawning over sleek and elegant couples, urging on them the benefits of Dunhill cigarettes, which claimed to be the preferred smoke for long flights. By modern standards the planes used even on transatlantic flights were quite small, and given the limited space in which to move about, or to prepare meals, it seems probable that smoking constituted one of the main sources of in-flight entertainment. In the early years of the decade, before commercial jet aircraft became widely available, piston-engined planes sometimes had to fly at altitudes which offered little opportunity to avoid turbulence in the atmosphere. Many of the meals at reasonable prices must have been consumed in circumstances of considerable discomfort. By 1951 both BOAC and its short-haul counterpart British European Airways (BEA) were both operating at a loss – £4.6 million in the case of the former – and announced that luxury services such as free drinks, free transport to the airport, and gifts for "special" customers would have to cease, a development which cannot have broadened the appeal of long flights. It was also a situation entirely of its time that, despite severe shortages of pilots, no airline would consider hiring women for duty in the cockpit, for reasons as various as the physical demands involved, the risk of a female co-pilot wanting to marry the captain, and the cancellation of bookings which would result if potential passengers were made aware of the awful truth that male hands might not be at the controls.

Some aspects of air travel were about to change however. In 1952 BOAC unveiled its secret weapon – the 40-seater de Havilland Comet jet airliner which was deployed on the 500 mph 'cannonball service' to Johannesburg. Even with stops at Rome, Beirut and Khartoum, and three changes of crew along the way, the trip was now possible in less than 24 hours. Equally important, the standards of comfort were higher, with a quieter cabin, less vibration, larger windows, a galley to prepare hot food, a bar and separate washrooms for men and women. By 1953 Comets were reaching Tokyo in less than 36 hours, compared to the previous time of almost four days, and the British aircraft industry had established a lead over all its rivals, particularly America. Then, almost literally, the wheels came off. Two Comets disintegrated in mid-air over Italy in 1954 due to what subsequently was diagnosed as metal fatigue, and the entire fleet was grounded during the investigation. There were local implications, because some of the Comet II craft were being built at Short Brothers, and production could not continue until the fault had been identified and eliminated. It was rumoured later that BOAC, de Havilland and the Air Ministry may have colluded in incomplete test procedures in order to get the Comet into service before the American competition, but no definitive proof ever emerged. The Comet did return to production, but it never regained the ground it had lost and by 1956 even BOAC was ordering Boeing 707s. A reporter on a flight by one of the new 707s in 1957 was impressed by its size and speed, but even more so by the fact that a normal conversation without shouting was now perfectly possible. The age of jet travel had arrived and suddenly the world was a smaller place.

Fliers from Northern Ireland did not deal in jet travel however, and the glamour of flight was somewhat diluted. The main airport was a converted RAF airstrip at Nutt's Corner, which had been given a civilian makeover and formally opened in November 1948, but the refurbishment amounted to little more than the addition of a ticket desk and a café/restaurant, and with no air terminal, it continued to resemble a collection of army huts. Being in Northern Ireland, there was no bar. Uniquely among UK airports, and despite the fury of those who sought to promote tourism, Nutt's Corner had no license to sell alcohol. No convincing rationale was advanced, but it seemed to be based on a belief that an airport was not regarded as an appropriate venue for relaxation and enjoyment. A bar would have been an enormous commercial success, because by the late 40s Nutt's Corner was said to be the fourth busiest airport in the UK, after Northolt, Heathrow and Glasgow, with an estimated 100,000 passengers per year arriving and departing. It seems safe to assume that at least some of them would have welcomed a drink.

The fare from Belfast to London was £11 return, Glasgow the equivalent of £4.50, Birmingham £8. Manchester, Liverpool and the Isle of Man were also served daily. It was noted that in 1937 the travel time to London was a surprisingly precise 4 hours and 35 minutes, and involved the passenger being picked up in central Belfast, driven to Newtownards airfield for a flight to Liverpool, a further flight to Croydon, finishing with a drive to Victoria station. In 1954 the route was more direct but the travel time from the pickup point at the BEA terminal in Belfast's Glengall Street was exactly the same. The Ulster Flyer departed from Nutt's Corner at 9.10 am and landed at 10.45 am, returning at 7.20 pm, and by 1955 BEA was running three flights a day. By then the glamour of flying was becoming tarnished and complaints were frequent about having to drink lukewarm coffee from plastic cups, and eating meals using half-size knives and forks, but here too, there was no turning back. By 1958 Nutt's Corner was handling 260,000 passenger movements a year and dealing with around 1,000 flights each month. The one million passengers a year mark was reached in 1969, and by 2006 the number had risen to five million. The causes of complaint have remained remarkably similar over the period however.

One of the recognised drawbacks of air travel was the time spent getting to and from the airport at all the major cities in the UK, and in 1951 the Interdepartmental Helicopter Committee of the Ministry of Civil Aviation concluded, perhaps unsurprisingly, that the future belonged to helicopters, "which must be regarded as the coming medium of commercial transport for distances up to 300 miles." A so-called 'rotor station' for access to helicopters could be built in an area of 90,000 square feet, which was regarded as obtainable in most city centres, and the Northern Ireland Transport Tribunal report of 1952 saw this as the next big development in flying from and within Northern Ireland. But even the rotor station might be unnecessary. In 1952 the head of BOAC predicted that by 1960 flights between Belfast and Manchester would be by helicopter, if buildings with suitable roofs could be found in city centres. In 1955 his successor predicted that helicopters and vertical take-off aircraft would make conventional airports redundant. Speaking to Portadown Chamber of Commerce the Northern Ireland manager of BEA suggested that it would be prudent in terms of planning to make space available in the town centre for helicopter landing pads, because in 10 to 12 years people would be commuting to Belfast by air. The Mayor of Portadown welcomed such forward thinking and pointed out that the town's prosperity in the past had benefitted from the fact that it constituted an important railway junction. If it did not prove feasible to have an airport in Portadown "we must at least have our own local helicopters to connect with the airlines."

Other visionaries predicted that the future lay with atomic powered flying boats, but these would be so heavy that no conventional runway would be able to support them, and land-based airports would become obsolete. Those with experience of flying boats might not have viewed such a prospect with delight, because although they were large, they were also slow, unpressurised, sometimes startlingly cold, and requiring frequent refuelling stops, often in choppy water, where seasickness could add to the ranks of the unwell. In addition embarking and disembarking had to take place by launch, sometimes in adverse conditions. The new generation of post-war flying boats were intended to travel to distant parts of the British Empire and were deliberately luxurious in design, but impracticable in operational terms and were never developed beyond prototypes.

The arguments about future trends helped explain why by the mid-50s Nutt's Corner was still little more than a dilapidated collection of huts. There was also an on-going debate about whether Nutt's Corner or Sydenham should be developed as the international airport. The former was remote from Belfast, with poor transport links, and vulnerable to flights being disrupted by fog; but the major – and decisive – drawback of the latter was the risk posed by aircraft taking off and landing over built-up areas. As part of the continuing debate it was pointed out that Sydenham airport had been opened in 1938 by no less a personage than Mrs Neville Chamberlain, who suggested that it would serve Belfast the way Croydon did London. It was also noted that in 1924 Belfast Corporation had spent £15,000 on acquiring a site for an aerodrome in the Malone area, but the cross-channel service, which utilised small, single-engined aircraft, had been discontinued after a few months. The Parliamentary Secretary to the Minister of Transport stated that if Nutt's Corner was to close, it should not be assumed that Sydenham was the automatic alternative, but it was to be several years later before Mr John Profumo dominated the headlines for entirely different reasons. Alternative sites for an international airport at Millisle and Comber were considered more suitable, but would have cost £2–3 million to develop. A crash by a BEA Viscount craft in October 1957 when it overshot the runway at Nutt's Corner, killing five crew members and a number of passengers, brought speculation that the airport's future was fatally blighted, and that operations would be moved to the old RAF airfield at Long Kesh.

In 1958 however, the decision was taken by the Ministry of Transport to spend £500,000 on developing Nutt's Corner, and even building a terminal. Undaunted by questions of transport links or access to Belfast, Coleraine Chamber of Commerce pointed out that the RAF station at Ballykelly would make an excellent alternative. In 1960 two air crashes over built-up areas, one in New York and the other in Munich, put paid to the idea that major developments should be permitted at Sydenham, but by then the decision had been taken to relocate from Nutt's Corner to Aldergrove, where the RAF would maintain a discreet presence and essential services could be shared. But even then speculation continued that with growth in numbers of big transatlantic jets flying between New York and London, Ireland as a whole would be bypassed and Northern Ireland would not need anything as grandiose as an international airport. Meanwhile the popularity of travel continued to increase. By 1959 it was estimated that there was a 500% rise in the number of Northern Irish people who wanted to travel abroad as compared with 10 years previously. With the currency restrictions eased people were prepared to pay, on average, around £50 for a Continental holiday, and take another £30 spending money. It was perhaps not coincidental that in 1959 Nutt's Corner was at last granted a liquor license. The Lord Mayor of Belfast formally opened the new bar in October that year, and although the dispensation also covered the restaurant, the transit lounge was excluded because women and children passed through it. There was some talk of running a railway extension to the airport from the Belfast–Antrim line but it came to nothing and connections to Belfast remained a weak link.

By the end of the decade direct flights from Belfast were being offered to a range of sunshine destinations – 15 days all-in on the Venice Lido for £63, the Italian Riviera for around £55, trips to Benidorm were priced in the lower £50s – and each year the full-page holiday promotions in the *Belfast Telegraph* became more elaborate, and ran throughout January. At the same time it was announced that, with tourists being allowed to spend up to £100 in America, a potential new market was opening. Double hotel rooms in the Broadway area of Manhattan could be had for less than £5 a night, and cheaper accommodation was readily available; while "excellent hamburgers and similar American dishes" made a sustaining meal for less than a dollar. With the dollar trading against the pound at almost three to one, and BOAC return flights from London at just over £150, it was a tempting proposition, and confirmed the belief that affordable long-distance travel was likely to see airport usage increase. Aer Lingus began offering flights to New York from Shannon at £149, with a £15 deposit and the rest repayable over two years. It was still more than most people could easily afford, but it was the beginning of the end of the era when taking to the air was an exclusive pastime reserved for the rich and famous.

For most people in Northern Ireland the prospect of foreign travel was remote. If advertisements in the newspapers are a reliable guide, the majority were content with day trips by bus or train at Easter, or at the Whitsun and August bank holidays. Belfast pleasure-seekers flocked to Portrush, Bangor, Newcastle, Warrenpoint and Whitehead, or to the zoo at Bellevue. Day trips by road and rail were available to Glendalough in Wicklow for the equivalent of £1.25 in third class, or to the Boyne Valley or Dublin for slightly less. Excursions to the Carlingford peninsula were available for the (post-decimal) sum of 55p, Buncrana for 87p, Portstewart for 40, Larne 23, Bangor 13, and Helen's Bay 10p. The Marble Arch caves in Fermanagh, now being illuminated by candles, were particularly recommended. Such advertisements were directed primarily at those based in Belfast, and offered the chance of a brief respite from the pressures of urban life. In this respect the provincial newspapers were far more restrained in their offerings – in many cases advertisements for day trips to Belfast for the Balmoral Show constituting the only evidence of interest in travel, creating the impression, rightly or wrongly, that gadding around the country was not a form of relaxation which appealed to simple country folk.

For those seeking relaxation on a more extended scale than was offered by day trips, cross-channel destinations were available. These were not necessarily cheap alternatives to Continental travel. In 1952 five days in Devon cost from 12–13gn (around £13), while 11 days in the Scottish Highlands could be had for 28gn (£29.40). The fact that prices were quoted in guineas was significant, and it is possible to detect a subtle hint of class. These could be seen as holidays targeted on those who did not wish to have their sensibilities assaulted by contact with unspeakable foreigners when abroad, or by having to rub shoulders with the populace at home. Wafting from these advertisements comes the aroma of middle-class respectability – the fixation with dressing properly for dinner, a meal which will be consumed in the hotel dining room in an atmosphere of delicately muted conversation and exquisite embarrassment if the cutlery by any chance should make a detectable noise. In 1960 when a strike by the national seamen's union led to the suspension of all shipping during the July holidays, fishermen in Northern Ireland did a lucrative cross-channel trade in ferrying stranded holidaymakers who could not get a seat, or who could not afford an airfare, to and from England and Scotland. Dresses may have got slightly creased in the crossing.

For less sensitive souls Butlin's holiday camp at Mosney, north of Dublin, beckoned. When it was first proposed in the late 40s the hierarchy of the Catholic Church in the south were strongly opposed to the importation onto Irish soil of an institution which was (a) British, and (b) held the promise of young people of both sexes mingling unsupervised in a moral cesspit. It was reported that opposition was only moderated when Billy Butlin promised to build a church as an integral part of the camp's attractions. Whether or not that was a factor, the camp was immensely popular with people from Northern Ireland. It held just under 3,000 campers and promised "A week's family holiday for a week's wages". The camps in Britain cost around £7 a week, but Mosney was smaller and may have been less expensive. Newspapers carried a series called Butlin Answers, where supposed queries from prospective holidaymakers received supposed answers from Billy Butlin himself.

Will there be enough food for the children? Will we be able to afford the amusements? I am not very sociable and am not good at mixing: will I be lonely? I am travelling on my own: will I be obliged to share a chalet with someone else? At the end of the July holidays in 1952 when 12 extra trains from Dublin were laid onto bring back holidaymakers from the south, an additional two were required for the Mosney contingent alone. People of a certain age still remember with enormous affection their weeks spent at Butlin's in an environment of boating lakes, Redcoats, knobbly knees contests, bonny baby competitions *et al* which was so utterly removed from everyday life. In the later years of the decade an annual Butlin's reunion dance in Belfast was a recognised part of the social scene. Given the popularity of Mosney it was not accidental that a rival should be established nearby. Red Island, at Skerries, described itself as "Ireland's happiest holiday camp" and promised a range of activities but "no regimentation, no insistent loudspeakers, no annoying restrictions, no organised gaiety." Despite being resolutely everything that Butlin's was not, the camp survived into the late 1970s, and was reputed to be very popular with British campers. New Butlin centres continued to be opened in Britain even in the 60s, but with the growth of package holidays to the Continent the popularity of holiday camps went into irreversible decline. Mosney did not escape the blight which afflicted the Butlin business empire and was eventually purchased by the Irish government in the 90s. In a surreal adjustment of its original purpose the site, still with much of its original infrastructure intact, now houses refugees and asylum seekers from around the world.

In a survey of British holidaymakers in 1952 it was claimed that 19% travelled by car, 14% by air, 8% by coach but 57% used the train to get to their destination. There might have been a few variations on those figures in Northern Ireland, but it was undoubtedly the case that the vast majority would have travelled by train. This was more than a little ironic, because by the early 50s, the railway era in Northern Ireland was almost at an end. A railway map of the 1920s shows almost 250 stations, halts and junctions in Northern Ireland, mostly in Antrim and Down, but even the west of the Province was comparatively well served, and with some 700 miles of track there were very few towns or villages that were unable to gain relatively convenient access to the system. The threat posed by the internal combustion engine was recognised even then however, and the first public inquiry into road traffic in 1934 recognised that the railways could not compete in the longer term. Just over 10 million passengers had been carried by the railways in 1933, but almost 40 million by road. During the war years both road and rail systems had been fully employed, and were even profitable, but the respite for the railways was temporary. In many ways the railway system was far too elaborate for a geographically small area, with an extensive road network, no major industrial centres to be connected, no requirement for freight transportation over long distances, and few heavily populated areas from which people would commute to work. It was a system designed for a different age; but even today many villages still have their Railway Terraces or Station Roads, the countryside has remains of bridges and embankments, and occasionally the distinctive red and cream brickwork of a private dwelling will betray its origins as a station house or converted offices. They are reminders of a system of transportation which was demolished with what many believe was ill-considered haste.

The trains belonged to an era when public transport was of paramount importance. When the trams were finally taken off the streets of Belfast in early 1954 it was calculated they had carried over four billion passengers since the system was inaugurated in 1905, with a peak of 155 million in 1945. At first glance that last figure seems incredible, but in a city of 440,000 (to say nothing of visitors), many of them making multiple journeys each day for work or pleasure it becomes more comprehensible. By way of comparison, in 1950–1951 the Ulster Transport Authority (UTA) operating outside Belfast carried 99 million bus and nine million train passengers. If the figures seem difficult to grasp, the reality behind them is simple – most people in Northern Ireland travelled by public transport.

The UTA was created in 1948, and was made up of the Belfast and County Down Railway, the Northern Counties Committee of the London, Midland and Scottish railway undertaking, plus the road services of the Northern Ireland Road Transport Board. It was a conglomerate intended to bring co-ordination to public transport, ensuring that road transport was used sparingly in support of the railways in areas where services were strong, and taking the strain in those locations where the trains did not run. Unfortunately the UTA operated under handicaps which militated against its ever fulfilling its remit to provide economic and efficient public transport. First of all it was not inclusive. Outside the conglomerate was the Great Northern Railway (GNR), the largest railway company to operate within Northern Ireland, together with a handful of small railways servicing local areas: the Dundalk, Newry and Greenore Railway; the Londonderry and Lough Swilly; the Sligo, Leitrim and Northern Counties lines; and the County Donegal Railways Joint Committee which operated the Strabane and Letterkenny line. In

1948 the UTA had around 400 miles of track, the GNR and the other companies slightly less. The second cause of weakness in the UTA was the fact that its operations were subject to the statutory authority of the Transport Tribunal for Northern Ireland, a body chaired by a former Appeals Court judge, which was firmly of the view that higher fares were no substitute for business efficiency, and which routinely refused to sanction the increases the Authority insisted were essential. The GNR, which was privately-owned and operating in both parts of Ireland, was not subject to the same constraints, and was able to operate in ways which maximised its advantages over the state-owned organisation. Overall, it was not a structure which guaranteed a prosperous future for railways in Northern Ireland.

As the economic realities which had been concealed by wartime activity became plain, the axe began to swing against the UTA's holdings. In the first six months of 1950, among the lines closed or with services drastically curtailed were those between Belfast and Newcastle, Belfast and Donaghadee, Ballymoney and Ballycastle, Limavady and Dungiven, Larne and Ballyclare, and Magherafelt and Draperstown. These were lines which the operating companies declared to be unprofitable, and with no prospect of ever becoming so. It was claimed that the eight-man crew of a train could transport the same number of passengers between Bangor and Belfast as 146 drivers and conductors by bus, and even if the figures were exaggerated for effect there appeared to be some logic in the argument; but the wider truth was that if lines operating in the most populous areas of Antrim and Down could not be persuaded to yield a profit, then it was highly unlikely that those serving more remote areas could reverse the trend. In the mid-50s, the price of a season ticket for rail travel between Belfast and Bangor was raised from £38 to £44 – an indication that even the Transport Tribunal realised that additional revenue was essential – but unprofitable lines could not be made solvent by such means. The UTA was forced to shed around a quarter of its line mileage in the first five years of operation.

Even the GNR was not immune from these considerations. In the early years of the decade it was making a loss of £250,000 a year on its operations within Northern Ireland, and requiring cross-subsidisation from its road transport function in the south in order to avoid a similar embarrassment there. Since the company operated on both sides of the Border any decision as to its future was one upon which the governments in Belfast and Dublin both had to agree. As early as 1950 proposals were being brought forward for the UTA and its southern equivalent CIÉ to jointly purchase the GNR, but questions of affordability and overall control ensured that negotiations were protracted, and it was not until the end of 1951 that it was announced that the two governments would purchase the assets of the GNR and lease them to a Joint Board. Thereafter, any losses incurred in either jurisdiction would become the responsibility of the relevant government. It was an accommodation, but it was not a solution. Within two years the accumulating deficits of the GNR had led Ministers in Northern Ireland to the conclusion that scrapping steam engines and replacing them with diesel locomotives with lower operational costs might help reduce the rate of loss, but could not eliminate it, and that there was no alternative to providing state subsidies. By 1955 it was reported that investment of £5 million would be required in order to create even the possibility of the railway system achieving profitability by 1964, and that possibility was itself predicated on the government writing off the accumulated debts which had occurred in the interim.

In Stormont in March 1956 the Minister of Finance declared that even the rapidly diminishing network was unsustainable. The government, he said, would act "swiftly, strongly and ruthlessly. A great part of our railway system must be scrapped without delay." In effect the government had taken the decision that the rail network in Northern Ireland was to be reduced to little more than three lines: Belfast to Dublin; Belfast to Derry; and Belfast to Bangor. Ministers might have regarded it with either amusement or despair, but at the Unionist Party conference in March a resolution was debated, calling on the government to ban the use of buses for all long-distance transport, obliging travellers to use trains and thus make the railway system economically viable. Before the end of the year the Cabinet was debating essentially two options: whether the introduction of diesel locomotives might achieve operational economies which could reduce the deficits of a minimalist system in the long term; or whether to accept that there was no prospect of ever achieving economic sustainability and scrap the entire system. In either event, closures would go ahead, and it was clear that the casualties would be concentrated in the south and west of the province.

Rail closures on a large scale was not a project which could be carried out immediately – job losses for railway employees, and the provision of alternative road transport services were just two of the issues upon which public opposition focussed once the government's plans were announced. The government in Dublin presented a convincing case that the contribution made by railways to the life of the community was one that should not be measured in financial terms alone; and simply in the geographical context of Northern Ireland the effect of the proposed closures would be to cut off all rail links with the west of the province, leaving only a narrow interconnected strip along the eastern rim. All kinds of questions were raised about what would happen in the event of a future war when large-scale mobilisation would be required, and there were serious concerns about the chances of economic development being spread throughout Northern Ireland if an effective transportation system was to be so circumscribed.

Local opposition to closure was fierce. It was an issue which crossed the usual political boundaries, and cross-border alliances were put together to co-ordinate resistance, with Enniskillen and Derry feeling particularly vulnerable to the effects of losing major linkages. The government was deaf to entreaty however, and after the round of closures in 1957 there were 338 miles of track left in Northern Ireland. In October 1957 the Fintona horse tram was towed to Belfast for a possible home in the Transport Museum, and it was hoped that Dick, the last in the line of the horses who had provided the locomotive power, could be found a final home with a local farmer. By the early 60s the rail network had been reduced to less than 300 miles of track and was fast becoming the skeleton which exists today.

Whether more could have been done to save the railways in the 1950s remains the subject of debate, but it seems clear that without a radical adjustment of how the problem was perceived, it was a battle the railways could not win. Even a basic point – that the roads were subsidised by all taxpayers but the railways had to finance their own infrastructure – seemed to be disregarded. The government based all argument around the goal of profitability, or at least minimising losses, thus setting the bar at a height the railway companies would find difficult, if not impossible to clear, and refused to give significant weight to the wider considerations of social value. Soundings taken in Britain indicated that the government there recognised that the rail system was destined to continue operating at a loss, but that a programme of substantial investment might help to at least manage the scale of the inevitable deficit. When in 1955, as already noted the Minister of Commerce brought forward the proposal for £5 million to be invested in the Northern Irish system, his colleague, the Minister of Finance, dismissed the idea out of hand, declaring it to be "the very mid-summer of madness", and that judgement prevailed.

Deprived of investment, therefore, the railways were caught in a downward spiral. Because they operated with older and less efficient locomotives and rolling stock, using sub-standard facilities, the travelling public was discouraged and passenger numbers declined, thus making it easier for the government to make the case that the quality of service being provided did not justify the levels of investment required to ameliorate the situation. Whether the newspapers helped to create a sense of fatalism, or whether they merely reflected the prevailing mood is difficult to say. The closures certainly created resentment in those areas where services were withdrawn, and even Lord Brookeborough faced political repercussions for his failure to oppose the closure of the Enniskillen to Omagh line. But somehow the opposition failed to translate into lobbying which was sufficiently effective to make the government change its mind.

By the late 1950s the buses and coaches of the UTA were the most visible sign of the competition faced by the railways, but they were not the only one. Perhaps the railways suffered ultimately from a perception that in the new scientific post-war world, where individual freedom would flourish as never before, the future of transport should of right be based on private mobility. Despite having already intervened in the public transport arena, the Northern Ireland government in the 1950s had a visceral dislike of anything which could be called nationalisation, and tried to avoid intervention where possible. As the age of the train was allowed to move into history, the age of the private car appeared to offer a more than adequate substitute.

The government certainly bought in to that vision. By the mid-50s, even as the railway system was being dismembered, it was made apparent in Stormont that the new priority would be roads. In 1956 the Minister of Commerce, Lord Glentoran, announced the new strategy in Parliament. It was, not unnaturally, based on getting traffic into and out of Belfast. There were to be a number of what were designated Approach Roads. The Northern Approach was to consist of a dual carriageway into the city from Ballyhenry in south Antrim; the Eastern Approach would feed in traffic from Tillysburn utilising the much-delayed Sydenham Bypass; and the Southern Approach would perform the same function from a vaguely-designated location in the vicinity of Lisburn. In all cases these Approach roads were to link up with new trunk roads which eventually would extend the network to Cultra in County Down in one direction and Dungannon in County Tyrone in the other. The total cost was estimated to be in the region of £7.5 million, a sum significantly greater than that which was suggested might save the railways. In a symbolic act – the old making way for the new – the bed of the disused Lagan Canal, which had been conveyed to the Ministry of Commerce in 1954, was now adopted as the course of the Southern Approach between Lisburn and Moira.

Whether such a roadbuilding strategy was affordable or even justifiable was not made the subject of prolonged debate. It seemed taken for granted that the future of personal transportation was on the road. One of the recurring fantasies of the 1950s was the idea of a tunnel under the North Sea so that people could drive from Northern Ireland to Scotland and northern England. It was an idea which resisted all attempts to kill it by financial, engineering or geological logic, because it embodied the ideal which for many people was becoming a reality – the capacity to abandon public transport and get around by private car. As Northern Ireland adjusted to the second half of the century a grandiose scheme for a new road network fitted perfectly with the mood of the times.

CHAPTER 6

TRANSPORTS OF DELIGHT

IF THE IDEA of an extensive motorway system for Northern Ireland seemed ambitious there was certainly room for an improved road network. The province already had over 13,000 miles of road, which arguably was more than enough for such a small area, but the quality was decidedly variable. At the top of the pyramid of excellence were trunk roads, which were those designated by the Ministry of Commerce as main through routes; then came Class I roads which ran between main towns; Class II roads connected smaller towns and villages; Class III comprised minor roads serving agricultural and industrial premises; and below that were unclassified or district roads where only agricultural vehicles dared to venture. In terms of quality however, there were severe imbalances. By 1954, out of the 13,000 miles of road, only 346 were rated in the trunk category – and a remote area like County Fermanagh had only 18 of them – while 7,500 miles, or more than half the total, were so unsatisfactory as to remain unclassified. These latter roads were capable of being used by cars in an emergency, but not by buses or lorries, but many even in the Class III category were denounced as being in such disrepair as to have those vehicles using them reduced to scrap in a short period of time.

The practical consequences were not difficult to discern – it was claimed by one of the Fermanagh MPs in 1956 that it took him five hours to get by road from Enniskillen to Belfast, and Omagh to Belfast by bus was a four-hour journey. Reports of deplorable conditions abounded. Around Coleraine in 1953 there were over 100 miles of roads surfaced with nothing but gravel and rolled-in sand, and it was estimated that it would be the 1970s before the deficiencies were remedied. A stretch of road in south Armagh ran on a high but unfenced embankment through a bog, where it was freely acknowledged that any mistake by a driver was liable to prove fatal. The hospitals in west Tyrone had to be supplied with a small ambulance because the regular model was too large for the roads it had to use. While the main roads were maintained by central government funds, the minor ones were the responsibility of the local Councils, with costs being borne on the rates, so reasons could usually be found for not remedying anything but the most unavoidable hazards. In 1947 the County Surveyor for Tyrone dismissed out of hand reports that the government was proposing that major roads should be 26 feet wide: "Autobahns might be desirable in the future but they are not desirable now." It was a road system which over the years had proved perfectly adequate for horse-drawn transport, but which was now being subjected to increasing usage by motor vehicles, and in particular by private cars.

Car ownership was not automatic in the early 50s. Production had been scaled back as Britain entered the Cold War era, and steel and other raw materials were diverted to fulfilling defence contracts. For Northern Ireland in the first six months of 1951 the allocation was less than 1,200 vehicles: 627 for Belfast, 37 for Derry city, 36 for Fermanagh, and 480 for everywhere else. Then there was the question of eligibility. To stake a claim to ownership of a new car it was necessary for the potential purchaser to have his or her name on a waiting list for up to six years in advance. Once acquired, a covenanting system precluded the owner of the new car from profiteering by selling it on within a two year period. The system had been introduced in 1946 and was finally phased out in 1953. Whether or not the profiteering fear was well-founded, it added an extra bureaucratic burden to car ownership, and enhanced the attractiveness of the second-hand car market. The Belfast papers in the early 50s were full of advertisements for cars, some of them dating from the late 30s, and often selling for prices not far short of new models. By the early 50s when there were 54,000 cars in Northern Ireland, 70% of them were pre-1947 models.

Much excitement was generated by the report in 1954 that Harry Ferguson was going to build a 'people's car' in Northern Ireland, using the same principles which had been so successful in the construction of his tractors. Ferguson had for a number of years been associated with promoting car and motorbike racing in Northern Ireland, but unfortunately for an equal number of years he and the Ministry of Commerce had had unsatisfactory dealings. Ferguson had a record of tempestuous business partnerships in America and Canada, and on more than one occasion had claimed to be developing projects which could be located in Northern Ireland if the Ministry would provide an appropriate level of funding. For its part the Ministry claimed the funding applications were seldom supported by a satisfactory business case. One example quoted in the Ministry files claimed that a proposal made by Ferguson in 1937 involving funding of between £100,000 and £200,000

Circuit of Ireland Rally 1955
The winner Robin McKinney faces the elements with flair and a flat cap.
(Courtesy of the Belfast Telegraph)

Coronation Party 1953
Plenty of adults are present to prevent the revelry getting out of hand, although boys
appear to be absent.
(Courtesy of the Belfast Telegraph)

Royal visit 1953
The new Queen and her consort meet their loyal subjects.
(Courtesy of the Belfast Telegraph)

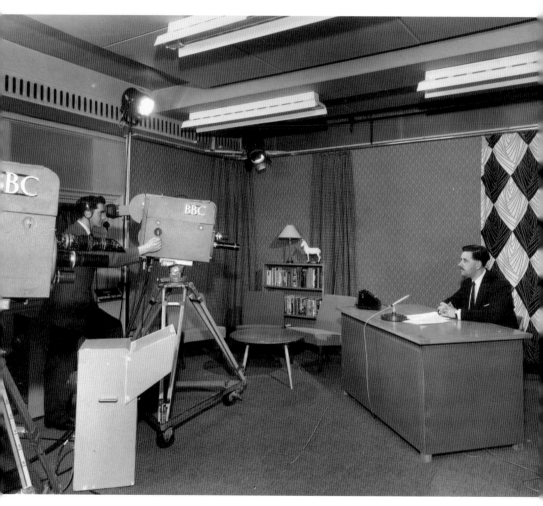

Presenting a programme on the BBC in 1957
After four years of broadcasting the studio avoids unnecessary visual distraction.
(Courtesy of the Belfast Telegraph)

Arrival of the commercial rival
Laurence Olivier launches UTV in 1959 and opens a new world of entertainment.
(Courtesy of the Belfast Telegraph)

The glamour of flying
Nutt's Corner without security checks, long-stay carparks, baggage carousels and shops.
(Official UTA photo; Colourpoint Collection)

Horse power
The horse tram which ran between Fintona Junction and the town. It must have been a formidable load for a single horse.
(Courtesy of Norman Johnston)

Bangor Station
The imposing architecture gives and indication of Bangor's status as a major destination.
(Official UTA photo; Colourpoint Collection)

Despite the absence of traffic, urban murk prevails
The old nineteenth century toll house seen here at the junction of the Lisburn Road and
Bradbury Place was demolished in the early 1960s.
(HOYFM.BT.311, © Belfast Telegraph, Collection Ulster Folk & Transport Museum)

Travel in an earlier age
Shaw's Bridge in Belfast, when a 17 foot wide roadway could cope with the traffic flow.
(HOYFM.BT.761, © Belfast Telegraph, Collection Ulster Folk & Transport Museum)

Belfast's Royal Avenue in the late 1940s
Trams and buses outnumber private cars, but pedestrians demonstrate their famous
disregard for road safety.
(HOYFM.BT.396, © Belfast Telegraph, Collection Ulster Folk & Transport Museum)

Primary education
Cloy Public Elementary School, County Fermanagh, celebrates its one hundredth
birthday in 1956. One teacher for 30 pupils was not considered remarkable.
(HOYFM.BT.1246, © Belfast Telegraph, Collection Ulster Folk & Transport Museum)

Secondary education
A technical college class pays rapt attention to a chemistry lesson. The presence of a the
camera may have induced untypically good behaviour.
(Public Record Office in Northern Ireland, document number INF/7A/18/10691)

The Sydenham Bypass shortly after its opening
A curiously tranquil picture, with little traffic on the road or at Sydenham airport, and
only the power station Belfast West sending its smoke into the peaceful air.
(Courtesy Roads Service)

Belfast Gasworks in 1950
The gasometers of Belfast Gasworks provide a striking urban landscape.
(Courtesy of the Belfast Telegraph)

Belfast's lamplighters
It was their task to turn the city's 16,000 gas lights on and off each day. In the background
are a line of old raid shelters, some of which remained for years after the war.
(HOYFM.BT.1202, © Belfast Telegraph, Collection Ulster Folk & Transport Museum)

had by 1951 been resurrected with a price tag of £10 million. Perhaps unsurprisingly, on this latest occasion the Ministry took the view that the taxpayer's money would be at too much risk in such a venture, and it was to be a further two decades before John DeLorean was able to produce a car-building project which would unlock the official coffers. For Northern Ireland there were to be two other ventures into the automotive industry (see page 131) but neither of them was able to free local drivers from their reliance on imported vehicles.

In terms of prices, in 1953 the range extended from the Ford Popular at £390 through to the Bentley exhibited at the Earl's Court Motor Show for £6,929. In between were the Ford Anglia at £515, the Morris Minor at £582, the Austin Somerset at £720, and the Ford Zephyr at £873. Around 2,000 new cars were brought into Northern Ireland in 1951: 523 Austins, 433 Fords, 303 Morrises, 94 Vauxhalls down to 21 MGs, 14 Jaguars, seven Bentleys and a single Rolls Royce, plus a small handful of Citroën, Daimler and Renault for those adventurous spirits who defied the conventional wisdom that British was best. The comparable figures for 1955, when 10,563 new cars were sold, indicated that tastes had not changed, with almost 3,000 Fords, 2,300 Austins, 1,800 Morrises and so on down to 231 Volkswagens, 43 Fiats, 12 Renaults, six Mercedes, four Citroëns and a single Alfa Romeo.

The list of vehicle marques from the 50s – Humber, Hillman, Alvis, Rover, Triumph, Wolsey, MG – summons up a vision of dedicated teams of British craftsmen in Coventry and Dagenham turning out cheap, well-built and reliable vehicles that were free from rust and which, with the appropriate application of oil and grease would run for ever. In terms of performance however, nostalgia can be misleading, because the performance of these 1940s and 1950s cars was positively primitive by our standards. The Ford Popular had a top speed of 60 mph, took 24 seconds to accelerate to 50 mph, and returned 36 mpg; plus it had totally ineffective headlights and wipers which refused to operate if the engine was pressed too hard. The Austin A40 cost £505, did 0–60 in 37 seconds and gave 34 mpg. The Austin A70 cost £845 and did 0–60 in 22 seconds and cruised comfortably at 65 mph, and for the driver's peace of mind was fitted with safety glass and what were referred to as "powerful brakes". As its name suggests, the Jowett Javelin was billed as a sports car, cost £819, had a top speed of 80 mph, but took 25 seconds to reach 60, and gave only 29 mpg. It was soon losing out to models such as the new Vauxhall Victor of 1957 which "sweeps you up to 50 mph in 14.5 seconds". In terms of performance however, the Bond Minicar enjoyed a unique place. With its 175 cc engine the promotional literature promised that it could be driven from Belfast to Dublin and back for less than 10 shillings' (50p) worth of fuel. What the literature did not specify was how long the journey would take, since the Minicar had a top speed of 40–45 mph only under the most favourable conditions, and lacked any reverse gear. In a road test in 1957 a Volkswagen was commended for attaining 60 mph on the flat, and for the fact that only on very steep hills was it necessary to change down into second gear, most inclines being manageable in third.

By 1952 it was predicted that the next big developments in cars would be automatic transmission and power steering, and as soon as a few minor snags had been ironed out, gas turbine engines would make petrol obsolete. The Standard Vanguard had tubeless tyres, and among its other extravagances listed courtesy lights, self-parking wipers and a heater, all being necessary to justify a price of over £900. Most car manufacturers regarded heaters as luxury items, while cigarette lighters were essential – as a Christmas present one year a device could be fitted in a car which not only held cigarettes but also dispensed them already lit when required – and seatbelts as less necessary than a starting handle. If a radio was fitted it was claimed that Dunlop Gold Seal tyres had non-static properties which gave improved reception. The Standard 8 cost £480 in 1955, but for an extra £28 came with coloured interior trim and wind-down windows, a level of extravagance which prompted one commentator to observe that "motorists are prepared to spend quite substantial sums for details that add nothing to a car's mechanical efficiency and little to the physical comfort of driving it." How typical the sample was is difficult to say but in a survey of commercial travellers carried out in 1957 comfort was rated as the most important aspect of a car's worth, effective brakes second, acceleration sixth, and fuel consumption ninth.

In 1956 the Vanguard Sportsman offered leather-covered foam pads on the fascia, but such a faint nod in the direction of driver and passenger safety only came in the model costing £1231. By the following year seat belts were being offered as an option, but like door locks which offered some resistance in the event of a collision, were a safety feature which seems to have attracted little interest. It was suggested at one stage that 'one legged cars' (in other words automatics) might appeal to ladies who found gear changing a challenge. In 1960 Vauxhall announced with some pride that all their models now came with a plastic undercoating to keep out damp and draughts. By inviting potential buyers to have a test drive during winter weather, they gave the impression that their competitors were less able to deal with water and wind. For those who wished to hire, rather than buy a car, models in Belfast in 1958 were offered at £2 a day,

£5 for Monday to Friday, or £8 for the full week. Alternatively, a taxi from Belfast to Dublin and back cost just under £8 (plus an undisclosed sum for waiting time) in 1951; to Derry and back for £5 12s 6d (£5.62½); for the round trip to Enniskillen £6 12s 0d (£6.60); and for Hillsborough and return 19s 6d (97½p).

For a brief period it looked (the failed Harry Ferguson venture notwithstanding) as if Belfast might make its own contribution towards automotive excellence. Towards the end of 1958 it was announced that Cyril Lord (of carpet fame) in an extension of his activities was going to manufacture small, lightweight 'bubble' cars. Although initial reports suggested that these machines would be produced in part of his Donaghadee carpet factory, the Short Brothers facility at Newtownards was soon introduced as the assembly line of what became known as the York Nobel 200. Built under license from its German parent company, the car was a three-wheeler, with a 200 cc engine imported from Germany, a fibreglass body based on new aircraft construction materials, a 50–60 mph cruising speed, and the capacity to return 80–90 mpg. Displaying it at the Paris Car Show in September 1958, Lord, who was chairman of York Nobel Industries, claimed that massive interest in the car was being displayed in America, and that the initial production run would be for export. By February the following year the first model was rolling off the Shorts assembly line, destined for display at a London press conference, and going on sale at less than £400, making it the cheapest car in Britain. It was expected that production would soon rise to 50 a week, and when the car was proclaimed as "a fantastic success" at the New York Motor Show shortly afterwards, it was confidently expected that production at Shorts would be stepped up. Then in August a terse statement from Shorts said that, with regret, at current costs construction of the Nobel was no longer viable and production had been terminated. In an equally brief statement Cyril Lord maintained that Shorts had consistently failed to meet production standards on the Nobel, and under no circumstances would he continue the relationship: assembly would be shifted to Fairey Aviation in England. No explanation was given for the fracturing of the relationship, but it could be assumed that there was a conflict between Shorts engineering standards and Lord's marketing requirements. The cars, not least because it was possible to engage four reverse as well as four forward gears, became cult favourites among their handful of owners, but they were not destined to be a success story for local industry.

A further flicker of automotive optimism took place in 1960 when it was announced that Triumph Heralds were to be assembled in Belfast by the Clarence Engineering concern, and it was hoped that up to 1,000 cars a year could be turned out. The decision was made as a result of the British government 'encouraging' car manufacturers (although in reality threatening financial sanctions for non-compliance) to expand operations beyond their traditional bases, and was responsible for creating thousands of new jobs in Scotland, Wales and some of the economically depressed areas of Britain. There was reluctance on the part of the car companies, whose assembly lines required a precisely timed delivery of components, to risk the transport links with Northern Ireland, and the government in London was not prepared to force the issue. For a time Heralds were certainly assembled in Belfast, but the economic realities of shipping components from Coventry and shipping the assembled cars back to the mainland (or at least those not bought locally) created long-term difficulties which it was impossible to overcome.

The price of petrol was then, as now, a source of contention. The 1950 General Election corresponded with a period of such severe petrol rationing that the political parties had to resort to horse-drawn transport to bring their supporters to the polls. Petrol cost the equivalent of 15p a gallon in 1950, but that compared very unfavourably with the price of 10p only a few years previously. By 1952 the price had risen still further to around 22p, and during the Suez crisis in 1956, when the amount of oil being imported was drastically reduced, the price rose to around 30p a gallon, and rationing was introduced to restrict private driving to 200 miles a month. The quality of the petrol itself probably contributed to the modest performance of the cars noted earlier. Before the war, the octane rating was 80, but by the early 50s that had been reduced to 70 (compared to the 95 to 98 now available) and led to the spluttering performance of many engines. In the days before fuel management systems motorists were constantly confronted with a range of unfortunate side-effects, such as 'pinking' and 'engine knock' as the ratio of fuel to air became unbalanced and led to undesirable noises from under the bonnet.

Until 1953 all petrol stocks were pooled and Shell, Esso and other household names were unable to advertise their own particular product, but after that came a rash of advertising for 'premium' grades which were claimed to give cleaner engines, easier starting, enhanced acceleration and more miles per gallon. Most petrol stations were also garages, and Shell and BP ran advertising campaigns which emphasised the benefits of the driver getting petrol from a man who knew not only him but also the idiosyncrasies of his car (and also his family and the people in the neighbourhood). It is not a comparison which would now be made, but this local approach was on occasions presented in terms of the experience of calling into one's friendly local pub compared with going into an anonymous and faceless purveyor of alcohol. 1953 also saw the introduction into some of Northern Ireland's 1,350 filling stations of pumps which recorded the amount and price of fuel delivered – a development which removed the hideous mathematical difficulties involved when amounts of less than full gallons were required, and calculations were necessary to determine fractions of shillings, pence and farthings.

Towards the end of the decade Messerschmitt and Heinkel three-wheeler cars (the latter assembled in Dundalk for a short period) were offering around 100 mpg and top speeds of 50 mph with engines of less than 200 cc, but these, although a rational response to the requirement for cheap motoring, never captured the public imagination. Both were produced by the famous German aviation undertakings which were temporarily barred from aircraft production, but it was scarcely an advertising bonus to have names so strongly associated with the Luftwaffe. In August 1959 however, the birth of a legend took place when the first Austin and Morris Minis were launched. They were promoted as "wizardry on wheels", 10 feet long, capable of 70 mph and 50 mpg. They were affordable at just under £499 for the basic and £537 for the deluxe model, but were not remarkable for either build quality or reliability. They arrived on the scene however just when young people had enough disposable income to afford a car and they democratised driving. The rich and famous, and even members of the Royal family were seen driving Minis and suddenly they became the epitome of cool.

As increasing numbers of Minis and other models took to the roads of Northern Ireland they highlighted a problem which had been growing throughout the decade. During a Bank Holiday in April 1951, on what was reported to be the warmest day of the year so far, hundreds of motorists felt inspired to drive and it was calculated that they created the greatest volume of traffic seen on the roads since 1938 – no fewer than 400 vehicles an hour (or around seven per minute) being recorded to the Belfast to Newcastle road. When the fuel rationing brought about by the Suez crisis ended in 1957 and motoring became affordable once more, a new record was set when, over the Whitsun weekend around 2,000 vehicles an hour were reported on the Belfast to Bangor road. (By way of comparison, in 2003 a traffic density of 50,000 vehicles per day was recorded on some stretches of the same road.) By 1958 there were 103,000 cars on the roads, plus 87,000 other registered vehicles, and 1,500 were being added each month. The traffic density was now 15 to the mile, double what it had been at the beginning of the decade, although this must be seen in comparison to the 45 vehicles to the mile which was the average for the rest of the UK.

As the number of vehicles on the road rose, so too did accident statistics. In 1948 around 1,700 people were injured or killed in traffic accidents. By 1953 that figure almost doubled to 3,200, and by 1958 rose to 4,500 including 141 deaths. By 1960 there were 172 deaths, or just over three per week. (Again by way of comparison in 2007, when there almost 900,000 vehicles on the roads of Northern Ireland, there were 6,000 accidents but only 113 deaths.) In 1957 however, accidents were already being blamed on "a lack of courtesy and a spirit of antagonism" among road users – 'road rage' was about to be invented. The Professor of Child Health at Queen's suggested that the use of seatbelts in cars, particularly for children, was "highly desirable", but even better, he suggested, would be for accident-prone individuals to voluntarily surrender their licenses. Although overly optimistic in his assessment of human perfectibility, the Professor had a point, because in the four years 1952–1955, 134 children under the age of 15 were killed in road accidents. It should come as no surprise to learn that, even in 1957, insurance premiums in Northern Ireland were among the highest in the UK, with the province being regarded as being as risky for drivers as Glasgow or London.

A number of factors lay behind the accident statistics. One was that many of the major roads were not only congested but also dangerous, with the Belfast to Bangor road often cited as a particularly bad example. It was described as being little better than a country lane, and so narrow in places that large vehicles could barely squeeze past each other. The Belfast to Newcastle road was stated to be an insult to a civilised society, and so full of bumps and twists that on one occasion a double-decker bus overturned and killed the driver. There was much confusion over lanes and markings. In 1954 it was decided that on trunk roads a single white line should be painted down the middle to indicate that two lanes existed, counteracting the established custom and practise of every motorist to occupy the crown of the road until forced to the side. In 1958 lane markings were upgraded, with double white lines being used to indicate potential danger spots. Drivers on lesser roads had to improvise with little or no lane guidance.

Drunken driving was not regarded as a major cause of accidents – it was rated tenth on a list of 22 causes drawn up in 1954 – although what constituted drunkenness was not specified, and was regarded as difficult to measure objectively. In the post-war years pedestrians were held responsible for causing 40% of all accidents on the road, while motorists were blamed for less than 30%, and it was not until 1961 that motorists asserted themselves and hoisted their share to 51%. By then the level of pedestrian responsibility for accidents had fallen significantly, either through exercising greater care or else by virtue of there being fewer of them around. In the early 50s Belfast had 138 pedestrian crossings, each consisting of a line of studs set into the roadway and marked by unlit beacons, an arrangement which failed to impinge on the consciousness of either motorists or pedestrians. One irate correspondent in the *Belfast Telegraph* insisted that using one of these crossings "would tax the agility of a top-rate matador." As that comment implied, there was confusion on the basic issue of who had right of way on crossings, and even judges in Britain handed down conflicting rulings which did nothing to clarify the situation. Accordingly pedestrians regularly stepped onto the roadway in a manner which gave motorists no warning and little reasonable chance of stopping, while motorists reciprocated by refusing to slow down or stop unless in circumstances where carnage seemed inevitable. Castlereagh Council toyed with the idea of painting white circles at designated spots on the roadway, the theory being that anyone standing in one of these circles was indicating an intention to cross the road, and expecting the oncoming traffic to respect his or her wishes. The now-ubiquitous zebra crossings were introduced in Belfast as an experiment in 1953 and introduced on a large scale by 1955, but even these caused confusion, with frequent complaints from motorists that people paused in the middle of the crossing to talk to acquaintances, or to light up cigarettes. An experiment was tried in 1959 to introduce two-lane crossings, with pedestrians to use the left-hand lane to avoid collisions with other users. Even under the supervision of police with loudhailers, pedestrians failed to see the logic of the arrangement and confrontations continued. Another experiment in Lisburn where pedestrians controlled the traffic lights was reported to have caused confusion among 98% of those attempting to use the crossing. On the main road from Belfast to Lisburn the idea of a pedestrian crossing at Dunmurry was rejected on the grounds that the road was 30 feet wide, and an elderly person would require nine seconds to make the crossing: given the absence of a speed limit this would necessitate a gap of some 200 yards in the traffic, which was regarded as unfeasible. The idea of erecting traffic lights to slow the traffic was not favoured by the Ministry of Commerce, even, it was claimed, in towns like Lisburn where through traffic on the notoriously busy road to Moira was regularly reported doing 60 mph. Some thought was given to the idea of creating pedestrian islands in the middle of busy roads – they were referred to without irony as 'pedestrian refuges' – but in most cases it was felt that they would interrupt the flow of traffic and cause congestion.

The absence of a speed limit was another significant factor in the accident statistics, but there was considerable resistance to the idea of introducing such a restriction. When the idea was under discussion by the government in 1952 it was argued in the Cabinet that a 30 mph limit in built-up areas would produce traffic congestion; would cause traffic to divert onto unregulated roads; would oblige drivers to watch their speedometer rather than other vehicles on the road and hence cause even more accidents; and above all, would place an unreasonable restriction on careful drivers in the interests of curtailing the behaviour of a few bad ones. It was clear that the government felt speed limits would be unpopular, and were prepared to devote some ingenuity to finding reasons not to introduce them. Carrickfergus, Antrim and Bangor had their own 10–20 mph speed limit, but in every other town and village children playing in the street were threatened by cars driving through at whatever speed seemed feasible to the drivers.

Yet it was not just politicians who were nervous. Officials in the AA and RAC agreed that it was the responsibility of the driver to determine the speed which was appropriate for the immediate circumstances, and advanced the rather contrived argument that while 25 mph in Belfast at midnight might be acceptable, it would be ridiculous to make the same assumption in heavy traffic at noon. The Belfast Insurance Institute rowed in behind this assessment, stating that only 4% of the traffic in the city travelled at 25–30 mph, and everything else at rates which made speed limits superfluous. The Lord Mayor disputed these figures, suggesting that since tramlines were being lifted throughout the city, and the old cobbled surfaces of the roads were being replaced with tarmac, motorists now regarded the streets as a racetrack. He cited reports of cars travelling at more than 60 mph on the Antrim Road. At a Chamber of Commerce dinner in Ballymoney in 1953 the Minister of Commerce warned that road safety was "a most complex problem" and advised that it would be unwise to "delude ourselves into expecting too much from such measures as speed limits." He neglected to outline the nature of the complexities that might arise from obliging drivers to exercise a greater degree of caution when driving in built-up areas, leaving the impression that it was the inalienable right of the citizen to kill or be killed on the road without government interference. When the issue was being debated in Stormont one of the arguments he advanced was that in Belfast, the times when there were most pedestrians on the streets – when leaving work or coming home from the cinemas – they used pedestrian crossings to an extent that made speeding by motorists impossible.

It was 1956 before the nettle was grasped and on 1 October 1956 a speed limit of 30 mph in built-up areas was nervously introduced, almost on a trial basis, because the provision was built in for the Minister of Home Affairs to cancel the limit during certain hours, or de-designate roads where he felt a limit was unnecessary. Britain had operated speed limits in towns since 1935 and was now contemplating national limits for open roads, so there was a danger of Northern Ireland getting seriously out of step, but the idea was still put forward with a degree of caution. After an intensive publicity campaign and the erecting of some 2,000 warning signs in towns throughout Northern Ireland the limit was introduced at midnight on 30 September. The first £5 fine for breaking it was handed out in mid-October to an indignant motorist who claimed that the police had promised a two-week amnesty until drivers had become used to the new system, and this was only the thirteenth day. The motoring correspondent of the *Belfast Telegraph* doubted whether the roads would be made safer under the new regime, but acknowledged that the scale and severity of the damage caused in accidents might be reduced.

There was a similar reluctance to introduce a driving test. Once again a range of arguments were deployed to counter the proposal that people who drove potentially lethal machines should be required to demonstrate some competence in controlling them before taking to the road. A driving test would be difficult to devise, and it would be administratively difficult to impose a uniform set of procedures. It would be expensive to implement. It would have no immediate effect since it would apply only to new drivers and existing ones would remain untested, so it would be many years before the overall levels of driving competence were significantly raised. There was no guarantee that the person who was careful enough to modify his behaviour for purposes of passing the test would not turn out afterwards to be a reckless driver. It was claimed that most accidents were caused by over-confident drivers who had years of experience behind them, rather than by nervous beginners. One former Minister favoured what he called a "mild test", which would require the candidate to have "a good rudimentary knowledge of what he was doing and a full appreciation of his responsibilities as a driver", but deprecated "a severe and strict test" which would include such manoeuvers as compulsory parking, at which he himself was incompetent. Some experts claimed that a driving test was unnecessary: all that was required was a medical test which would eliminate those with bad eyesight or a physical disability, or who lacked knowledge of 'the rule of the road', and raising the permissible driving age from 15 to 17.

What exactly constituted 'the rule of the road' was difficult to say. A Highway Code existed, but it was not an extensive document, and in the early 50s was still offering guidance on the signals by which those driving carts gave warning of their intentions to other road users – the whip being rotated above the driver's head before pointing left or right being one example. Most of the Code consisted of friendly advice rather than mandatory rules. It was recommended for instance that a motorist should sound his horn when overtaking another vehicle, but should not do so in an aggressive or intimidating fashion. How this particular requirement was to be met was not explained, and in numerous cases before the courts it was a matter of contention whether the overtaking motorist had in fact "blown for the road" before colliding with the vehicle in front making an unexpected turn. Cyclists were advised to ride as steadily as possible and not wobble about on the road. Even the Minister of Home Affairs, who was theoretically responsible for road safety, admitted that he could think of no general rule for who had the right of way on roundabouts, and merely recommended that drivers should enter and leave these "gyratory islands" with as little disruption as possible to other users. It was acknowledged that the Code was not legally enforceable, and it was not an offence in law to have failed to observe its provisions, but it was regarded as a source of helpful advice, and to make it legally binding would be difficult and unhelpful. It was a sign of the times that, in an age when the Code required the use of hand signals to indicate the driver's intentions, the joke could be made in Stormont that a woman extending her right arm through the driver's window might be signalling that she was preparing to make a turn, or was slowing down, but could equally well mean she was flicking the ash off her cigarette, drying her nail polish, or merely checking whether it was raining. In fairness, the politician who passed on this witticism acknowledged that most male drivers didn't know what hand signals meant either.

Both the driving test and the speed limit were introduced in the Road Traffic Act which took effect in 1956. The Act recognised that existing legislation was out of date (some provisions of the Locomotives on Highways Act of 1896 were still in force) and that the consequences of higher volumes of traffic needed to be recognised. It was said at the time that the ideal solution would be to build four separate road systems for fast traffic, for slow traffic, for cyclists and for pedestrians, which in a sense was the original inspiration behind railways, but it was recognised that such provision was unaffordable. During the Bill's passage in Stormont comments which had been made in Westminster by the Bishop of Carlisle were quoted with approval, and set the tone for much of the debate: "I believe that in the eyes of Christian men bad driving is a sin against God's creatures." Besides introducing the system of provisional licenses, driving tests and L-plates, the legislation made it mandatory for all vehicles to display red lights and reflectors at the rear. It was decided however, not to bring on a system for testing the safety and mechanical reliability of cars, but to rely instead on the existing arrangements whereby the police could satisfy themselves at any time as to the roadworthiness of a vehicle. A new range of offences was introduced, including driving without insurance, or failing to stop in the event of an accident, and the police were given the power to require driver identification. Also included were new provisions to prevent drivers from parking on corners, on bridges or opposite another vehicle where the road or street was sufficiently narrow for traffic congestion to be caused, and the courts were given flexibility to determine whether a driver who recognised that he was too drunk to drive and slept in the back seat of his car should be treated as harshly as the driver who decided that his chances of being apprehended were lower if he drove. The fact that such provisions were felt to be necessary says a great deal about the standards of driving behaviour which were the norm.

It was not until 1952 that the government got round to erecting warning signs on trunk roads, one idea being that it would be helpful if Stop signs were to be placed at all junctions with major roads because of the high number of accidents caused by motorists emerging from side roads without taking any precautions. It was also suggested that it would be a good idea for local authorities to begin erecting signs giving directions and distances to towns in their area, if only to help tourists. As it was, even experienced local motorists got lost when diverted from the main roads, having little to rely on other than occasional signposts erected by the AA. To be fair, Northern Ireland was not uniquely deficient in this respect. Britain had muddled along with a regime of local signs primarily designed to assist cyclists before the advent of motorways in the late 50s made it imperative that a uniform set of rules applied, and the current system of circles, triangles and rectangles was adopted. It was yet another example of the state intervening to regulate what had until then been private behaviour.

Driving tests were introduced in Northern Ireland in September 1956, just before the imposition of the speed limit. News of the imminence of the new regime triggered a frantic rush of applications for licenses in advance, some of them from people who admitted to not owning a bicycle, never mind a car, but who were determined to avoid the agonies of being tested in the future. The first L-driver passed his test in October, and within a year an entire new industry had been created of driving instructors charging £1 an hour for tuition. True to form, the local insurance companies acknowledged that the absence of both tests and a speed limit had been responsible for pushing premiums in Northern Ireland to high levels, but said that, despite these safeguards now being introduced, it did not automatically follow that premiums would be reduced. The situation would be reviewed in the light of developments.

One of the fundamental differences in attitudes between the 1950s and our own age is the extent to which the idea of official intervention was then regarded with distaste. With the introduction of the welfare state and subsequent reforms in education and social services, together with industrial development grants and aids to industry, central government acquired throughout the 50s a far more prominent role in regulating the life of individuals than had ever been the case before. It was not a transition which was universally welcomed, and fears were expressed about the insidious effects of people losing their sense of self-reliance and social responsibility. On one occasion in 1952 the Minister of Home Affairs opposed a regulation making it mandatory for all gas and electric fires to be sold with protective bars on the front: "For my part I am opposed to any legislation which seeks to impose further restrictions on the populace merely for the purpose of saving them the labour of using their own intelligence." It was a statement which nowadays would be regarded as unacceptably elitist, but which then encapsulated a widespread view that it was not the responsibility of the state to protect people from acts of personal folly.

As has been seen, similar considerations applied with regard to regulating the behaviour of the motoring public. It was clear that seatbelts could play a role in reducing injuries in the event of an accident, as could motorbike helmets, but there was a genuine reluctance on the part of the government to impose restrictions on individual freedom of action. By 1959 it was recognised that alcohol was liable to affect drivers' capabilities even without the physical evidence of staggering or slurred speech, but although breathalysers were being used in other countries such as Germany and Canada, there was ambivalence in Britain about devising scientific tests which drivers would be obliged to take. When Westminster debated the possible introduction of a drink-driving test in 1960 three double whiskies was suggested as the safe limit, but it was a limit which seemed based more on the personal experience of its supporters than on any scientific evidence. In Northern Ireland it was recognised that the police could, in theory, sit outside public houses and pick up motorists who were visibly affected by what they had consumed, but such behaviour was regarded as underhand and unacceptable. There were protests in Stormont at reports that the police were using cameras and electronic devices to monitor speed limits, with one MP insisting that the use of such devices constituted a form of trespass and assault to the person. Because there were so few laws applying to the conduct of drivers, the police relied instead on a policy of what was quaintly referred to as 'admonition and advice' for drivers whose habits were suspect, and some 70,000 friendly chats were delivered in 1950 alone. It was widely held that the relationship between police and motorists should be based on respect, rather than fear, and the evidence suggests that this was not an entirely utopian view.

Other contributions to road safety were discussed. Most Councils outside Belfast refused to grit roads in icy weather, although Antrim County Council did send out lorries loaded with grit which was scattered from the back of each by a man with a shovel. Cat's eyes were known to be helpful in foggy weather, but placed at 12-yard intervals cost £110 a mile to install, and on winding roads their closer spacing increased the price to £130 or £140 per mile. Teaching road safety in schools was suggested from time to time, but rejected on the grounds that there was already enough pressure on teachers.

The same reluctance to intervene also applied to traffic congestion in Belfast. In 1954 over a two-hour period at Holywood Arches a survey logged the passage of 192 UTA buses, 310 Corporation buses (an average of a bus every 15 seconds), plus 1,200 private cars, all conveying passengers into Belfast, to say nothing of the numerous lorries and vans competing for their share of the road. Other arterial routes were experiencing similar densities, and it was said that commuting times were slower than when horse-drawn trams were operating in 1904. What could be done to ameliorate the situation was the subject of debate, with Belfast Corporation and central government each declining responsibility, the former refusing to consider any schemes which would involve additional burdens on the ratepayers, and the latter refusing to become involved in a problem which it felt was of the Corporation's own making.

Parking in Belfast was governed by an 1845 by-law which prohibited vehicles from remaining static on the street unless for the purpose of unloading goods or passengers. The police took a surprisingly tolerant view of motorists breaching such regulations, giving 20 minutes grace before leaving a note on the windscreen of the offending vehicle inviting the driver to drop in to the nearest police station for an enlightening chat about the regrettable necessity of parking restrictions. The fact that the Belfast courts imposed fines totalling just over £300 in 1957 suggests that the police were open to reasonable, or possibly inventive explanations.

It was noted in 1953 that while there had been 823 on-street parking spaces available in 1938 there were now only 550, and capacity was being squeezed further by virtue of the fact that buses, unlike trams, needed to pull in to the kerb in order to pick up and set down passengers, so parking along main routes was no longer unrestricted. Parking meters were considered but rejected, despite their proven capacity to generate revenue, and surprise was expressed when in 1960 Westminster introduced legislation which allowed traffic wardens to levy on-street fines.

By 1956 Belfast was home to 43,000 registered vehicles and as wartime bomb sites were redeveloped during the decade, it became an increasing problem to find parking space for them. A number of solutions were proposed, some drawing on the American model of multi-storey carparks. One ingenious idea was a Ferris-wheel device, the idea being that a large number of vehicles could be lifted 120 feet into the air on a structure occupying a small area of ground. Besides fears as to the stability of the contraption, it was acknowledged that returning motorists wishing to reclaim their vehicle might be faced with some delay if the wheel was at an inconvenient stage of its storage cycle. Other proposals included the conversion of all open spaces in the city into parking lots, culverting all or part of the Lagan and using the space thus created for parking, or building concrete platforms above all the railway lines coming into the city for the same purpose. Staggered working hours to ensure that all employees did not arrive and depart at the same time was another proposal which was felt to be too radical for adoption. A £7 million scheme for a tunnel under the Lagan was suggested as a means of easing traffic congestion on the Queen's and Albert bridges, but suffered from the drawback that, despite charging tolls, it would merely have moved the congestion closer to the city centre. In Derry, little regard was had for such sophisticated exercises in congestion management and it was proposed instead that breaches should be made in the historic walls in order to allow traffic to flow more freely. By early 1959 it was noted that, partly thanks to traffic densities, smog and pollution in Belfast were getting to the stage where legislation might be needed to deal with the problem. Motorists protested, but not as loudly as business interests who felt the expense of new plant and fuels would cripple industry. It was another demonstration of the inconvenient truth that in the second half of the twentieth century no problem could be dealt with in isolation.

Arguably it was to the government's credit that, rather than attempt piecemeal improvements which would be contested with Belfast Corporation, a more strategic approach was adopted, and from the mid-50s attention turned in earnest to the plan for Approach Roads referred to earlier, with a view to creating a co-ordinated system allowing traffic to enter, leave and bypass Belfast as required. The plan was given its first practical expression in the Sydenham Bypass, which had begun in the 1930s but had been temporarily abandoned due to the War and the post-wars shortage of construction materials. By the mid-50s work had resumed again, and in a display of optimism in 1956 the government announced that some thought was being given to the possibility of creating a fourth Approach Road, this one running from Carryduff to somewhere in the vicinity of Annadale embankment. At the same time it was stated that the initial scope of the new roads was too limited. The Eastern Approach was now to extend to Cultra with dual carriageway from there to Bangor; the Northern was to be continued with dual carriageway from Glengormley to Ballymena; and the Southern would reach Moira, and possibly beyond that to Dungannon.

When the Sydenham Bypass opened in November 1959 it had cost £800,000 instead of the original estimate of £250,000. A 30 mph speed limit was applied, and a welter of preliminary advice was issued that people should not walk, cycle or park their vehicles on the new road. It was also advised that if when driving it was felt necessary to change lanes, signalling in advance and ensuring that the other lane was clear were useful preliminaries. Despite, or perhaps because of these precautions there was gridlock on the first morning of operation, and calls were soon being made for the road to be extended across the Lagan to terminate at Victoria Square. A key consideration bearing on many motorway projects was already becoming apparent: even before completion came the realisation that the solution they represented was already inadequate.

Thereafter the priority became the Southern Approach, largely on the grounds that the road from Belfast to Moira was claimed to carry more traffic than any other in Northern Ireland. On the other hand it was difficult to ignore the fact that both the Northern and Eastern roads were providing access from areas of greater population density and with greater concentrations of industry. One unkind suggestion hinted that the Southern Approach would mean easier access to Lord Brookeborough's Fermanagh constituency, but the government may also have been influenced by the decision of Armagh County Council to replace an extensive section of trunk road near the Birches, which, at 16 feet wide, crossing boggy ground and subject to a 25 mph speed limit, was accorded the accolade of worst trunk road in Northern Ireland. Co-operation between Tyrone and Armagh County Councils raised the prospect of the new Approach extending to Moira, but then proceeding as a dual carriageway to Dungannon. For whatever reason, the Southern Approach became the focus of activity. The original idea that the new carriageway should extend from Lisburn to Moira along the existing trunk road was abandoned. In 1957 the first contracts were signed for building the bridges which would carry traffic across the motorway on the stretch between the Donegall Road in Belfast and the Saintfield Road in Lisburn, and work was put in hand for the draining of the Bog Meadows where the new Approach road would reach Belfast. Progress was held up by protests over the compulsory acquisition of houses and land. The acquisition of 14 houses in the Roden Street area to allow the creation of what was termed "the collection and dispersal point" for the new carriageway at Donegall Road caused such delay that plans for an extension through to Grosvenor Road had to be abandoned for the next decade. By the middle of 1959 however, it was announced that what was still officially referred to as "the new trunk road" would be developed in three phases: the first, a seven-mile section from Donegall Road to "a point south of Lisburn" which was already in hand; the second, a further seven miles from Lisburn to Moira, was at the detailed planning stage; and the third, the 22 miles from Moira to Dungannon, would be built in a number of sections with initial work possible by 1960. Planning for the Moira to Dungannon section was greatly facilitated by the engineers discovering, after inspecting motorways in Britain, that the carriageway would not have to be built as a series of gentle curves to eliminate headlight dazzle. It was a juxtaposition noted by very few that 1960 also saw the proposal to demolish the old toll house which had stood on the corner of Belfast's Bradbury Place since 1810, when the new road to Lisburn represented what was then the latest endeavour to make transportation more efficient.

By then roadbuilding appeared to have become fashionable. If Armagh Council envisaged 19 miles of dual carriageway the other County Councils were anxious not to be left behind. In 1958 the roads programme for County Down included a dual carriageway from Knock to Newtownbreda, plus 22 other major schemes; County Londonderry balked at the idea of widening the road over the Glenshane Pass and felt the money would be better spent on acquiring a first tentative section of dual carriageway; and Antrim proposed spending £1.4 million, some of which would prepare the way for the proposed Northern Approach. Tyrone meanwhile decided that motorways and dual carriageways were futuristic visions unsuited to a county with an estimated 2,000 miles of minor roads in poor repair and little by way of through traffic, while Fermanagh Council, never to the forefront in such matters, appears to have registered no plans at all.

In the event, it was July 1962 before the first section of the new motorway opened, and late 1967/early 1968 before the final two sections were finished to complete the link with Dungannon. Lord Brookeborough was treated to a private drive on the first stretch of the motorway before the official opening and declared that the M1 was the most wonderful work he had ever seen. By then there were some 250,000 vehicles on the road network, and the Belfast newspapers speculated breathlessly about what the new roads would mean in the future, with people and industries being able to locate in places previously considered to be inaccessible. The prospect of Portadown being brought within an easy drive of Belfast was considered semi-miraculous. It was predicted that the accident rate would be reduced because the main causes of accidents (cyclists, parked cars, crossroads, pedestrians) had all been removed. Delivery times for goods would be reduced, as would wear and tear on vehicles, and fuel efficiency would be increased. A social revolution seemed to be in sight.

The motoring public took a less romantic view. At 6.00 am on 10 July 1962 a motor cyclist was first in a group of 14 vehicles on the Donegall Road access lane when the motorway was opened with no official ceremony. Since no speed limit had been set, a police officer in the group reached Lisburn in five minutes, but many vehicle drivers distrusted the prospect of so much open road and announced their intention to continue using the old Lisburn Road. By the second day of operation three motorists had contrived to run out of petrol and were rescued by AA and RUC patrols, since the system of emergency telephones had not yet been installed. The carriageway had changed, but human nature remained the same.

Incomplete as it was the M1 pointed the way forward and by the mid-60s the government was so entranced by the concept that no less than 100 miles of motorway were proposed, including an M11 to Newry, and an M23 from Ballymena to Derry. The planners remained dubious however, about the wisdom of motorways in Tyrone, Fermanagh and south Londonderry, and most of the proposed miles of asphalt were destined to be laid east of the Bann. Before long it became apparent that an elaborate network of motorways was as unaffordable in Northern Ireland as the extensive railway system which had been abandoned, but by that time it was clear that there would be no return to the privations of the 1950s either. The sense of entitlement to private transport and the freedom that car ownership brought could not be reversed, and the urge to go further and faster could be indulged as never before. The days were passing when a horse and cart could amble along a country lane, or a farmer could safely drive his herd of cows across a road at milking time. From now on, even remote country districts would rarely escape the insistent sound of traffic on quiet summer nights.

CHAPTER 7

THE GETTING OF WISDOM

IT CANNOT BE ignored that Northern Ireland in the 1950s was divided along religious lines. By and large Protestants and Catholics wore the same style of clothes, ate the same food, drove the same cars, suffered the same health problems and spoke the same language. Radio programmes from Radio Éireann had more appeal to Catholic listeners, and the *Irish News* was not often read with approval by Protestants, but the only way of distinguishing the religious bias of a cinema crowd was when outrage was periodically triggered in Unionist circles as patrons refused to stand for the National Anthem played at the end of the performance. Yet distinctions were apparent in the games and recreations adopted by either clan, there being relatively few Catholic cricketers or Protestant camogie players, while the Orange Order and the Ancient Order of Hibernians each celebrated memberships which were exclusive in religious terms. There were differences too in religious observance, with Catholicism preferring a monolithic approach to how worship should be conducted, and the Protestant faith being disseminated through dozens of different denominations and sects. On a single weekend in 1950, besides advertising 120 services for the three main Protestant denominations, the *Belfast Telegraph* carried an additional 115 notices for Sunday services in the greater Belfast area featuring other Protestant groups. Exactly what points of theology distinguished each of these groups from all the others was a matter capable of explanation only by members of the participating congregation, but it was a graphic demonstration of the point that religion mattered deeply to many people in Northern Ireland, and could inform all aspects of life.

Despite the decline in conventional religion brought about by wartime experiences, Northern Ireland's was still a conventionally religious society, with levels of church attendance which were among the highest in Europe. In the 1951 census, out of 1,371,000 people enumerated, fewer than 6,000 failed to state a religion, 221 claimed to be freethinkers, and 64 said they were atheists. Determining the levels of church attendance was not straightforward – those who claimed to be in regular attendance might have attended every week, or once every month, or regularly at

Christmas and Easter over a number of years. Attendance, too, was more of a duty for Catholics than Protestants, but one estimate in 1961 put Protestant attendance at around 50–55% and the corresponding figure for Catholics at well over 90%.

Such piety was not accompanied by a high degree of interest in each other's religion, each side being content to rely on a handful of assertions which were never closely examined or debated. In broad terms Catholics tended to believe that Protestants were heretics, whose dubious spiritual and moral values were a threat to true Christianity. In a typical example of the kind of rhetoric which was deployed on the issue the Bishop of Derry in 1951 warned his community of the risks of mingling: "If their young people went into dangerous surroundings, if they had to seek their amusement among non-Catholics, in non-Catholic halls, where the standard of purity was not as high as it was among Catholics, could they expect their young people to come out of those halls as good as they went into them? … If you allow your children to be contaminated by those who are not of the Fold, then you can expect nothing but disaster…" For their part Protestants were happy to believe that Catholics were priest-ridden members of a monolithic international conspiracy intent on imposing its doctrines on a global scale, and eternal vigilance was the only defence against their wiles. Fear and loathing of 'Romanism' as a religion, and distrust of its adherents had been an underpinning of Protestant thought in Ireland for the past three centuries. When members of the Orange Order gave thanks for the inestimable virtues of civil and religious liberty it was understood that it was the Protestant exercise of those liberties for which gratitude was being returned. Sectarianism came at an early age and generations of children playing in the streets "skipped to songs of cheerful hatred." Most towns of a size sufficient to warrant a newspaper ensured that there was a Catholic and a Protestant paper, each giving its interpretation of local, national and international affairs in ways which accorded with the prejudices of its readership.

Each community had its own distinctive religious ethos. There were exceptions of course, but for the most part the Protestant clergy kept a low profile, and unless on issues such as drinking and gambling, seldom made public comment on the spiritual affairs of their flock, whereas the Catholic Hierarchy seemed permanently involved in the task of providing moral guidance. Occasionally there were public demonstrations of Protestant devotion – for instance, when 30,000 attended a Youth for Christ rally in Windsor Park in the summer of 1952, and 45,000 people and a choir of 6,000 filled the same stadium three years later to hear an American evangelist, Dr Jack Shulia – but such outpourings were comparatively rare. Protestants could celebrate the Queen's Coronation and the doings of the royal family, but regular expressions of religious fervour were usually confined to occasions when the more fundamentalist sects issued their denunciations. On the other hand, the celebration of 1954 as a Marian year, the blessing of grottos, the consecration of new churches, pilgrimages, retreats, 'rosary rallies', Corpus Christi, first communion, Holy Days of Obligation and numerous other acts of veneration were among the devotional aspects of religion which gave the Catholic Church a high and permanent profile in the community, with a concomitant emphasis on the spiritual dimension of everyday life. Reports made the front page of the *Irish News* for several days in October 1951 when it was announced that the Pope had experienced visions of the Virgin on five occasions during the Holy Year of 1950. When the same newspaper issued a special supplement to mark its centenary in July 1955, the feature was introduced by a specially commissioned article from the Catholic Bishop of Down and Connor. The inauguration in Armagh of the Patrician Year in 1960 was attended by four Cardinals, 43 Archbishops and Bishops, the Papal Legate and 200 other senior figures, and was described as "one of the greatest ecclesiastical events in our time and land." There was simply no equivalent on the Protestant side. As Seamus Heaney put it, the Catholics in Northern Ireland were "saturated in religious values", but beyond the purveying of those values the Church also acted as unifying force in both social and political terms, with its basic conservativism permeating the Catholic community.

It was little wonder that marriages between Catholics and Protestants were rare, and never a cause of celebration. Catholics were not as obsessively hostile to Protestant clerics as Protestants were to the Catholic clergy, and there was no equivalent of the almost hysterical anti-papal rhetoric which was trotted out by some Protestants, as if it was a necessary component of their identity. Catholics as a matter of courtesy had little difficulty in expressing some regard for the British monarchy as head of a neighbouring state. Condolences were offered at the death of George VI in 1952, shopkeepers on Belfast's Falls road received threats from Republican sources for selling Coronation souvenirs the following year, and messages of congratulation and goodwill to the new Queen were issued on behalf of various Catholic organisations. There certainly was resentment at the Union flag being used as a political emblem by the Unionist Party, and frustration at successive British governments underpinning what was seen as the injustice of a partitioned Ireland, but insofar as it could be separated from the national obsession with the Irish suffering 800 years of persecution by England, overt anti-Britishness was comparatively rare. Such fine distinctions however, were rarely recognised on the other side of the religious divide, where Catholicism was equated with Irish nationalism, which equated with anti-Britishness, which equated with a threat to Northern Ireland's constitutional connection with the rest of the UK.

The differences in spiritual emphasis inevitably carried through into the field of education, where the Catholic Church saw the lessons provided in schools as an extension of the religious and moral teaching imparted in the home, to be delivered in an appropriate ethos by persons already well instructed in the Catholic faith, and emphasising distinctively Irish cultural and historical values. It was not accidental that one of the cherished images of Catholic identity was a romanticised notion of the hedge-school, where the schoolmaster imparted the myths and legends of old Ireland to reinforce among his young charges the sense of a superior culture enduring despite centuries of persecution. The Catholic Hierarchy issued frequent warnings, not just of Protestant dancehalls, but of the dangers to members of their flock attending non-Catholic educational institutions (Trinity College being a case in point) where they would be exposed to influences detrimental to their faith and morals. In 1950, indeed, the Bishop of Derry insisted that it was imperative that Catholic children were sent to Catholic schools to preserve the faith of the next generation, and that those who neglected this fundamental duty were in danger of encouraging, in his view, a generation of "perverts". On the Protestant side there was less stress laid on spiritual teaching *per se*, but it was supplemented by a belief that the purpose of education was to reinforce the values embodied in the Northern Ireland state, and the development of an essentially British world view. A Ministry of Education circular issued in 1952 and directed to all teachers gave a flavour of what was expected on 24 May, Empire Day: "The enclosed Empire Day message from the Earl of Gowrie ... might be read at an appropriate opportunity during the day, or at least that part of the message which has been specially addressed to young people. The reading of the message could be followed if desired by an address on the significance of the Empire ... Lessons suitable for the day could be arranged and songs appropriate to the occasion could be sung, and it might also be possible to hold a parade of the pupils ..." It was very far from the ethos of the hedge school. Given the fundamental disagreement which existed about the legitimacy of the Northern Irish state, it was unsurprising that there should be little meeting of minds about the ultimate purpose for which children were being educated.

In the immediate post-war years education for most children

began at age five and ended at 14. Those years were spent in the Public Elementary schools. By today's standards, many of those schools were primitive, particularly in rural areas. Overcrowding was routine, and the report of 165 pupils being taught in a three-room school in Antrim so congested that at times half the pupils had to stand while the rest were crammed in three to a desk was not untypical. Many schools had huts rather than classrooms, and one, near Ballyclare, occupied a building originally designed as a Civil Defence mortuary. Others were in poor repair, with leaking roofs and draughty windows, and were damp and rodent-infested. Even in 1952 there were examples of parents organising mass protests and refusing to send their children back to school after the summer holiday because promised repairs had not been made, oil lamps gave insufficient light, and rats still ran across the floors. Childhood ailments were transmitted with effortless efficiency, and since handkerchiefs, particularly for boys, were often regarded as an unnecessary luxury, running noses and gummed-up eyes were so common as to elicit little notice. As late as 1956 the Divisional Medical Officers in County Londonderry visited 175 schools and inspected 5,212 children. Of these 1,131 were categorised as "grossly defective in bodily cleanliness" in terms of hair and bodily infestation with lice, and if dirty feet had been taken into account, the figures would have been significantly higher. As it was, the figures were regarded as evidence that in at least some schools washing facilities were being used, and in others bottles of DDT hair lotion were being employed. Overall, the situation was felt to be improving.

By the late 40s, of the almost 1,700 schools within the elementary system just over half were in the scheme which provided for necessitous children to be provided with free milk, and for the rest to pay a nominal sum. Out of the 185,000 pupils enrolled in the sector only 11,000 had access to school meals however, and everyone else lunched on whatever gastronomic miracle their mother had conjured that morning from white bread and home-made jam. Books were sometimes in short supply, as were maps and other visual aids, and slates were used when writing paper ran out. It was said that no one who had heard the eldritch screeching sound as a class of children scraped pencils across slates ever forgot the experience. The desks used were of sturdy wooden construction, and by tradition were incised with the initials of every bored schoolboy in possession of a penknife. In country areas the children were often absent during periods when farm work took precedence over education, and some regarded schooling as a winter activity, sometimes pursuing their interrupted studies well after the statutory leaving age of 14.

Lessons were graded in complexity to match abilities from the so-called 'infants' class' through to the older classes taken by the senior teacher, but the core curriculum throughout was based around the 'three Rs' – reading, writing and 'rithmetic' – as delivered through instruction in English, Arithmetic and Geography. Additional subjects such as Drawing, Domestic Economy, Needlework, Nature Study or elementary Science could be used to lend variety, but it was assumed that at least two-thirds of the pupils' time would be devoted to the three staples. There was also a daily act of communal worship, sometimes little more than a collective recitation of the Lord's Prayer, although some schools offered a more intensive course of moral instruction. In terms of curriculum delivery variations existed between schools, as individual teachers had some flexibility in regard to the means by which their lessons were delivered, so long as the basics were covered to the satisfaction of the inspector from the Ministry of Education, whose periodic visits were a test of nerve for pupil and teacher alike. Utilising the three Rs to inculcate a love of learning for its own sake was not regarded as a necessary or even a virtuous outcome, provided the pupil was provided with a set of basic skills and values which, all other things being equal, would be a foundation for good citizenship.

Reading was practiced using a variety of sources, usually beginning with the simple Janet and John stories (or some variation of them), based on middle-class English children, copiously illustrated and incorporating words which were intended progressively to develop reading skills. More advanced books drew on history (how James Watt discovered steam power by observing his grandmother's boiling kettle) or morally uplifting stories (the boy who stuck his arm into a leaking dyke and prevented the city of Harlem from being flooded) until the apprentice reader was deemed to have sufficient skills to manage entire books from the approved canon of children's literature. For the most part these were the same books that had been read by his or her parents – *Treasure Island, Black Beauty, Little Women, Robinson Crusoe* and their like – and made no attempt to be relevant to life as experienced by their young readers. Accompanying the reading exercises were lessons in grammar, explaining the rules by which the individual words related to each other so that the structure of a sentence could be understood. This 'parsing' was generally agreed to constitute one of the more acute forms of mental torture that a pupil could be asked to endure. Chunks of approved poetry were learned by heart ("If I want to be happy and quick on my toes, I must bite my food slowly and breath through my nose" was just one uplifting example) and if comprehension of the piece accompanied the feat of memory, that was regarded as a bonus. Geography in many cases consisted of little more than memorising the names of the counties and principal towns of Ireland, together with a brief statement of what they produced by way of industry. Of course, to an extent which would be regarded today as counterproductive, all learning was by rote, everything from the multiplication tables to speeches from Shakespeare. How effective it was as a means of learning remains the subject of debate, but many people today who have difficulty in recollecting the events of the previous week can recite with exemplary accuracy the poems they learned at the age of 12.

Handwriting was taken seriously. In some schools ink was distributed from a communal bottle to recessed ceramic inkwells in each desk, and the use of cheap steel-nibbed pens required advanced powers of concentration if the page of the copybook, which was marked with pink and blue lines to indicate the appropriate size of the letters being transcribed, was not to be desecrated with blots or punctured with holes. Writing on unlined paper was reserved for advanced practitioners of the art. Ballpoint pens or biros were miracles of technology available to only the fortunate few, and fountain pens were regarded by parents and relatives as the Christmas present which marked a child's coming of age. The skills of calligraphy were demonstrated to practical effect in 'the composition' or essay, where budding authors were required to describe in their own words how they spent their holidays, or enjoyed a birthday party, or imagined what it would be like to take a space ship to the moon.

Arithmetic also made considerable mental demands. In a non-metric, non-decimal world measurements and money were capriciously designated by units which in many cases were mediaeval in origin, and the absence of overall logic meant that relationships had to be learned and memorised. The measurements designating length included inches, feet, yards, chains, furlongs, poles, miles and occasionally leagues; those for measuring area comprised square feet, square yards, rods, poles, perches, roods and acres; weight was calculated by reference to ounces, pounds, stones, quarters and hundredweights; capacity included gills, pints, quarts, gallons, pecks and bushels; and currency consisted of farthings, halfpence, pence, threepence, sixpence, shillings, florins, half-crowns, crowns, half sovereigns, pounds, sovereigns and guineas. These were bewildering on their own, and terrifying in combination. Calculating the gain or loss to the bank balance of the farmer selling four acres, three roods and 14 perches of land at £12 17s 6d an acre, but buying five acres, two roods and 24 perches at £11 18s 9d an acre was the stuff of nightmares for many poor unfortunates.

There were over 7,000 teachers in the elementary system, which indicated an average class size of around 30 pupils per teacher, but it could be assumed that in country schools numbers could be lower and in towns and cities often considerably higher. The shortage of trained teachers was recognised, and the President of the Ulster Teachers' Union deplored the necessity of bringing in untrained staff, mostly young inexperienced girls, to help spread the load. "He thought a more useful source would be motherly souls who just love to be among children … their influence would be productive of nothing but good." The implication was that academic qualifications were less important. The vast majority of pupils would have endorsed the view that motherly souls would have been welcome, because in many schools teachers enforced their authority by physical means. For purposes of disciplining boys, the use of the cane was almost universal. It was a form of punishment borne with stoicism in the knowledge that chastisement usually carried full domestic approval, parents in the 40s being almost unanimously of the view that a teacher would not have inflicted such punishment without good cause. The Ministry of Education laid down guidelines which recommended that punishment should never be inflicted for excusable ignorance on the part of the pupil, and reserved instead for dealing with acts of moral turpitude, but monitoring of the rules was minimal and ill-disposed teachers were seldom held to account for inflicting a reign of terror. Some of those who survived such a regime were retrospectively grateful, acknowledging that respect for authority and acquiring a disciplined approach to intellectual activity were useful lessons for later life. Many more, of course, in such circumstances were mentally scarred, and acquired a lifelong detestation of learning. It was not an educational regime which as a matter of routine inflicted Dickensian levels of brutality on the pupils, but for many children school was a purgatorial period involving little but the acquisition of useless information, and which had to be endured before a meaningful life could be undertaken. In such circumstances, the maintenance of discipline was an essential part of the teacher's repertoire. It is worth noting that it was only in 1952 that regulations were issued for the special schools dealing with delinquent children, forbidding the use of the cane on those less than eight years old, and restricting its use on older pupils.

Pupils were subjected to yearly examinations so that their progress could be measured. Those coming up to their final year could sit the Elementary School Certificate exam, and if successful, use the certificate to either seek employment or pursue a further stage of education. Alternatively, pupils could sit the Secondary School Entrance Exam, on the basis of which the education authorities awarded scholarships.

These scholarships did not cover all the expense of secondary education however, and participation by those from a less affluent background was virtually non-existent. In 1945 out of the 185,000 children enrolled in elementary schools, only 1,655 won scholarships to secondary grammar schools, and 738 to technical and vocational colleges. For the vast majority of children, whatever formal education they had picked up after five or six years of elementary school was their quota for life.

Those who joined the grammar school regime could expect to continue their English, Arithmetic (now mutated into a number of disciplines under the title of Mathematics) and Geography, and be introduced, among other novelties, to at least one foreign language, plus the mysteries of different branches of Science. After three years of study an exam for the Junior Certificate of Education was undertaken, followed two years later by the Senior Certificate, which was recognised by a number of universities in Britain and Ireland as sufficient for matriculation, and by some professional bodies in lieu of their preliminary examinations.

In the immediate post-war years, there were just under 20,000 pupils in grammar schools; 28,000 in technical and commercial schools; around 400 students at the teacher training colleges of Stranmillis and St Mary's in Belfast, and Strawberry Hill in London; and some 2,000 students at Queen's University, where Medicine and Dentistry were more popular than the Arts, and both more favoured than Science. Overall, it could only be seen as a system which favoured the few and neglected the many.

In an attempt to address the shortcomings of this system the Education Act of 1947 was based on the English educational model. Primary, secondary and further education were identified as progressive stages of the system of public education, and it became the duty of the educational authorities "to contribute to the spiritual, moral, mental and physical development of the community by making available efficient education at each stage." While the leaving age remained at 14, the primary phase now was education regarded as suitable for children aged less than 11 years and six months, after which secondary education took over to meet the needs of those between 11½ and 19 years old, progression to further education being determined towards the end of that period. The Act, which became operative in April 1948, introduced two new concepts. First, the scope and value of the scholarship system were expanded enormously to ensure that free grammar school places would be made available to all those who passed a qualifying examination at age 11, or just over, irrespective of economic and social background. Second, provision of 100% state funding was on offer for all schools which would accept a management structure permitting a degree of official accountability for the subvention's use. Both developments were to prove highly contentious. On top of that the Act provided that the educational authorities in each county and city were now obliged to supply schools with free medical treatment, transport, milk, meals and other necessities. The education of young people in Northern Ireland was about to acquire a new reach and focus, and to present more opportunities for advancement than ever before. It was apparent from the start however, that this vision would not, and could not be achieved overnight.

The results of introducing selection at 11 soon became clear and in effect split the post-primary school population into three streams, with around 20% gaining grammar school places, a similar proportion progressing to technical or vocational education, and the remainder completing their education in intermediate schools. A high proportion of all available grammar school places were now reserved for those who passed the 11-plus exam, with the remainder to be filled by fee-paying pupils. Debate on the fairness (or lack of fairness) in this method of selection broke out almost immediately, with the proponents on either side arguing their case with the intensity of mediaeval theologians. But the prospect of free grammar school education opened up the possibility of giving thousands of children access to a learning environment where their abilities could be developed to the full. Even if the selection process could be debated, the outcome was a prize for which sacrifices were worth making.

One of the requirements for delivering the objectives of the Education Act was a vastly enhanced school building programme. In the late 1940s there were around 1,700 primary schools but only 118 secondary schools, grammar and technical. The new intermediate stream required by the Education Act represented the bottleneck, because in 1950, out of the 250 intermediate schools which were estimated would be required, only 11 were actually in operation. Four years later the figure had risen only to 17 and it was reported that while 55,000 children were eligible for intermediate education, only 7,000 places could be offered. Where circumstances allowed however, progress was brisk. In 1954 when Garvagh county intermediate in Londonderry was opened to accommodate 325 pupils, it had been built in 22 months at a cost of £107,000. One consequence of the blockage in the system was that, despite the cut-off at age 11 required by the Act, primary schools had to continue accommodating older children for whom no intermediate places were available. Even by the early 1960s there were still almost 500 schools in this category, attempting to provide secondary education in a primary setting, as if the Education Act did not exist. As was the case with public housing and other infrastructure projects in the post-war years, the building programme was held up by a lack of materials like steel and concrete, and education had to compete with the other post-war priorities. Short Brothers produced aluminium buildings which were quick to fabricate and comparatively easy to construct, and for a while these were urged as the answer to the accommodation problem, but they were not popular, even with architects, and their use did not become widespread.

Each county, plus Belfast, was charged with creating an Education Committee which would take forward the building programme, but as always, particularly as 20% of the necessary expenditure had to be funded from the local rates, some committees were more effective than others. By 1959 there were 73 intermediates, with more in the pipeline, but the geographic spread was uneven. Londonderry County Borough had 100% of the places it required, and Belfast and County Down around 80%, but that figure diminished to 38% in Armagh and 35% in Antrim. It was feared that the requirements of Fermanagh and Tyrone would not be fully met until the 1970s. Meanwhile many of the old primary schools remained little better than they had been a decade before. In 1960 reports were still being received of poor conditions in rural areas. A school in Glynn in County Antrim, with dry closets and a leaking roof, found that when the stoves were stoked in winter to an extent which provided even partial warmth, the stove pipes threatened to set fire to the wooden walls, so 45 children were regularly faced with either freezing or immolation. Another in Glengormley on the outskirts of Belfast had been condemned as far back as 1914, but was still in use and so crowded that children were using the stairs as desks: the floors were of stone, one classroom was below street level, and the toilets flooded during heavy rainfall. The accommodation requirements of the technical college in Antrim could only be met by taking over part of an adjacent hospital, and future plans included the annexation of a building used for training Council refuse collectors. Educational facilities in Northern Ireland had been neglected in the pre-war period, and the inherited deficiencies could not be rectified overnight.

An additional, if only temporary complication was caused by the government's wish to raise the school-leaving age from 14 to 15. While undoubtedly there were sound educational reasons for believing that an additional year's schooling would be beneficial to society as a whole, the government was more concerned with the attractions of keeping thousands of young people at school rather than joining the employment market, and hence in due course swelling the unemployment figures when jobs could not be found for them all. Besides increasing the pressure on available space within schools, it was calculated that the move would require 400 new teaching posts to cope with the additional pupil numbers, and it was feared that the demand would result in drawing experienced teachers from the primary sector. After much debate 1957 was eventually settled upon for the introduction of the new regime, condemning an entire cohort of young people to an extra year of academic endeavour and leaving them with the temporary conviction that theirs was a star-crossed generation. Three years later the Education Minister announced that, in line with developments in other countries, the school-leaving age would soon have to be raised to 16.

Under the circumstances the pace of the building programme was impressive, but undoubtedly it could have been accelerated had religion and politics not intruded. For different reasons, clergymen on both sides of the religious divide disliked the Education Act. The Protestant Archbishop of Armagh criticised the Act for being too closely modelled on the English legislation, which he insisted was in danger of producing a generation of educated pagans. He proposed that the General Synod should appoint an education officer to visit schools to ensure that the spiritual development of young Protestants was not being neglected, and to forestall the danger that such children might be taught – on what looked like a carefully graduated scale of risk – by "a Roman Catholic, an infidel or a Communist." Among Catholics the Bishop of Derry in 1950 observed that his Church had not asked for the Education Act, and thoroughly disagreed with parts of it, "but I maintain we are entitled to have it implemented", while the Primate, Cardinal d'Alton, who shared the reservations of his colleague, complained that sinister forces were at work to undermine the Act.

These last remarks were prompted by the provisions within the Education Act which allowed schools which chose to remain outside the state system to receive only 65% grant aid towards building, equipment and building costs, although salaries were still met in full. In order to qualify for 100% funding a school had to accept accountability via a management committee consisting of four representatives appointed by the school manager and two by the local education authority, commonly referred to as a "four and two" committee. Most schools under the control of the Catholic Church, but also a significant number of Protestant ones, refused to accept the principle of lay intervention in school management, and chose to make up the funding deficit by charging tuition fees, or by soliciting voluntary contributions. By the mid-50s there were just over 900 of these 'voluntary' schools, as compared to almost 800 in the state or 'controlled' sector, and of the 900 around 700 were managed by

Catholic authorities, the vast majority of them being primary schools. In other words, the financial restrictions bore down to a considerably greater extent on the Catholic rather than the Protestant community, and weighed heaviest on the primary school sector.

Catholics saw the situation as one where the Unionist government was attempting to use the financial provisions of the Education Act to impose their values on the development of Catholic children, and hence engender support for the Northern Ireland state by indirect means. In this analysis, Catholics paid taxes on the same basis as Protestants and it was inequitable that their children should be deprived of free education simply because of their religion; but given that reality, making up the 35% funding gap was a sacrifice the Catholic community was prepared to make. Protestants chose to interpret this stance in very different terms. To them, the Catholic Church and community were prepared to accept generous levels of funding from the government, but still withhold recognition of the state. This was seen as the kind of moral duplicity which raised questions about the entitlement of Catholics to be regarded as *bona fide* citizens, and calls were frequently made for funding levels to be reduced so far that schools would be obliged to come within the controlled system, or perish outside it. Such proposals led to the comments of Catholic clerics referred to earlier, insisting that the Act should be administered in a fair and transparent manner.

Even during the passage of the Education Act there had been protests from Unionists that the financial provisions were far too generous towards the voluntary sector, and in 1949 the Minister of Education, Colonel Sam Hall-Thompson was obliged to resign when opposition from the Orange Order threatened to split the Unionist Party. A review of educational provision was ordered, but in 1951 Sir Basil Brooke announced in Stormont that it had not been possible to identify any solution to the divisive issues besetting education, or as he put it in a memorable, if inelegant, metaphor: "To put the thing in a nutshell, we cannot unscramble the egg." Even some of the extremists who argued that funding levels and four and two committees should be used as an active inducement to bring all schools within the controlled sector, realised that such a move would be regarded by the Protestant voluntaries, including the more prestigious grammar schools, as an attack on their independence, and would have dangerous financial consequences for the Protestant controlled primary schools. For its part the government, while not above tweaking the education system for political purposes, realised that any attempt to reverse the financial provisions for Catholic schools would be patently unjust, as well as counter-productive in terms of public opinion in Britain and abroad, and was content to allow the controversy to die down. In 1956 when the radical Unionist MP Nat Minford tabled a motion in Stormont calling for grant aid to be reduced to 50% for schools refusing to accept a four and two committee, official pressure was applied to make him withdraw, and when that failed the government introduced its own amendment which committed it only to a further inquiry into the funding regime, but with no timetable for reporting back. By 1957 all the main Protestant churches had publicly made known to the government that any reduction in funding for the voluntary sector was to be opposed, not only for the impact it would have on the Protestant schools which remained within the sector, but also because with a new wave of IRA violence beginning to gain momentum, alienation of the Catholic community was impolitic as well as unjust.

By then it was becoming apparent to Unionists that the four and two committees were not a particularly effective means of managing a school, and that their universal adoption would not greatly contribute to a better or more accountable education system. At the same time, Catholics who looked objectively at the committees recognised that in practice the clerical appointees could always outvote the lay members and that the risk of spiritual values being undermined in any school adopting the system was remote. But as was the case with other aspects of life in Northern Ireland, once an issue achieved the status of a point of principle, logic and reason were set aside. Towards the end of the decade Nationalist MP Cahir Healy made a speech in Parliament regretting that Catholic schools could not accept the conditions which would allow full grant aid. It would be the equivalent, he said, of inviting him to dinner on Friday night and serving roast beef: an offer which was attractive but which could not be accepted as a matter of conscience. By that stage much of the heat had gone out of the debate. In 1959 it was announced in Westminster that grants to voluntary schools in England and Wales would be increased to 75%, but the fears that this would re-open the controversy in Northern Ireland were not realised. When the Catholic Church finally agreed to accept four and two management committees in the late 1960s the level of grant aid on capital expenditure had been raised to 80%, and it was inevitable that cynical remarks should be made about God and mammon, and the flexible nature of the human conscience.

It was undoubtedly the fact that the building programme for Catholic schools was hampered by the row over funding accountability, although in a perverse way the struggle to raise funds through weekly collections and social events had the effect of enhancing community organisation and the ethos of self-help. Arguably, too, the fact that some sacrifices had to be made to meet the costs of education gave schooling an enhanced value in the Catholic community. The figures suggest that the surge in construction of Protestant secondaries began in 1954, but the Catholic programme lagged behind until 1957. Certainly by the mid-50s only seven Catholic intermediates were operative as opposed to 43 in the controlled sector. In overall terms however, the government's record was not unimpressive. At the opening of a new school outside Derry in 1954 the Catholic Bishop publicly thanked the County Education Committee and praised the Ministry of Education for their efforts to ensure that suitable education was made available to the local children. And in terms of physical provision, even though by the early 60s the building programme was still incomplete, the major needs in both controlled and voluntary sectors had been met. Around 130 new schools had already been built since the passing of the Education Act, many more school premises extended, and the 27,000 pupils in secondary education had increased to over 80,000. Over the same period the education budget had more than tripled to around £16 million, and the aggregate contribution from government funds of 80% compared favourably with the 44% local authority funding in Britain. By 1960 over 32,000 children were being educated in grammar schools, 47,000 in intermediates, and just under 5,000 in technical colleges. It was coming from a low base immediately after the war, and progress was held back by unnecessary problems, but the record of the government in the field of education could be accounted a surprisingly good one. At one new school which opened at the beginning of 1959 the children were instructed to wear rubber-soled shoes to prevent damage to the wooden floor, acquire fountain pens to prevent ink stains, and were warned that harsh penalties would be visited upon anyone who attempted to carve his (or her) initials into the new desks. As the trade-off for electricity, sanitation and a waterproof roof, some traditional values had to be sacrificed.

The government, like all governments, was not above massaging the system in the interests of its own supporters, while also ensuring that its opponents suffered inconvenience and detriment. Despite a provision in the Education Act saying that education authorities should have regard to the principle that children were to be educated in accordance with the wishes of their parents provided the expense involved was not unreasonable, some of the Unionist-dominated County Education Committees refused to authorise travel or boarding grants for Catholic children to allow them to take a place in a grammar school of their own denomination. The government was reluctant to use its power of direction on such matters, and at times the threat of legal action by

Catholic parents, or the personal intervention of the Prime Minister, was required to break the stalemate. The management committee of a Belfast primary school was allowed to manipulate the government's own rule about ex-servicemen being given preference in employment, in order to avoid the possibility of having to appoint a Catholic teacher. A decision to build a new Catholic grammar school in Maghera, County Londonderry was agreed in principle in 1948, but was stalled by a succession of Education Ministers until 1959. In this latter case the government was forced to accept its responsibilities only when Ministry officials made it clear that in any public inquiry they would feel obliged to reveal that a number of Protestant grammar schools had been built having met criteria lower than those presented as an obstacle in the case of Maghera. Disparities in the funding for Stranmillis teacher training college (Protestant), and St Mary's college (Catholic) were justified on the grounds that the former was exclusively Protestant only because the Catholic Bishops had discouraged Catholic students from attending, warning that teaching qualifications obtained there would not be accepted in Catholic schools.

It was not that the government had malign intent towards Catholic education as such – although Harry Midgley, the Minister of Education from 1950 to 1957 was notoriously anti-Catholic in outlook – so much as lacking the stomach for a fight when their supporters on the ground proved aggressive in their opposition on educational issues. In the late 50s when the Ministry attempted to carry out a programme of rationalising primary school provision, sound economic arguments were put forward for amalgamating smaller schools and sharing services, with consequential closures. Where the closures threatened Protestant schools, the local Unionist constituency association was usually prepared to make the case that votes might be withheld at subsequent elections, or that the delicate voting balance might be affected, particularly in border areas, if Protestant families left the area as a result of schools closing down. In such circumstances even Ministers at Cabinet level were prepared to argue that educational considerations might be subordinated to political imperatives. To be fair, Midgley's successor as Minister, Morris May, usually ensured that the educational needs of the community were given priority, but he had inherited a legacy where, all too often, political expediency had been given precedence over civic responsibility.

The overall effect of these manoeuvrings on the provision of Catholic education was not insignificant, but neither was it catastrophic, and as noted earlier, in individual cases there was evidence of a very positive relationship between the Ministry and the Catholic authorities. On the basis of anecdotal evidence however, the general feeling among the Catholic teaching fraternity was that the bureaucracy of the state was to be kept at arm's length, rather than be treated as a potentially benign source of support. In that sense, it has to be recognised that some of the Church's difficulties were of its own making. If it insisted that Catholic children should be educated in a Catholic ethos, that Catholic graduates from Stranmillis (or Protestants) would not be employed in Catholic schools, and that a degree of official invigilation of school management was unacceptable, the effect was to create a wall of exclusivity around the education of its children which diminished the grounds for legitimate complaint if all its requirements were not met within a secular state. And of course the uncompromising attitude of the Catholic authorities on occasions made it all too easy for reactionary elements on the Protestant side to demonstrate their own brand of intransigence. The best that can be said is that the amount of unnecessary damage done to the education system by such encounters was less than it might have been.

One issue on which there was a surprisingly high degree of cross-party agreement was the pivot around which the entire system of secondary education revolved – the Qualifying examination, aka the 11-plus, aka 'the Qually'. The arrangements for the exam were set out in a yearly circular from the Ministry. It specified two intelligence tests, each of 45 minutes' duration, to be held in December and January; followed by examinations on a one-hour English paper, a 90-minute Arithmetic paper and a second 75-minute English paper, all to be taken on a single day in March. The English questions were to determine the ability of the candidate to understand the language and use it correctly, and would test skills in comprehension, vocabulary, sentence construction, spelling and punctuation. The skills to be tested in Arithmetic had an arcane basis which involved "the compound rules and reduction" as applied to units of money, avoirdupois weight, liquid capacity, length and time, with a top dressing of vulgar fractions, decimals and "the elements of simple proportion." It was clear that the underlying principle was intellectual rigour.

A few examples serve to make the point. In the exam set for 1950 in the two English papers the requirements included (quaint idea) an exercise in letter writing: a friend has issued an invitation to go on a picnic, and the response has to convey thanks in suitable terms, to state whether the date and time are suitable, and to indicate whether the seaside or the country is the preferred location for the event. There was a choice of essays: describe how a table is laid for breakfast; or describe how milk bottles are distributed and collected in the examinee's school; or describe a fireplace at home; or describe a day spent ill in bed. There was an exercise where a string of uncapitalised and unpunctuated words had to be turned into coherent sentences, including spoken dialogue. The first few paragraphs of an adventure story were given and the candidate was asked to complete it as he or she saw fit.

In the Arithmetic paper 19 questions were to be attempted in the 90 minutes. Among them: a child receives one penny a day in pocket money, but spends only three pence each Saturday. Before receiving her penny on Thursday 27 October she has six shillings and eight pence (about 33½p). How much does she have after receiving her penny on Friday 25 November? A joint of meat cooks at 45 minutes for the first pound and 15 minutes for each additional pound. If a five pound joint is to be served at 1.15 pm, at what time should it be put in the oven? No artificial aids to calculation were permitted, and the means by which the answer was reached was to be clearly set out in the answer booklet. Whatever such exercises may have lacked in promoting creative thought they more than made up for it in the application of logic and method.

Perhaps recognising that intellectual rigour had its own limitations, in 1955 the Ministry of Education published a new programme for primary education, in an effort to shift the emphasis away from a curriculum-centred approach to education, and towards a more child-centred one. Acknowledging all aspects of a child's personality – physical, intellectual, emotional, imaginative, social, moral and spiritual were specifically identified – the new programme with dreadful earnestness sought to develop aspects of character which previously had been neglected in the pursuit of mere intellectual achievement. Considerable regard was still had to "the paramount necessity of establishing the children's education on a firm spiritual basis", and there was no suggestion that the act of collective worship with which each day began should be scaled back, but health education and good citizenship were recognised as equally important aspects of the learning process. Within this enlightened approach, the importance of thrift, temperance and kindness to animals were emphasised: "training in the humane treatment of animals is necessary not only for the sake of the animals themselves but also as a means of inculcating a hatred of cruelty of every kind and a sense of compassion for the suffering and defenceless". As before however, the teaching of history and Irish were left as optional subjects, to be embarked upon only by the courageous teacher looking for professional excitement and stimulus. And while no mention was made in the new programme of what was regarded as the appropriate means of enforcing discipline, it is doubtful whether, notwithstanding the new focus on humane treatment and compassion, all canes were left to gather dust at the back of a dark classroom cupboard.

Even with the adoption of a more child-centred approach – and it could not be assimilated overnight – for those who undertook it the 11-plus examination remained a formidable obstacle to advancement, and almost from its introduction in the Education Act, debate had raged about its fairness, and its effects on both children and parents. For those who failed the exam by a narrow margin, provision was made to repeat the whole exercise the following year, but in most cases 'the Qually' had an ethos of finality about it. When introducing the measure in 1946 Hall-Thompson was unapologetically elitist in supporting the idea of selection based on academic ability, so that the brightest children would go to the schools best suited to develop their capabilities. He tried to give assurances that the exam would be selective, not competitive: "the essence of the examination was simply to determine the type of mind the child had ... if they were of an academic type they would be permitted to go one way and if they were not of an academic type they would go the other way" into technical or intermediate education. He failed to convince his critics. Some people complained that it was iniquitous that a child's course in life should be determined at so early an age, while others insisted that the focus on English and Arithmetic to the exclusion of other subjects would be injurious to the concept of a rounded education. There were even complaints that the timing of the exam was wrong, since in the winter months the vitality of children was low and their susceptibility to flu was high. A representative of the National Society for the Prevention of Cruelty to Children called the exam "the invention of the Devil", and claimed that history would compare it in infamy with the imposition of child labour in previous centuries.

Soon, too, emerged the criticism that children were being 'crammed' for the examination, and were being forced to attend night classes and Saturday tuition by parents terrified at the prospect of their child acquiring the stigma of failure. Teachers complained that they were being forced to drill children in English and Arithmetic (or their parents were sending them to professional tutoring establishments which did the same thing) to deal with anticipated questions to an extent which might get them through the exam, but which would leave some of them incapable subsequently of coping with the demands of grammar school education. One MP insisted that teachers were forcefully instilling knowledge until "at a certain point the children feel like hens under a hedge on a wet day", and even those not gifted with insight into the psychology of poultry agreed that he had a point.

The problem was, the new system had created pressures which were not easily relieved. Within a few years of the exam being introduced, teachers' organisations were pointing out that, despite Hall-Thompson's insistence that it was not a competitive exercise, it was being viewed in terms of success or failure, and even the epithet 'intermediate' when applied to a school had connotations of a different and lower standard of achievement. The advice offered to parents in 1952 in a newspaper article from "A Teacher" was well-intentioned: "do not for the sake of social prestige, which is little more than snobbery, allow a child to go to a secondary [grammar] school unless you are prepared to consent to that child's leaving it if the work proves to be too difficult." Well-intentioned and eminently sensible it might have been, but even by 1952 such advice already sounded hopelessly naïve. That year, of the 9,495 pupils who sat the Qualifying exam, 3,443 (just over one-third) were successful. The quantum of social prestige thereby gained or lost presumably was proportionate.

While the exam could be criticised, none of the critics could bring forward an alternative which was capable of winning a greater degree of support. One suggestion was that those who passed the 11-plus should be re-examined two years later to see if they were still suited to academic life, or whether an education more appropriate to their abilities might be delivered through the technical colleges. Another proposal was that the exam should be scrapped and selection made on the basis of reports from the pupil's teachers. A variant of that idea was that intelligence tests should be carried out every six months and averaged out when the child reached 11, and this to be followed by child and parents appearing before an interview panel to discuss options. There were advocates of an American-style system where all students undertook intermediate education until age 15 before deciding whether to leave or progress to high school and ultimately university.

The difficulty was that while all of these ideas had some degree of support, they also aroused greater levels of opposition. The idea, for instance, that the British model of comprehensive education should be adopted was flatly rejected by the Minister of Education on the decided but nebulous grounds that it was "out of harmony with Ulster traditions." Other proposals were rejected by the teachers because they would mean that it was they, rather than the exam itself, which would attract the wrath of disappointed parents. The Education Advisory Council made a preliminary report in 1952, finding that the examination system had worked reasonably well over the initial period of its operation, and suggesting that many of the problems associated with it would disappear if, among other desiderata, parents and teachers fully understood the objectives of the selection process. It was doubtful, even by that stage, whether such a shift in attitudes was possible. In a debate in Stormont in 1956 it was admitted that employers were reluctant to give jobs to applicants who had failed the 11-plus, believing that if they were academically unsound they were also likely to be generally incapable. In the same debate a Nationalist MP voiced the opinion that the system turned out children who were "cute" and capable of passing exams, but "these smart Alecs getting through the 11-plus examination with flying colours are not likely to be the best citizens in the long run." A Unionist Member agreed, suggesting that intelligence tests were better suited to urban children rather than to those from a rural background, because the former were "quick and slick" to an extent unknown to their country cousins. While the political coteries in Parliament disagreed on almost every issue, the future welfare of young people was one area where, just occasionally, common ground could be found.

Ten years after the exam system had been introduced, an exasperated Minister of Education was still complaining that "if many of the parents in Northern Ireland who are running about … putting themselves into a hysterical condition were to leave the children alone for a while … so that they can exercise their own mental balance and their own God-given capacity … there would be fewer candidates for mental treatment later on." Again it was a sensible statement, but one which was unlikely to be heeded. By the end of the decade the sound and fury showed no signs of abating, but one commentator probably summed up the consensus that was emerging: the Qualifying exam was "an imperfect but good instrument used for an impossible task." In 1960 the Education Advisory Council recommended that the exam should be retained, but that local experiments in alternative means of testing should be welcomed. It was entirely in keeping with the nature of the debate that even this tentative compromise could not be agreed by all members of the Council.

Given the intensity of the education debate, it was unsurprising that there should be some sensitivity about what was taught in class. This applied particularly among Protestant observers. There were protests in 1953 when an alert Tyrone Education Committee member discovered that Chaucer's *Prioress's Tale* could be read as possibly glorifying the Virgin Mary; and a few years later in Belfast a book was deemed unsuited for Protestant schools because it contained a story in which a juggler gave a performance in front of a statue of the Virgin. Grave offence was caused by a book designed for teaching Irish history at primary level because of an illustration showing a boy with a small Tricolour in his hand. When this was raised in Parliament a demand was made that all copies of the offending work should be withdrawn, because public funds were not to be used to subsidise disloyalty. The Ministry of Education had limited powers to influence teaching within the broad curriculum, but could refuse to sanction expenditure on books regarded as inappropriate, and authors and school authorities bombarded the Ministry with requests for books to be approved. Strict standards were applied, particularly in the field of Irish history. "The author in my opinion makes very little attempt to be impartial in his presentation of the facts" ran one report, "Irish history for him is very obviously an affair of black and white..." The personal predilections of another author were judged to have "so affected the atmosphere, language and in some instances the proportions of the book as to render it unsuitable for general use in Northern Ireland." Without knowing the content of such books it is difficult to pronounce on the accuracy of such judgements, but it could reasonably be inferred that they did not uphold the value system which was predominant in the Ministry.

The extent to which it was representative of general thought is difficult to say, but a glimpse of Catholic sensibilities was given by an enthusiastic review in the *Irish News* in 1960 of a book written by a priest who set out to disprove the theory of evolution, which he claimed had distorted the factual basis of much recent historical interpretation. The main line of argument put forward was that man as a species had existed for only 20,000 years, and so-called fossil finds suggesting earlier development could be dismissed as fakes or as mistakenly attributed. The Biblical Flood occurred around 7,000 years BC, and covered the inhabited surface of the earth, wiping out the Neanderthals who at that time were the predominant species, and were the race of Cain referred to in the Bible, paving the way for modern man to fulfil God's purpose. The review concluded: "I foresee that this book will have a deep influence, especially in the field of Catholic education."

When the matter was discussed in Parliament, both Unionist and Nationalist MPs agreed that history should be studied in schools, but disagreed profoundly on what that history should embrace. The subject was not completely ignored but was largely avoided in primary schools. At secondary level in Protestant establishments the emphasis was on modern European and British history, with Irish history only featuring where it impacted on the British story. In Catholic secondaries the emphasis was on the struggle to regain the freedom lost seven or eight centuries previously, emphasising the role of leaders, mythological and actual, in maintaining national pride.

In Stormont Protestant MPs insisted that an "approved" history of Ulster was necessary and should be made compulsory in all grant-aided schools. One Member asserted that the people of Ulster (by which he meant the Protestant people) had "a historical destiny" and it was necessary that children should be put in possession of the essential facts so that contrary ideas could be rebutted. Another MP felt that a reliable history was essential "so that instead of one child in 500 knowing about King William's progress in Northern Ireland and possibly one child in 10,000 knowing about Lord Carson and Lord Craigavon we will have educated children in our schools." (The fact that the speaker seemed unaware that Northern Ireland did not exist in the late seventeenth century when King William was progressing perhaps indicated that the lack of knowledge complained of was if anything understated.) Terence O'Neill took a similar line, arguing that knowledge of history, and specifically the story of how the Northern Irish state came into existence, was necessary to ensure that young people were made aware of the struggles of their forebears and respected the institutions of government which had been created. Nationalists MPs, probably recognising the futility of trying to argue a contrary point of view, relied mostly on sniping from the sidelines, insisting that any history of Ulster should recognise that it comprised nine counties instead of six, that the Presbyterian-led United Irishmen in the eighteenth century had rebelled against the British Crown, and that thousands of armed Protestants in the north before the First World War had defied the authority of both the British Crown and Parliament. One suggested that a comprehensive idea of how Northern Ireland was governed could be obtained by reading the slogans which adorned gable walls. In 1957 the Minister of Education acknowledged that if history in schools was to serve any useful purpose it would have to be objective, and an account written solely from either the Protestant or the Catholic point of view would not pass that test. He was correct in insisting that history should be an objective discipline which challenged, rather than reinforced, accepted mythologies, but given the state of history teaching in schools, he was probably wise to avoid addressing the question of where this objective chronicler was to be found.

Despite this high profile wrangling, much of which was carried out with displays of parliamentary theatricality understood and enjoyed by all the participants, a great deal of the wider public discourse on education in the 1950s was tempered by awareness that many of the issues arising in the classroom were reflecting changes taking place in post-war society. The Chairman of the Irish National Teachers' Organisation in 1951 complained that "instead of the 3 Rs we may find the 3 Ls – laziness, lassitude and luxury – to be the height of children's ambition." The same organisation complained about the growing lack of discipline in the classroom, and suggested that it arose from the fact that education had been taken over by experimenters and analysts: and proposed that the answer lay in the judicious use of corporal punishment for acts such as the wanton destruction of property, careless and slovenly habits, and bullying. The headmaster of a school in Ballymoney complained in 1954 that fewer children were now mastering the basic techniques of reading, writing and spelling, and blamed the increased availability of films, picture papers, and most of all "the so-called 'comic' or strip cartoon, commercially produced by mean and shoddy minds, often vulgar, sometimes corrupt, and always fantastic and educationally futile." And there were those who remained convinced that the older ways were better. Antrim County Committee debated the cost of sending a school group "to look at statues" in London because the trend towards providing pupils with visual stimulus was felt to be unlikely to produce such good citizens as had been turned out under the old and more rigorous regime. Omagh Urban Council in 1952 debated whether it was proper to raise the rates so that the Tyrone County Committee could supply schools with radios, pianos and film projectors. And despite no such service yet being available in Northern Ireland, one Councillor feared that it was only a matter of time before the level of pandering was reached where schools were demanding television sets. It seems safe to assume that at least some of these objectors had received part of their education in the school of hard knocks, and felt that learning by rote, with endeavour reinforced by judicious application of the cane, were necessary preliminaries on the road to merited citizenship.

The education system in Northern Ireland in the 50s was not flawless. Complaints about Protestants wishing to corrupt the spiritual integrity of Catholic education, and Catholics being ungrateful for the generosity of state funding, were never far from the surface and reflected the fact that for both sides, important issues of principle were at stake. On occasions the government's actions were morally reprehensible, but it was also the case that in refusing to come down from their own moral high ground Catholics accepted a role which at times seemed almost cherished as a badge of serfdom. In that sense, and given the centrality of education in the daily life of Northern Ireland, the wonder was that complaints were not more vociferous, or the disagreements more profound. Overall, while politics could never be stripped out of the policy debate there seemed to be a tacit recognition that the future of the youngest members of society was so important that displays of tribalism in their most extreme form were inappropriate. Speaking in the debate on the Ministry of Education expenditure estimates in 1959 one of the leading Nationalist MPs congratulated the Minister on his speech, saying that although it was like the curate's egg in being good in parts, in fact most of the parts were good. It was a fair assessment: anything more would have been hypocritical, but anything less would have been ungenerous.

As the new decade commenced, the arguments began to have a familiar ring to modern ears. The Belfast education authorities decided that all its intermediate schools should be equipped with television, despite a Nuffield Foundation study which claimed that the desire of children to watch TV was inversely proportional to intelligence, with the brightest children watching the least. In the newspapers exchanges took place between parents complaining that their children were ignorant of the basics of arithmetic and grammar, that discipline was lax or non-existent, and that teachers were trying to be too friendly with the children. Teachers claiming with equal fervour that the 3 Rs were not neglected, but were approached in a more intelligent way than formerly, and if discipline was less strict, the overall educational experience was happier, broader and better. In grammar schools it was noticed with some surprise that increasing numbers of pupils were staying on to attempt the new Advanced level of the Senior Certificate examination, increasingly being recognised as the standard for achieving major scholarships, and there was a slight uneasiness that the academic system was beginning to focus too much on exams and results for their own sake.

Along with the spread of affordable personal transport and the exponential growth of television, the provision of universal free secondary education was another of the crucial factors that marked the 1950s as the transitional decade between the pre-war era and the modern age. On the one hand it could be argued that implementing the reforms of the late 1940s had the effect of entrenching the system of religious separation in education, leaving with the church authorities a disproportionate influence on the value systems imparted to young people. On the plus side however, as more and more young people benefitted from the reforms introduced by the 1947 Education Act, and then made their way in the world, a new professional middle class was created which in its extent and diversity was fundamentally different from anything which had gone before. In one crucial respect it was revolutionary, because it created a playing field upon which Protestant and Catholic pupils could compete on a basis of relative equality, and if thereafter job opportunities were not distributed with impartiality, the educational status of the Catholic community in overall terms was in no sense inferior to that of its Protestant counterpart. In due course that would create a sense of self-confidence and a willingness to challenge the *status quo* which earlier generations had lacked. Perhaps the brightest colours began to fade in the image of the hedge school.

CHAPTER 8

POWER TO THE PEOPLE

CONTEMPORARY SOCIETY WOULD be impossible without electricity. Every individual, every house, every shop, every business, every street in every town or city in Northern Ireland depends on the constant availability of electricity. Along with water, it is a public utility which has become one of the fundamental requirements of life. The 1950s knew about electricity, and made use of it, but while on occasions its temporary loss caused inconvenience to many, there did not exist a level of dependency which meant that the structure of everyday life was threatened by its absence. As with many other aspects of modern existence, the availability of a continuous and affordable supply of electricity which developed throughout the 1950s came to fulfil a need of which previous generations had been unaware. Although most towns of any size were connected to the grid, in large swathes of the countryside, particularly in south Londonderry, and the greater part of Counties Tyrone and Fermanagh, oil-burning lamps, candles and open fires continued to serve the same purpose as they had done for generations. Latticed pylons made their appearance across the landscape, but they were not ubiquitous, nor was every home filled with electrical devices greedy for the power they carried. According to official figures, at the end of 1948 there were 83,066 electricity consumers throughout Northern Ireland, and that was an increase of 30,000 from two years previously. The term 'consumers' was flexible, covering everyone from individual households to shops, cinemas, hotels and industrial complexes, but it is known that less than 800 of them were on farms.

To a considerable extent therefore, the availability of electricity was an urban phenomenon, and even in towns and cities was still not a luxury enjoyed by everyone. By our standards the countryside was not only unbelievably quiet at night, but also incredibly dark, lit only by moonlight and the occasional gleam of light from a kitchen window or the headlights of a passing car. But here, too, change was getting under way. Agriculture was a major industry and in the eyes of the government modernisation was essential, so rural electrification was identified as a strategic necessity. If in the immediate post-war years very few farms in

Northern Ireland had electricity, the government was determined that the picturesque darkness of the countryside would soon be obliged to yield to progress.

By arrangements put in place under the Electricity Supply Act of 1948 the government retained overall control of electricity supply in Northern Ireland, largely on the same basis as had been put in place as an emergency measure during the War. On a day-to-day basis the generation, transmission and distribution of electricity became the responsibility of three bodies – the Electricity Board of Northern Ireland, Belfast Corporation, and a co-ordinating body, the Joint Electricity Committee (JEC). Londonderry Corporation had its own separate arrangements which were to some extent outside the new scheme. The Board and the Corporation were responsible for generating electricity via three power stations, one at Ballylumford on the Antrim coast and the other two situated in the Belfast harbour area. A small generation unit in Derry and one in Larne were also used occasionally as standby stations. The electricity produced went into a common pool which the JEC sold on for distribution to consumers at a fixed tariff. In practical terms, Belfast supplied the city and a considerable part of the surrounding area, while the Board supplied the rest of Northern Ireland apart from Derry. It seemed a cumbersome arrangement, but the objective was to ensure that roughly the same price was charged for electricity to users throughout the system.

Left to themselves the temptation for the Corporation and the Board would have been to focus their efforts on supplying Belfast and the larger towns, plus the bigger industrial complexes, where the output of electricity could be sold on with minimum investment in pylons, power lines and distribution infrastructure. Over a number of years the Board had sequentially acquired more than 50 of the pre-existing local electricity undertakings – Lisnaskea, Fivemiletown and Ballygawley in 1945 for instance; Limavady and Newtownbutler in 1946; Antrim, Carrickfergus, Glenarm and Portstewart in 1947 – and incorporated their distribution networks. By the end of 1949 there were 233 towns and villages in the network. An Electricity Board distribution map of that year shows the expected pattern of intensive coverage around Belfast, north Down and the Lagan valley to Portadown, with lesser coverage elsewhere. The major high tension cables extended south from Belfast to Newcastle; east to Bangor and the Ards peninsula; north via Antrim to Portrush and Ballycastle in County Antrim, and via Maghera to Derry in County Londonderry; and west via Portadown to Omagh, Strabane and Derry, with a branch from Ballygawley to Enniskillen. There were numerous low tension lines leading off these main corridors, with more than 2,500 miles of cable by the late 40s, but as already indicated, there were also huge tracts of countryside which literally were not within miles of a supply of electricity. Before the War there had been no public supply of electricity and the system was now being charged with expansion on an unprecedented scale.

Rural electrification – filling in the blank spaces on the map – was the government's priority. An electrified farming industry would be a more efficient farming industry, producing more food at cheaper prices and assisting the overall growth of prosperity. Electrification would make conditions on farms more attractive and hence help slow down the drift from the land. And of course if thousands of new consumers were added to the network, economies of scale would suggest that prices for everyone could be expected to fall. Although details of their location were not given, official sources claimed that 26 farms had been electrified by 1932, so the concept was not entirely new, and in the King's Speech at the opening of the 1947 Parliamentary session, the government pledged to push forward electrification "as fast as the present physical limitations of supplies and equipment permit".

Apart from severe shortages of wood and concrete for poles, and a scarcity of cables and technical equipment like transformers – the 'physical limitations' which the government had been careful to flag up – the major blockage in carrying out rural electrification was the lack of money. Before 1948 the arrangement had existed that rural consumers could be connected to the grid provided they entered into a five year covenant to purchase electricity to the value of 12½% of the installation costs. For many farmers this was simply unaffordable, and it was claimed that in many cases the costs involved would be greater than the value of the farm concerned. One farming MP quoted figures which showed that he would have to undertake to pay £1 a day for five years while not using more than a fraction of the electricity such a sum would buy. It was claimed that in a small village like Dromara in County Down, householders were charged only the price of wiring their property, but for the Catholic church and parochial house just over a mile away an undertaking of £150 a year was required. Farmers at Carnmoney, less than five miles from Belfast were each being asked for £200 a year. Such figures were no doubt quoted for their shock value as much as anything else, and were unlikely to have been fully representative, but they were used to argue that covenants were an obstacle to the more rapid spread of electrification. One of the major changes introduced in the 1948 Act was the abolition of covenants.

For Belfast Corporation rural electrification was not a critical issue, but it turned out that covenants were an essential component of the Electricity Board's ability to trade as a business. One example quoted from the numerous surveys undertaken by the Board related to Drumquin in County Tyrone, where 34 farms, 59 residences, two churches, a hall, a shop and a quarry would, if connected, have generated revenue equivalent to only 5% of the capital costs of installation. It was recognised of course that the Board could not be expected to run power lines across miles of bog and mountain to bring a supply of electricity to a lone cottage, but there was a feeling among the farming community and their representatives in Parliament that the Board was being over-cautious, and refusing to undertake schemes unless a healthy return on capital investment was guaranteed. Attention accordingly focussed on what arrangements the government had made with the Board to underwrite the deficits which might be incurred in pushing forward the rural electrification programme. One concession which overtly had been made was that the Board was freed of the obligation to balance its books each year, so long as the position was satisfactory after 10 years. But another concerned an undertaking which had been given in a less public manner, and which could be interpreted as meaning that the government would not allow the Board's work to be held up because of a lack of funds. Ministers argued that all that had been promised was that the government would support any scheme which seemed like a reasonable business risk, provided the advantages to be gained made the risk justifiable. What that meant in practice remained a matter of contention, and there were suggestions that the Board was attempting to manipulate the situation to force the government to subsidise rural schemes. The Ministry of Agriculture confessed that it had a scheme to make grants towards the installation of generators on farms which were unlikely to be connected to the grid, but it was unable to implement it until the Electricity Board had completed its surveys and it became known which areas were least likely to be connected. There was little point in assisting a farmer to purchase a generator if within a short period of time mains electricity was to become available to him.

The Board did not immediately throw in the towel, and in the first two years of the decade spent almost £4.5 million in connecting to the grid 2,335 farms and 7,810 rural dwellings, figures which in themselves (averaging well over £400 per installation) demonstrated the economics of the project. But subsequent usage of power was low, because even the farmers who were connected insisted on using electricity as sparingly as possible, mostly only for lighting rather than operating equipment. It was claimed with some bitterness that the average farmer used only enough electricity to run two light bulbs plus enough to allow him to listen to the radio on a Saturday night. Enthusiastic MPs spoke of the number of sheep which could be sheared, the number of cows which could be milked, the number of chicks which could be raised, and the tonnage of root crops which could be chopped up for feedstuffs by the use of electricity. To keep prices down, it was suggested that farmers might be allowed to use suitable trees off their land for the poles which would carry the necessary cables, and that other unnecessarily strict safety precautions might be relaxed. It was all to no avail. The Board was able to produce figures which demonstrated that the financial burden of rural electrification was such that the obligation to balance the books would become permanently impossible. The shortage of materials persisted too, and by 1952 the programme simply ground to a halt. The following year legislation was introduced which allowed the Board to accept guarantees from customers that they would purchase predetermined amounts of power, or else make a contribution towards the capital costs of the lines and equipment necessary to ensure installation. Ensuring that those who could afford it got first choice was a departure from the basic principles behind the 1948 arrangements, but it was the only way to keep the project afloat. In Stormont there was a sense of irritation that farmers did not realise the enormous potential of electricity, and insisted instead in hanging on to their hurricane lamps, Aladdin table lamps, candles and Tilley storm lanterns, together with the pre-war way of thinking that they symbolised. For the government, it might have been the beginning of a realisation that managing the electricity industry was not as straightforward a task as it might seem. Whether it was wise to leave such a complex task as just one of the myriad of functions carried by the Ministry of Commerce, or whether a dedicated Ministry of Power should manage so crucial an undertaking became an unspoken question in the next few years.

If the farming community liked its paraffin lamps, the town dwellers depended on gas. Gas was still the most widely available source of energy in urban areas. The largest gas works were in Belfast, Derry and Bangor, but there were around 30 other undertakings, mostly owned by the municipal authorities, and others operated by private concerns. Industrial usage and domestic cooking accounting for the major share of the output, and street lighting absorbed the rest. The image of foggy, gas-lit byways was by no means a forgotten relic of the Victorian era, and lamplighters with their ladders, cleaning gear and other paraphernalia were a familiar part of the urban landscape. On each light, when required, lamplighters had to clean the glass, change the fragile mantles (the sacks of chemically treated fabric which became incandescent when heated), wind the clockwork mechanisms which controlled the flow of gas and identify maintenance requirements, in many cases while standing on a ladder. In the early 50s there were over 100 lamplighters in Belfast alone, each responsible for around 140 lamps out of the 16,000 which lit the city streets, and even by 1960 it was acknowledged that it would be some years before all of Belfast's streets lost their Victorian and Edwardian gas lamp standards. In Omagh, the local gas supply was so unreliable that the street lights went out when domestic usage rose, and it was suggested that the Electricity Board should be invited to convert the system, having already carried out successful projects in Lisburn, Portadown and Newtownards. Ballymoney's new electrified system was hailed for giving street lighting for less than £400 a year. When in 1950 the lighting in Coleraine was described (with dubious precision) by the local Chamber of Commerce as being reminiscent of the fifteenth century, the Board offered to convert the system for £30,000.

For most of the decade gas production continued to rise, but it became increasingly difficult to compete with the economies of scale the Electricity Board could offer. By the early 60s there were still 16 gas undertakings, but it was clear that only in Belfast, which by now accounted for over 70% of total production, was there any hope of a long-term future. Gas was laborious to produce – essentially, heating or 'carbonising' coal in coking ovens or retorts, and collecting the gases and other by-products which were given off – and there were limits to how much could be stored. Every undertaking had its huge circular gas holder or gasometer, sometimes the largest structure in the town. The larger gasometers were contained in water-filled reservoirs – the water providing a seal against leakage as well as a means of support – rising and sinking as the volume of gas varied. By the late 50s gas increasingly was being seen as smelly, nasty and dangerous, responsible for explosions from leaking pipes or appliances. Apart from fires and water heaters, there were few domestic appliances which could run off gas, and other than being easier to control for purposes of cooking it had no practical advantages over clean, instant and versatile electricity. The industry limped on until the 80s, but in terms of competition, it was the steam train versus the automobile all over again.

Given the sheer convenience of electricity for domestic purposes, and the desire of the government to attract new industries and improve existing ones, it was clear that the demand for electricity was going to keep rising. Planning for how this demand was to be met was not straightforward however. Power stations were massively expensive in terms of capital outlay, and most cost-effective when subsequently used to near full capacity. Too much capacity was uneconomic, but too little led to localised outages. Losses occurred in transmitting energy over long distances, and reserve capacity had to be fed in from time to time to maintain the transmission system in some kind of overall balance. Demand for capacity varied throughout the year, and even throughout each day depending on the weather. Generators had to be taken out of service for periodic maintenance and eventual retirement. All in all, while it was possible to predict what the growth in demand was likely to be in broad percentage terms, commissioning power stations to meet that demand was a complex process. It was the function of the JEC to make the calculations and advise the Ministry of Commerce accordingly.

Additional complications arose in regard to where power stations should be located. Because they burned coal which had to be shipped in, and required copious supplies of water for cooling purposes, coastal locations were preferred. And since the main market for electricity was the greater Belfast area, it made sense to minimise transmission losses by ensuring that generation capacity was located close to where it would be used. Belfast already had two power stations in the harbour estate, known prosaically as Power Station East and Power Station West, and the addition of any further capacity would create the danger that any attack on the city (memories of the Blitz remaining fresh) would disable the greater part of the province's entire electricity system. Indeed one MP in 1951 suggested that having two power stations so close to the city centre was in itself an inducement to a nuclear attack. In 1950 however, the JEC predicted that new capacity would be necessary for the winter of 1953–1954, and after considering possible locations in Newry, Warrenpoint, Derry and on the shore of Lough Neagh, came to the conclusion that the best choice was another station in Belfast harbour.

Advice from the British government's Key Points Planning Committee was that it would be unwise to put so much generation capacity in one area, and a debate ensued whether it would be safer to build only a small station in Belfast and put additional generators into Ballylumford; or whether, since Belfast was regarded as a 'defensible area' and capable of resisting attack to some extent, an isolated power station was more at risk. By 1951 the Cabinet had decided that plans for meeting demand up until 1958 should be based on a new, large-capacity station in Belfast harbour's Victoria Channel, with an estimated cost of at least £4 million, and Belfast Corporation was instructed to proceed with the project forthwith.

Due to faction fighting within the Corporation it was not until early 1953 that invitations to tender for the new station were issued. Proceedings then became farcical. On the advice of the Corporation's consultants, the invitations were issued only to a small group of engineering companies who were felt to be capable of undertaking a contract of this size. In May 1953 the contract was awarded to one of these firms, Babcock and Wilcox (B&W). This resulted in a protest from one of the firms which had not been invited to tender, and who complained that by not using an open tendering process the Corporation had acted in breach of its own Standing Orders. The contract was withdrawn and a new tendering process begun. The Ministry of Commerce, concerned at the delay which had already taken place, insisted that in the interests of making progress the contract awarded to B&W should be reinstated. This was done but when the contract was brought before the full Corporation for ratification, it was noted that the B&W price was more than £250,000 higher than the next highest bid, and legal proceedings were commenced to block the contract being awarded. A new public tendering exercise was then launched, only for it to be discovered that the specification included equipment that only B&W could supply, and the invitations to tender had to be withdrawn and re-written to include specifications for equipment equivalent to that manufactured by B&W. By February 1954 even the Corporation recognised that the only possibility of procuring the generating capacity which would be necessary for 1957 was to allow the Ministry of Commerce to assume responsibility for placing the necessary contracts. There was concern within the government that a situation had arisen whereby in order to meet the deadline the more expensive B&W contract would now have to be accepted, and that the government would attract the criticism that the Corporation through its mismanagement deserved. But if the lights were to be kept on, there was no alternative.

Taken together with the need to intervene in the rural electrification programme, the power station dispute convinced the government that strategic planning for electricity was too important a task to be left to the bodies with a vested interest in the outcome. If possible, alternative sources of generating capacity should be found, and surveys were undertaken to see if there were viable supplies of coal at Coalisland in County Tyrone, or whether the numerous peat bogs throughout Northern Ireland could be exploited, or indeed whether wind-generated electricity could assist in the quest for diversification. The possibility of using the waters of the Bann and Mourne rivers seemed worthy of consideration, and the tidal flows of Strangford Lough were felt to posess some potential. From the early 50s the government was actively involved in the Erne hydro-electric scheme being undertaken by the Electricity Supply Board in the Republic, although the Northern Irish interest was primarily in the opportunity this presented to undertake an extensive drainage scheme in an area notoriously prone to flooding. Asked in 1954 whether the two electricity authorities had any plans to trade power across the border, the Minister of Commerce, perhaps fearing that a political trap was being set, stated blandly that the question did not arise because neither system had surplus generation capacity to share. Most alluring of all however, was the vision of a nuclear power plant in Northern Ireland. The announcement in 1954 that Britain's second nuclear reactor would be built at Dounreay in Scotland caused tempting parallels to be drawn with Northern Ireland: an under-developed area, thousands of construction jobs, and cheap power at the end of the project. For supporters of the idea the logic seemed to be unchallengeable.

The vision was attractive on a number of other levels. First, although a nuclear plant would be disproportionately expensive in terms of capital costs – around £20 million was a conservative estimate – once established there would be no need for constant supplies of coal or oil. Second, the establishment of such a plant would send a very positive message to the world that Northern Ireland was at the forefront of the technological developments which would drive the wheels of industry in the future, and this selling point could be used to attract inward investment. Third, and by no means the least important consideration to a Unionist government, the location of such a project in Northern Ireland would demonstrate that the province was an integral part of the UK, playing its part in cutting-edge technology where Britain was among the world leaders.

These attractions were not immediately grasped by many people however. Among politicians it was Brian Faulkner who emerged as the champion of atomic energy as early as 1951, when his question in Parliament about the government's attitude towards constructing an atomic power station was met with derisive laughter. The *Irish News* gleefully speculated that in the near future new slogans would have to be devised, with "Not an Atom" replacing "Not an Inch", and the Grand Atomic Lodge of Ireland authorising atomic drums to be beaten on the Twelfth. It was not subtle, and perhaps was not intended to be. Two years later when Faulkner returned to the charge in November 1953, the Minister of Commerce, Lord Glentoran, seemed unenthusiastic, claiming that he had recently attended a confidential briefing on the matter, and the prevailing wisdom was that coal-fired generation would be cheaper than any alternative for some time to come. Behind the scenes however, Glentoran was preparing to open negotiations in London with the Lord President of the Council, Lord Salisbury, whose remit included electricity, and was urging the case for Northern Ireland to be given permission to build a nuclear station as soon as possible. Atomic energy, as a spin-off from the research which had produced Britain's atomic bomb and missile capability, was a policy area reserved to London, and London for understandable reasons was not prepared to relinquish control without proper safeguards. Whether it was visionary, opportunistic or merely blissfully deranged, Coleraine Borough Council resolved to mount a campaign to have any nuclear station located on the banks of the river Bann, in or adjacent to Coleraine. In February 1954 at the start of the new Parliamentary session, it was stated that Ministers now attached the highest importance to the potential benefits of atomic power and were closely monitoring developments in Britain.

What that might mean in practice was not revealed, for the very good reason that there was still considerable uncertainty surrounding both the costs associated with atomic power, and doubts as to whether the Northern Ireland system was capable of taking advantage of the benefits it might offer. Nevertheless there was surprise and disappointment in Belfast when in February 1955 the government in London announced a 10 year programme to build 12 nuclear stations at a cost of some £300 million, but none of them were to be located in Northern Ireland. Although public assurances were given that the position of Northern Ireland would not be overlooked, Glentoran's officials had already been given fairly unambiguous advice from the Ministry of Power in London that a conventional power station was more likely to suit the requirements of the Northern Ireland electricity system, and a nuclear station could prove to be an expensive liability. Glentoran in Parliament made a statement which suggested that, while Northern Ireland had not been included in the 10 year programme, neither had the province been specifically excluded, and the Electricity Board had been listed among the authorities which might own and operate a nuclear station. Faulkner interpreted this as a positive indication of intent and urged Glentoran and his colleagues to capitalise on whatever opportunities were offered without allowing financial considerations "to guide them too strongly in this matter." A few days later Glentoran attempted to introduce a note of realism into the debate, pointing out that the 10 year programme was concerned with the design and development of new stations, but the earliest commercial model would not be generating electricity until 1961. Only then would design faults and operational shortcomings become apparent, and a clear picture of costs begin to emerge. While those anticipated teething troubles could easily be carried within the extensive British electricity system, given the centrality to the Northern Irish system of the proposed nuclear plant, any such hiccups could be disastrous. Despite such caveats however, Glentoran could not resist the temptation to gild the lily. The new Belfast station in Victoria Channel would meet immediate requirements, and although he could not say for certain that the additional capacity Northern Ireland would require for 1961 would be nuclear, "it is my intention and expectation that an atomic station will be provided here within the period covered by the programme recently announced." Faulkner gratefully accepted this as an assurance that Northern Ireland would be included within the British scheme.

In reality, Glentoran was much less sure of his position than his bullish pronouncements had indicated. At a Cabinet meeting in March 1955 he argued that the benefits to be derived from nuclear energy "were so tremendous that the inherent risks were worth taking", but since the capital costs of a nuclear station were now put at £25 million, or one quarter of Northern Ireland's entire public expenditure budget, it seemed sensible to try and quantify what the balance might be between risks and benefits. The Minister of Finance stated without equivocation that he would not be prepared to sanction expenditure on this scale unless it could clearly be shown that nuclear-generated electricity was cheaper to produce than power from conventional sources. Glentoran was forced to admit that the experimental stations in Britain had not been in operation for long enough for reliable data to be collected on production costs, and confessed that he now felt uneasy that his comments in Parliament might have been misconstrued as meaning that Northern Ireland was committed to playing a part in the British 10 year programme.

His uneasiness was justified. Despite protracted Ministry of Commerce lobbying which came as close as protocol would allow to begging for Northern Ireland to be given a place in the 10 year plan, officials in the Ministry of Power and in the Atomic Energy Authority (AEA) were letting it be known that they regarded such a bid as being emotional rather than practicable, and urged Salisbury not to allow his personal sympathies to lead him astray by encouraging Glentoran to believe there was any realistic possibility of gaining access to the programme. The best that Northern Ireland could hope for was that a decision on a nuclear station should be deferred for at least another 10 years.

The arguments put forward in London were unassailable. The costs of a nuclear station were unpredictable, but undoubtedly would be high, and overall generation costs would possibly be greater than from conventional sources. Reliability was unproven, and a small electricity system like Northern Ireland's could not afford the risk of losing so substantial a proportion of generating capacity at any given time. To make a nuclear station profitable it would have to operate at a capacity which was in excess of what the entire market in Northern Ireland required, or was likely to require in the near future unless large-scale industrial development were to take place. Northern Ireland possessed no personnel with the skills to operate a nuclear station, and lacked any educational capacity to produce people with the requisite knowledge. In short, the advice concluded, Glentoran and the Ministry of Commerce were to be told definitively, although as tactfully as possible, that the development plans of the AEA were unlikely to include Northern Ireland for the foreseeable future. In September 1955 Salisbury wrote to Glentoran to explain that the British programme was based on the construction of a series of inter-connected stations whose operations would complement each other, and it was impossible to fit a stand-alone Northern Ireland station into this framework.

Despite this setback, Glentoran and his expert advisers in the JEC continued to think positively. In March 1955 the JEC had issued a report which stated that, while reliable data were not yet available, there were good reasons to believe that nuclear power would turn out to offer substantial cost advantages over coal and oil-fired generation. A few months later the Committee was consulting with engineers to identify a suitable site or sites on the shores of Lough Neagh which should be acquired and held pending a final decision to proceed with a nuclear project. In September, and notwithstanding Salisbury's advice, Glentoran ordered the purchase of two sites, one at Ballylumford and the other on Lough Neagh, to be held until a decision could be made as to what kind of station would best meet Northern Ireland's needs when the next increment of generating capacity was required. It was clear that Glentoran remained attracted to the nuclear option, and officials were instructed to open negotiations with the relevant local authorities about building the new roads which would be necessary if construction were to begin at Washing Bay, on Lough Neagh. Lobbying was also taking place at the highest levels, and in October the Ministry of Power received a tactful query from the Prime Minister's Office in Downing Street conveying the hope that a place in the nuclear programme could be found for Northern Ireland. While the Ministry of Power did not immediately drop its opposition, politically aware officials recognised the wisdom of preparing to change tack should the need arise. Opening a new school in Cookstown, Brookeborough appealed to boys throughout Northern Ireland to begin studying for degrees in nuclear science, rather than medicine and the arts. It could have been read as an indication of his hopes for Washing Bay.

Despite these omens, Glentoran (or his officials) recognised that the electricity supply industry was too complex to risk dependence on a single source of generation capacity and that all the options deserved to be explored. In a White Paper published in the middle of 1956 attention was drawn to other potential sources of power. Peat was discarded as a fuel source because it was unlikely to be available in sufficient quantities to make it economic for a power station, and reserves of native coal were predicted to be too insignificant to break reliance on imported supplies. Oil was beginning to be used in some British power stations, but seemed to offer no real price advantage over coal. Tidal and wind power were examined, but the conclusion was that such projects were too capital-intensive to be attractive. Hydro-electric schemes on the Bann and Mourne rivers were suggested at a capital cost of some £6.5 million. This was greater than the cost of a conventional station, but once operational could save £135,000 and 75,000 tons of coal a year. It had to be recognised however, that such schemes would be opposed strongly by farmers and fishing interests, and the compensation which would have to be paid for the loss of agricultural land would nullify part of the savings on fuel.

All this provided the backdrop against which the nuclear stall could be set out. According to the White Paper, nuclear stations were 'inherently safe' and although it was felt desirable to avoid building one in a populated area, this was in the nature of a precaution which could be discarded once public confidence had grown. A number of drawbacks were acknowledged: nuclear stations could not be stopped and started at will, were most economic when operating with high generation loads, and in that sense existing demand levels in Northern Ireland were still too low to be ideal. Finance was also a factor. The cost of a 200 MW station was now estimated at between £25 and £30 million, with a further £5 million for the uranium fuel which would be needed. Reliability was also a concern, because any nuclear station would be generating a high proportion of the province's total requirement, and stoppages would be an expensive embarrassment. The White Paper concluded on a positive note however, insisting that the technical difficulties could and would be overcome, and the government was proceeding on the assumption that by the early 1960s a more accurate view could be taken about when a nuclear station would become fully viable.

It was consistent with this mood that a meeting between Ministry of Commerce and engineering experts in the summer of 1955 should conclude that there would be no serious hazards associated with the disposal of nuclear waste. The spent uranium fuel removed from the reactor would have to be stored under water for some weeks until its inherent levels of radioactivity had fallen sufficiently to allow it to be transported by road to a processing facility. The water in which it had been stored would become "slightly" contaminated, and would have to be discharged into a large volume of fresh water in a controlled fashion so that dilution could take place. It is difficult to say whether such an optimistic assessment was shaped by the wish to uphold the government's political and economic imperatives, or whether it reflected a determinedly positive interpretation of the limited scientific knowledge available at the time. In either event it represented an attitude to overcoming obstacles which verged on the cavalier.

A warning note should have been sounded in the early months of 1956 when an electricity strike brought Northern Ireland to a standstill, and demonstrated the government's limited understanding of the industry they were determined to enhance. Negotiations on a pay increase which had been taking place – the employees demanding an increase of 4d an hour which they claimed was the rate in Britain while the employers were offering 3d – broke down when, without recourse to arbitration, the 2,300 workers in the industry walked out at 8.00 am on 14 March. The strike was called off the following day when, after a meeting lasting 11 minutes the workers' claims were met. The cost of the stoppage was estimated at £500,000, with those hardest-hit being the chicken hatcheries throughout Northern Ireland which lost thousands of incubating eggs and just-hatched chicks. It was suggested at one stage that the strike had been Communist-inspired, but it seemed generally accepted that a flexing of industrial muscle was responsible, rather than a significant degree of political motivation.

The government had been taken by surprise, and the initial reaction was to complain loudly that the strike was unofficial, since it had taken place without observing the requisite 21 day period of notification required by law. Whether the government would have been better prepared had notice been given was doubtful, because Glentoran reported to the Cabinet that the supervisory staff in the industry who had co-operated with the Army and Navy personnel during a strike in 1949 refused to do so now, and without such assistance, it was impossible to operate the generators and transmission system. An additional complication was that, even if supervisory staff had been willing to help, Service personnel in 1949 had shown considerable reluctance to become involved in an action which would be seen as strike-breaking, and were unlikely to prove more amenable now. Compelling the armed forces to assist the civil power in this way was not within the competence of the Northern Ireland government, and it was not certain that London would take the view that Service intervention was justified until a general state of emergency and hardship threatened. Some of Glentoran's fellow Ministers were uneasy at the thought of the government becoming involved in a dispute between employers and workers, although others felt that electricity was so important to commerce, industry and the general wellbeing of the community that there was no option but to intervene. There were recriminations between the Ministries of Labour and Commerce, each of which had been monitoring the situation but was now inclined to blame the other for failing to anticipate that a strike had been imminent. The best that could be done was to make a reassuring statement in Stormont, claiming that the dispute would be carefully investigated, and that plans for maintaining essential supplies in the event of future industrial action would be re-evaluated as necessary. A small Ministerial committee was set up to examine how such a promise might be delivered.

As officials drew together the information for the committee's consideration it became clear that while existing arrangements for coping with a strike were unsatisfactory, it was impossible to suggest anything significantly better: "basically the operation of electricity plant with the aid of Service personnel remains the only known approach to the maintenance of supplies." It was also clear that the employers – the Electricity Board and Belfast Corporation – had no contingency plans of their own in place, apparently believing until the last minute that a strike would not take place.

When the committee reported towards the end of October 1955 it endorsed that preliminary judgement. The emergency provisions which had been agreed in 1949 were based, as in Britain, on the assumption that the co-operation of key members of the Electrical Power Engineers' Association (EPEA) would operate with the assistance of Service personnel to keep the lights on. That co-operation had been withheld during the March strike and one of the report's main conclusions was that the future loyalty of the EPEA should be secured, by financial inducements if necessary. There was also a rather fatalistic recognition that in the event of a future unannounced strike, no provision would prevent emergency supplies of electricity from being unavailable for at least 48 hours and possibly longer.

A few weeks later Glentoran brought forward details of how electricity supplies would be distributed in an emergency. This envisaged that co-operative arrangements were in place and a minimal amount of power would be generated in the hours after a properly notified strike had been declared. In the first instance electricity would be made available to identified hospitals, water and sewerage-pumping facilities, the BBC and other critical users in the Belfast area. For technical reasons the power could be distributed only on an incremental basis, by designated districts, and it would probably take 24 hours before bakeries, creameries, cold storage plants and similar facilities would be re-connected, and after that supplies to undertakings and individuals would be shared out on a rationed basis as supplies allowed. It was acknowledged that the scheme had serious and possibly fatal flaws. In the first place there was no guarantee that Whitehall Ministers would sanction the use of Service personnel unless they could be convinced that their deployment was essential to maintain supplies of electricity in a civil emergency. Even if that co-operation was forthcoming, the process by which the distribution system was activated district by district was a delicate one, and if users in the designated areas attempted to draw down power in excess of the prescribed limits, the entire system could collapse. Glentoran noted wistfully that hydro-electric stations required very little manpower for their operation, but otherwise was unable to offer any reassurance that another electricity strike would not have serious consequences. He refrained from pointing out that the more dependent Northern Ireland became on electricity, the greater would be the adverse consequences if the supply was interrupted, and the effects of a strike which could be accommodated in 1956 might well be unsupportable ten years later. He also, and perhaps understandably, refused to speculate on what would happen if key workers were to walk out of a nuclear power station for any reason, without making provision for its operation under emergency circumstances. Events in Northern Ireland less than 20 years later during the Ulster Workers' Strike would have rendered that possibility even more disturbing.

By the end of 1956 Glentoran was not particularly optimistic about the prospects of nuclear power coming to Northern Ireland. In a statement in Stormont he admitted that three factors would have to change significantly before a nuclear station became a viable proposition. The demand for electricity would have to increase significantly, the capital costs of a station would have to come down, and the practicable size of reactors would have to be reduced. None of these developments was impossible, but neither were they within the gift of the government, and until they were brought about there was a danger that Northern Ireland would end up with a power station which would be under-utilised and capable of producing energy only at prohibitively expensive prices. The government remained committed to the concept, but its realisation might have to be deferred. Early in 1957 the JEC retreated from its earlier position of enthusiastic support and now professed itself to be unable to recommend nuclear power.

If the project was to survive it would be because of Glentoran's championship. In January 1957 he received notification from the head of the AEA, Sir Edwin Plowden, to the effect that, if there was found to be a substantial cost advantage over conventionally-produced power, he was prepared, on balance, to recommend that Northern Ireland should be authorised to proceed with a nuclear station. It was a carefully-worded endorsement, and it placed on the authorities in Northern Ireland the responsibility of assuring themselves that the economic arguments stood up. It was a challenge Glentoran and his officials were prepared to accept and in February he brought to the Cabinet a number of determinedly optimistic propositions. First, that it could be anticipated that by 1963 an additional 150 MW of capacity would be required. Second, that on anticipated unit costs nuclear-generated electricity could be produced more cheaply than by conventional means. Third, that the Reactor Location Panel in Britain which adjudicated on the siting of nuclear stations had approved in principle two locations on the shores of Lough Neagh. Fourth, and perhaps the most surprising of all, that the Ministry of Finance had undertaken to help the Electricity Board raise the necessary funding, which even though it had shrunk to £24 million was still a massive slice of the public expenditure cake. He admitted that electricity could be produced from hydro-electric schemes on the Bann and Mourne at even cheaper rates than nuclear, but the requirement for their comparatively small output diminished in light of the capacity of the nuclear station, and he recommended that they should be removed from the capacity equation. The future energy strategy was being built around nuclear power. Some reservations were expressed by other Ministers – the massive capital investment could siphon off funds from industrial development, and doubts were expressed about the capacity of the Electricity Board to control such a project – but one of them remarked that it would be as well to make progress quickly before the Republic brought forward proposals for an all-Ireland nuclear station. If that argument was not decisive it was certainly persuasive, and Glentoran was given permission to make a public announcement that Northern Ireland planned to have nuclear generating capacity by 1963–1964.

Early in March 1957 therefore Glentoran announced the good news in Stormont, and described it as "a happy day for Ulster." The reservations of the previous autumn were banished, and he claimed that on the basis of the most recent calculations he was confident that there would be sufficient industrial and domestic demand for electricity to justify the new station. He ended with a declaration that "it has been estimated that the cost of current from nuclear fission will be lower than that from either coal or oil." It was a slightly ambiguous statement, but it was well received, both in Parliament and the country, and offers of possible sites for the new station rolled in from local Councils, including Tyrone, Limavady, Cookstown, Newry, Magherafelt and Ballymena. In addition private submissions were made in respect of locations on the Quoile and Lough Erne. Electricity was suddenly exciting. Over the coming months objections were raised that the Washing Bay site, which now moved to the front as the government's preferred location, was not ideal from the security point of view, the area having experienced some IRA activity, but Glentoran stated that for technical reasons the location offered economic advantages which no other site could offer, and the Inspector General of the RUC had pronounced himself satisfied as to security. The four year project would employ around 1,000 construction workers, and give permanent employment to 160. By October he was in a position to seek Cabinet approval to enter discussions with the Reactor Location Panel and with the local authorities in the Washing Bay area.

Days before Glentoran's critical Cabinet meeting news came through of a fire at the AEA facility at Windscale in Cumbria, and of the emergency procedures subsequently deployed to ensure that food and water in the area had escaped contamination. The AEA was quick to issue reassurances that no damage had been done, and apart from having to dump all supplies of milk produced in an extensive surrounding area, insisted that no threat to public health had resulted. It was probably true, but for Glentoran the damage had been done. At the Cabinet meeting where he had hoped to get the green light for Washing Bay, it was clear that his colleagues had succumbed to a collective attack of nerves. The main ground of rejection, inevitable in the light of Windscale, was that the discharge of nuclear material into Lough Neagh was seen as presenting an unacceptable risk to public health. The Lough was due to become the main source of drinking water for Northern Ireland when the Mourne reservoirs reached their capacity in the late 1960s, and in the light of the AEA response to what looked like a minor incident at Windscale, it was clear that nuclear emissions posed a significant risk of contamination. Nuclear discharges from a coastal site would reduce that risk, and in the event of an accident would also minimise the area which had to be evacuated, besides cutting out the dangers of transporting nuclear waste along public roads. Shortly afterwards the political card was played in. According to the Unionist Party Whips, there had been strong opposition in Party circles to the Washing Bay location, where a large number of construction and operational jobs would probably go to non-Unionists. The view on the ground was that such considerations should be given at least equal weight with whatever economic and technical reasons Glentoran had advanced in favour of the location. His colleagues in the Cabinet did not reject Glentoran's proposals, but he could not dismiss the public health argument and agreed, after much debate, to put Washing

Bay on hold while the possibility of a coastal site was investigated. Suddenly, for Glentoran, all the lights had turned to amber. He might have appreciated the irony if, a few months later, he had seen a letter to the Minister of Home Affairs from a priest in the Washing Bay area. Far from expressing disappointment at the loss of potential jobs, it was claimed that the whole idea of a nuclear power station in the vicinity constituted nothing less than a vicious plot by the government to exterminate the local people as an act of revenge for the IRA activity which had taken place there.

The pursuit of a nuclear station did not end there, but never again did it seem so close to realisation. Throughout 1958 advice was received from the AEA and the Home Office experts, the burden of which was that, even if the Lough Neagh site posed a small public health risk, why should it be incurred when a coastal site would be risk-free? It was rumoured that Belfast Corporation, although realising that a nuclear station would never be built within their jurisdiction, were opposed to its being located elsewhere, and had lobbied discreetly against the project. Experts advising the Ministry of Commerce felt that the risks identified with Washing Bay could have been overcome, or at least managed to the point where they became insignificant, and that professional opinion could have been mustered in favour of the project proceeding if the political will had been present. One of Glentoran's colleagues expressed the sense of unease which still existed in the Cabinet however – "I feel that in this grave matter with all its attendant technical problems we are rather like children playing with a toy which could destroy us." There was continuing support on the government back benches in Stormont, but it was scarcely persuasive, one MP referring, apparently without facetious intent, to the political prestige which remained attached to the project "and the warm glow that radiates in our hearts when we think about an atomic power station."

Despite maintaining his belief that Washing Bay was, and would remain, the optimum site for a nuclear station, Glentoran authorised the search to be made for a suitable coastal location. By the middle of 1959 a possible site had been identified near Kilkeel, which although it lacked some of the advantages of Lough Neagh was still felt to be capable of providing electricity at rates fractionally cheaper than were offered by fossil fuel. It was then claimed that, although it would add significantly to the capital costs, the long-term economic advantages could be enhanced if the nuclear station was built in conjunction with a pumped storage facility – water pumped up to a dam at night when demand for electricity was low and released during the day to generate current available for sale. (At one time Cave Hill in Belfast, using water from Belfast Lough was proposed as a suitable site for the same arrangement.) But by that stage it was becoming clear that the demand for electricity in Northern Ireland was not reaching the levels predicted in the White Paper of a few years previously, and that a conventional power station would best be suited to provide whatever additional capacity might be required until the mid-60s. At the same time suggestions were being put forward that an interconnector between Scotland and Northern Ireland would allow trading arrangements for surplus energy at costs with which nuclear could not compete. The preliminary geological surveys and engineering reports on Washing Bay were filed away in the hope – or in Glentoran's case the expectation – that they would one day provide the basis for a new venture on the site.

In the circumstances the arguments in favour of a new oil-fired station at Coolkeeragh in County Londonderry became compelling, and the Northern Ireland electricity industry would enter the new decade still embracing the technology of the old one. In retrospect it was the right decision. Even 20 years later the Northern Ireland Economic Council in putting forward its ideas for a long-term energy strategy recognised that a nuclear station of a suitable size and with the right characteristics for the Northern Ireland system simply did not exist, and if one had been installed earlier its costs would have placed an unsupportable burden on consumers. Coolkeeragh was officially opened in November 1960. By then there were 179,000 consumers, more than half of them located in rural areas, and almost 23,000 of them farmers, so the programme of rural electrification had recovered from the hiatus of the early 50s. By the later years a chain of Electricity Board showrooms had sprung up in all the larger towns, and an expanding range of electrical appliances was being offered to housewives. It was still a relatively restricted range of products, with cookers and boilers for laundry being the most popular, and food mixers and refrigerators at the bottom of the list, but it unmistakably pointed the way forward. The link between electricity, convenience and labour-saving devices was being forged on a daily basis.

Yet despite the miles of cables which now ran in profusion along the side of every major road Northern Ireland entered the 60s still far from being fully electrified. In order to boost generation output there was talk – although not from any seriously-regarded sources – of electrifying the railways. Given the economics of the railways that was never a realistic proposition, but it was noted with a degree of wistfulness that a promising market segment had been lost when Belfast Corporation decided to phase out its fleet of trolley buses, which had used power from overhead cables.

The number of farms and houses connected to the grid looked impressive when compared to the situation in the immediate post-war years, but was still only around one quarter of the total, and represented the most accessible segment of the market. The remainder would be more difficult to penetrate, and predictions were made that at the current rate it would be at least 80 more years before everyone was connected. Complaints continued to be made about the guarantees required before connection could take place. Saul church outside Downpatrick was unable to afford the £130 per year required and was instead fitted with gas lighting and heating supplied by Calor gas, which was then expanding its distribution of Liquid Petroleum Gas (LPG) in containers, and was increasing its popularity with caravan owners and smaller households who appreciated the convenience of energy which came in manageable yellow cylinders. But as always, the finger of blame was pointed at the farmers. If 23,000 farms had signed up they still used only 12% of the electricity generated, while another 50,000 remained unwired. Perhaps their attitude was summed up in the anecdote told in Parliament about a bachelor farmer who was very fond of attending dances in the local hall until electricity was introduced. After one visit he announced his intention to quit, claiming that while his appearance had passed muster when oil lights had been used, it would never survive electric lighting where his dance partner would be able to see the very fleas on his person.

It was an unorthodox view, but it reflected the underlying belief of the cautious Ulsterman that perhaps not all change was for the best. As the *Telegraph* had observed at the imminent arrival of television, progress could be disturbing.